SHALLOW ROOTS

By

ELIZABETH WEHMAN

Summit Street Publishing

Shallow Roots
Published by Summit Street Publishing
131 West Grand River
Owosso, Michigan 48867

This book is a work of historical fiction based closely on real people and events. Details that cannot be historically verified are purely products of the author's imagination.

ISBN 978-1-7377539-2-6
ISBN 978-1-7377539-3-3 (ebook)

Publishing in the United States by Summit Street Publishing, Owosso, Michigan

Library of Congress Cataloging-in-Publication data
Wehman, Elizabeth
Shallow Roots/Elizabeth Wehman-1st ed. 2022911235
The Newburg Chronicles - 3

Printed in the United States of America
2021

I would like to dedicate *Shallow Roots* to my newest love.

Baileigh Jo Lawson

Your creation has brought me great joy. You are wonderfully and beautifully made by the ultimate Creator.

I'm so happy God chose me to be your Grammy.

ACKNOWLEDGMENTS

Welcome back.

In this third edition of the *Newburg Chronicles* series, I am excited to bring in a new member of the Baker family. Researching this character brought me so many emotions. I was ecstatic to find someone related to the Baker family. I loved her story from the first paragraph I read about her, and then as more and more information surfaced, I realized how great of an addition she'd be to the series. I believe you'll soon agree.

Shallow Roots has me believing that Hosea Baker had a rough life. Perhaps he didn't. As only fiction can do, it's made me question whether I have made him famous in my imagination or was he really a prominent figure in Shiawassee County in 1833? His mention so many times in the history books makes me assume he was famous, but as I write and imagine what his life could have been like, perhaps he was just a simple man born during a prominent time in our county's history.

I believe Hosea was recorded in the history books for my benefit. As snippets of information I've gleaned about him unfold, there is a pattern I'm required to pursue. Like a responsibility, of sorts. You can decide for yourself whether that's true or coincidental, yet the more I learn about him and find out about his family, the more I believe the family's adventures need to be told.

My *Newburg Chronicles* series is fiction, yet woven throughout this book are facts and truthful stories. Some are definitely believable, but some sound unreal, like I made them up, but I didn't. Be sure to read the Author Notes in the back to learn more.

My thanks for the production of *Shallow Roots* go to you, my readers. I'm so thankful for you. You keep me writing. Your encouragement to get another copy of the series into your hands keeps me digging into research and writing even when I'm not sure what should go on a page. And as always, a special thanks to my faithful editors, Kathryn Frazier, Beth Hafer, and Emily Lawson. You all make it read better, become more understandable, and often whittle off my bad ideas and make them pretty again. Thank you.

After much thought, I'm choosing to add one more book after *Shallow Roots* to end the series. Be waiting for book four. But, for now, enjoy *Shallow Roots.*

Elizabeth

Psalm34:8

SUMMER 1836

CHAPTER ONE

Rhoda Seymour pulled tight on the braid she'd just woven in her daughter Philinda's hair. The child's shoulders scrunched. Rhoda patted her head. "Stop it now. I didn't pull that hard."

"But Momma, it hurts when you braid them so tightly."

"We need these braids to stay. We've got a long trip ahead, and I don't want to keep fixing your hair each morning on the trail." Rhoda stood up, brushing off strands of hair dotting her skirt. "Get around now. Put your things in the satchel on the bed. We need to be ready at the crack of dawn. I can see light starting over the horizon."

"It's so early..." Philinda got off the bed and began placing her nightclothes in the bag, along with her younger siblings' garments.

"No complaining now. Just get to it!" Rhoda grimaced at her stern voice. She hated scolding her children so, but they had more than enough journey left that if she didn't push her children, it would make their trip harder to endure. Truth be told, she'd love to sleep in for a spell herself.

"You help dress Martha and Rhoda Ann and I'll wake Giles." For a five-year-old, he was at the age that he was harder to manage than his older sisters, especially when still tired.

Rhoda watched her eleven-year-old strip the night clothes off her two younger sisters and put their day clothes on them. The children had circles under their eyes. This trip had caused them to fight between fatigue and hunger. The food she'd brought to eat along the way was long gone after she'd shared some with other travelers on the steamboat into Detroit.

Picking up her satchel, she dug inside a sewn-in pocket where she stored their extra money for the trip. She pulled out the last twenty-dollar gold piece. Fumbling in the pocket of her dress, she retrieved another two dollars. Surely, it would be enough to get them to the doorstep of her brother. She'd skimped and planned the best she knew how for months to pay for this trip. It would be so sad to be this close yet not have the resources to finish the trip.

She placed the gold piece deep inside the satchel pocket. Adding her children's clothes to the top of the pile of her belongings, she crimped the edge of the bag shut. Sighing, she helped Philinda braid the girls' hair. More complaints came because of the tightly woven braids. She hushed the girls and encouraged them to budge by reminding them of breakfast awaiting them in the dining room of the boardinghouse.

"I hope they have flapjacks!" Giles bounced on the bed so Rhoda couldn't tie his shoes. "Stop squirming, child." She forced herself to smile. "If the food from last night is any sign of what will be on the table this morning, you should be pleased."

Miss Haddy, the boardinghouse owner, had set out a pleasant feast the night before for their dinner. The children had eaten with gusto, putting a smile on the elderly hotel owner's face.

"I love to see children eat so well," she'd commented.

Rhoda had smiled at the cook but didn't dare tell her that at this point in their travels, they'd eat dog meat if they had a chance. The boat ride had been hard on everyone's queasy stomachs. Anything tasted better, knowing they wouldn't see it again within an hour. The children were starving. If she weren't a proper lady herself, Rhoda would have asked for another heaping spoonful of the fluffy mashed potatoes.

"Now let's get a move on! We need to finish our breakfast in time to head to the local stable to hire a teamster to take us deeper into the territory."

The children squealed in delight, eager to reach their destination.

Rhoda watched Giles eye the large plate of flapjacks placed in front of him. "Only take two, for now, Giles. I'm afraid your stomach isn't as big as your mind's eye." The young boy scowled at his mother, but obediently used his fork to stab at the stack on the plate.

"Thank you so much, Miss Haddy, for another wonderful meal." Rhoda handed the plate off to the plump woman standing beside her on the right.

Miss Haddy tipped her head back and laughed. "I love to feed the young'uns just off the boats. They seem to have not tasted food for ages."

"I've heard those boat trips can be quite the swaying experience," commented another boarder sitting across from Rhoda and her children at the long table.

"It unfolded into a completely new way to travel. You get to your destination faster by steamboat, but it requires considerable stamina to endure the rocking ship." She placed a pat of butter on the two pancakes she took from the enormous stack now offered to her by Miss Haddy.

"Is your husband on the trip with you, Mrs. Seymour?" Another female boarder asked her from farther down the table.

"We've come first. My brother lives inland and we're heading there to meet him and get settled in the new territory." Rhoda smeared butter on Giles's pancakes, too, adding a drop of marmalade to his stack. His mouth seemed to salivate at the thought of his first bite. Rhoda thought to pick up his napkin to wipe his mouth but instead chose a knife to cut his flapjacks into pieces he could easily stab with a fork.

"That's very brave of you. I don't think I could come from New York by myself, let alone with four children in tow." The woman seemed to say with disdain, with one eyebrow raised, then looked at the others seated at the table.

On the steamboat, Rhoda had grown used to looks from other women. She was the only parent on the journey, and a woman traveling alone. She hadn't been all that afraid, knowing family would be at their destination. Prices for traveling had gone up in the past year, and if part of the family didn't come now, it could be even more costly in the future. Her husband, Sidney, could finalize the selling of their store in Sodus, New York, and then he'd follow with their three eldest children.

"So, you have other children in New York?" Miss Haddy sat at the foot of the table after serving each guest.

Rhoda had just taken a bite of her breakfast but wiped her mouth before speaking. "Yes." She wiped again to be sure she wasn't spitting food. "I have three older children." Before anyone could ask more, she added, "Harriet is eighteen, Lucinda is fourteen, and George is thirteen."

Everyone at the table chuckled.

"You have your hands full, Mrs. Seymour." Miss Haddy smiled as she took her selection of jams from the table to smear lavishly on her stack of flapjacks.

"I'm grateful for each one, but yes, I lead a busy life."

Thankfully, the conversation then went around the table of twelve for the next few minutes, so Rhoda could concentrate on eating as much as she could consume. She had no clue when their next meal would come, and she'd paid a high price to stay the night.

Many of the guests at Miss Haddy's boarding-house had also come off the boats, but most were staying there to work in town. The enormity of Detroit surprised Rhoda. Whenever she asked about living here, it seemed travelers believed the area was still quite primitive. Yet Detroit was civilized, like their towns back East, only much larger.

Finishing up her breakfast, Rhoda took advantage of a lull in conversation to ask about the next stage headed into the territory. Would there be one available to take them to her family?

One man at the far end of the table spoke up. "Mrs. Seymour, I'm afraid many of the stagecoaches don't head that far north just yet. I'd be more than happy to escort you and your children to the stable in the back part of town. There are teamsters there who can take you farther interior, but I have to be truthful with you—" The man wiped the crumbs off the front of his shirt. "I'm not sure even they will take you to Knagg's Place. Is that the location you told us about last night?"

Rhoda nodded. "Yes."

"That's rough country, ma'am. Infested with Indians and mosquitoes. It will be a rough go for a lady with children."

Rhoda watched Philinda stop eating to give her a panicked glance.

"We've come this far, sir. I don't have any other choice than to make the journey."

"Well then, may God be with you." The man stood up. "I'll be waiting outside for you and the children." He motioned to the little ones finishing up their morning meal. "And please. There's no rush. I need to have a smoke and Miss Haddy hates me to do it in her delicious-smelling dining room, so take your time finishing up." With that gesture, the man left the table.

"Such a dreadful habit," Miss Haddy whispered to the other guests when the door shut behind the man on the porch. "Any more flapjacks, children?" Miss Haddy lifted the plate that only held two more fluffy cakes.

For once since leaving home, the children shook their heads slowly. Rhoda raised the napkin to her mouth to not laugh out loud and then announced, "Their eyes are always bigger than their stomachs."

Miss Haddy cackled again. "I love feeding my guests and I'm even happier when they leave satisfied."

Rhoda picked up the heavy satchel and handed each child something to carry as they went out onto the front porch to find the kind man who had offered his services.

As soon as he saw them approach, he snapped the tip of the cigar he'd been smoking into the bushes at the front of the house. "Ready to head out?"

Rhoda smiled at the short man. Gray hair edged the outline of his tall hat. "Thank you for helping us. I appreciate it."

"No problem." The man held out his hand. "Name's Cooper. Cooper Martin."

Rhoda moved her satchel to her other arm and shook the man's hand. "Where are you headed, Mr. Martin?"

"Pontiac. Not as far as you, but inland—just the same. I have to rent a teamster myself." Mr. Martin raised his voice to be heard over the commotion on the street in front of the boarding house. As he stepped off the porch, he slipped easily into the rush of residents heading in both directions on the wooden sidewalks. On the dirt street, men rode into town on horseback amidst teamsters shifting wagons around them. The wagons were loaded with all kinds of goods, headed for—who knew where? Despite the early hour, the town was alive with activity.

The sun now illuminated the once dark-street with streaks of light as Rhoda looked north. Sliding her satchel to her elbow, she took the hands of Giles and Rhoda Ann and beckoned Philinda and Martha to follow her. Moments like this made her wish she'd talked Sidney into allowing Harriet to come with them. Her eighteen-year-old daughter was a great help with the younger children, but she was needed to pack up the store with Sidney and her older siblings.

Rhoda hoped the negotiations to sell the store in Sodus went as planned. If not, she would need to earn more money to feed and house the family once they arrived at Knagg's Place.

She hoped the twenty-dollar gold piece in her satchel would be enough to not only rent the teamster, but also to shelter them once they arrived at their destination. Hopefully, her husband wasn't far behind. As she'd done the entire trip, she thought about her brother Hosea's response to her arrival. Would he be happy or upset that she'd made the trip, especially without Sidney? If she knew Hosea at all, she wanted to assume he'd be pleased. But what if he rejected her instead?

CHAPTER TWO

"A dollar and how much?" When Rhoda heard the cost of hiring a teamster to take her as far as Pontiac, she panicked.

"Thirty cents, ma'am. That's a dollar and thirty cents a day." The man turned his head and spit tobacco in the opposite direction. At least Rhoda had a teamster with manners. She'd dodged the other men along the way who spewed in any direction they found suitable.

"And how long will it take us to get to Pontiac?"

"Three days."

Rhoda struggled to count up in her head how much it would be. She was good at ciphering, as long as she could do it on paper.

"That's nearly four dollars, Momma."

The teamster winked at Philinda. "That it is, young lady."

While the man complimented her daughter, Rhoda was still figuring the total in her head. "How long will it take to get from Pontiac to Knagg's Place?"

The man scratched his head. "Well, I can't take you near that far. I only go to Pontiac and back, but I reckon it will take maybe a week or more to get you North. The trails are quite primitive north of Pontiac and are still hard to maneuver a team through. Might be hard to find a teamster to travel that far up."

Rhoda bit her bottom lip. If she was figuring it correctly, it would take nearly half her twenty-dollar piece to pay for their transportation, but what choice did she have? What could she do if she became stranded and did not reach Hosea? Would Sidney even be able to find her? Could she manage the children and also work to feed them all? As fast as fear filled her thoughts, she put it aside to shake the hand of the man who would get them closer to Hosea. Confidence in her capabilities had never been an issue for Rhoda—but at that moment, broad strokes of doubt washed over her soul.

She held out her hand. "My name is Mrs. Seymour and these are my children."

"Augustus Drake, ma'am." The teamster took off a glove to shake her hand.

"Are you sure this is how you want to go about this endeavor?" Ambrose Baker placed his hands on his hips, looking his Pa in the eye.

"What's wrong with my idea?" Hosea Baker folded his arms, squinting against the bright sun.

Ambrose looked away. "I don't know. Seems risky!"

"Risky?" Hosea stepped back. "Son, I don't know another way to do it."

"Asking all those men to not only travel here but then to be that close to the river, pushing enormous logs into place—" Ambrose shook his head. "I just wonder if you're taking on too much responsibility for other lives."

"Lives? What are you sayin', Ambrose? When somethin' has to be done and we're without the added manpower, we ask for help. We can't manage something so tedious by ourselves. You know that."

"I know Pa, but perhaps we should wait until we get more oxen for the job or head to another sawmill to ask them how they went about it." Putting his hands on each side of his head, Ambrose added, "Pa, you've never put together such a large sawmill, have you? And so close to a river?"

"It's the only way. I have men coming from all over. We need a sawmill. We need it soon. This is the only way, and you know it." Hosea seemed to grow disgusted at Ambrose's lack of confidence. "Sides...I gotta find a better way to put food in the mouths of my family."

Ambrose turned to leave, raising his hands in the air in resignation. "Okay. Sounds like you've made up your mind. What time do you want me here on Saturday?"

"Daybreak. Can you get up that early?" Hosea snickered behind him.

"Horace and I will be here." But as Ambrose walked away, he grimaced. Pa always had outrageous ideas about how to continue the progress of this little town in the Michigan Territory. This time Ambrose worried he'd taken on too much. His pa had been in failing health ever since losing his adopted son, Alexander, to the Indians just the year before. With that loss and endeavoring to turn his piece of land into a farm—the toll was showing in the deep lines on his face and the way he shuffled when he walked. Ambrose's otherwise strong parent had begun to show his age. Yet when he thought of the benefits of the sawmill, he knew his pa was right. It was necessary and, with enough men, they should be able to get the job done.

The jarring of the wagon headed north made every bone in Rhoda's body hurt. They'd only been traveling a day, but Giles had managed to crack his head against the wagon's side more than once. The girls just stared up with large eyes and frightened looks, especially after the last night's wolf howling serenade. They'd heard coyotes back in Sodus, but these were long, drawn-out, life-shaking howls. The children had crowded around her so tightly she couldn't shift positions to make herself comfortable. She got little sleep and her hip was still sore from the hard wagon bed.

The wagon driver had little to say to her. He'd helped her fix breakfast that morning, offering what he had to add to what Rhoda had purchased in Detroit. It wasn't much, but it satisfied their gnawing stomachs. Through the rocking of the steamboat and the money getting slim, Rhoda knew how to go without, but the children always seemed hungry. She'd scolded them too many times for requests she couldn't fulfill.

As a wagon wheel dipped again into a rut on the road, Rhoda thought back over her decision to come ahead of Sidney to secure their property in the New Territory. She'd convinced her husband she could take the younger children and head into the new state without him. He'd wanted to finish selling the last of their possessions and have the new store proprietor take ownership of the store before the family left. Sidney always desired to have his to-do list complete before embarking on the next venture. The older children would help pack up the supplies they'd need to ship to start a new business near Hosea. She just hadn't realized how hard it would be to go without Sidney, nor how costly it would become.

The lingering journey gave her too much time to think about what she was doing. Philinda's voice interrupted her thoughts.

"Momma!"

"Philinda! You don't have to use a scolding voice to speak to me."

Her daughter's shoulders slumped, and she looked away.

"I'm sorry, Ma. You didn't seem to be here with us. With the look on your face, it seemed like you were miles away."

Rhoda knew it to be true. Instead of apologizing, she acknowledged her daughter. "What do you need?"

"Can you tell us again about Uncle Hosea's cabin? About where we're going? I need something to distract me from thinking the worst about what we are doing going this far without Papa."

Rhoda could only imagine the fear in her child's heart. Philinda had always been her skeptical child. She needed specific plans to get her through the moments when fear overtook her heart. For just eleven years of age, Philinda's apprehensive character made her seem much younger. "Yes, let's talk about what awaits us at Uncle Hosea's house."

"I can't wait to see Jillian." Hosea's child, Jillian, was just two years older than Philinda. They'd been childhood friends since both families had lived in New York.

"Don't forget about Ambrose, Betsey, Caroline, and Etta."

Nine-year-old Martha asked, "Who are they?"

"They're our cousins." Philinda tucked a strand of hair behind Martha's ear, pulled her bonnet up, and then tied it tight under her chin. "You'll love having cousins. They're like sisters and brothers, but they don't live with you."

"Will they like us?" Seven-year-old Rhoda Ann wanted nothing more than for everyone to like her. She was Rhoda's pleasing child.

Rhoda smiled and pulled her youngest daughter into her lap. "Yes. They've met you and loved you since the day you were born, but just haven't seen you in a long while." She squeezed her daughter close to her. "We'll live near Uncle Hosea until Papa arrives. You'll see. It will be the greatest adventure you've ever had. From all that Uncle Hosea writes to me about the New Territory, it is a hard country, but will open soon to many new residents. The land is cheap, and Papa will follow soon to purchase a store here for us to do business—just like home."

"Will our store be as nice as it was in Sodus?" Philinda had been a big help at their home business. Each of the Seymour children worked to make the store a delightful place for the residents of the small town to shop.

A close-knit family was important to Rhoda and her husband, Sidney. Because of that, they had put each child in charge of a specific aspect of running the store. That way, they could be together while they worked. Rhoda insisted working as a team kept them close and dependent on each other. It also saved a lot of earnings by not having to hire workers.

Rhoda realized she hadn't answered Philinda. "We'll just have to wait and see. From what Uncle Hosea tells me in his letters, a store is desperately needed in the place where he now lives. Coming in early will help us get established, and soon, perhaps, we'll have just as nice a store as we had in Sodus." She smiled at her children. "With all of your help."

Hitting another jarring bump, Rhoda placed Rhoda Ann into the bed of the wagon. The weight of her on her lap made her hip hurt worse.

Suddenly, the wagon stopped moving. The teamster driver hollered a command to the snorting oxen.

The wagon stood still for a moment before Rhoda asked, "Augustus? Why are we stopping?"

"The team needs a rest, ma'am. We've been going uphill for over an hour. And, from what it looks like, there's a log across the road up ahead, too." Augustus pulled back on the wagon brake and tied the reins to the brake's lever. "I'll be right back."

If they continued to have to stop like this, Rhoda wondered if her bill for transportation would rise. What if it took more days than expected to arrive in Pontiac? At least the stop helped give her side some relief.

CHAPTER THREE

"Day after tomorrow?" Hosea answered his daughter's question as she scurried to scoop up Richard as he edged his way toward the cooking fire just outside Betsey's house. When Hosea approached, Betsey was dipping clothes into a large boiling pot to wash.

"I'm not sure Aaron will be back in time, Pa. He had to head north to help with an Indian dispute. You know if he's available, he'll be there to help." Betsey blew a piece of hair out of her eyes as she struggled to hold the child, who wriggled to get out of her grasp.

Hosea took the squirming child. The day was hot, and Betsey looked to be suffering the ill effects of having to chase two young'uns, so close in age, and still manage her daily chores. He placed a kiss on the cheek of his one-year-old grandson. "That's enough, boy. No more squirming."

Baby Richard loved his *Bopa* as Julia called him. Soon he stuck his thumb in his mouth and leaned his head on Hosea's shoulder.

"I have several men coming in next week to put the logs in place for the mill. We need all the help we can get from everyone. Including Aaron."

"So that's what you've decided, Pa? Using as many men as you can find to do the heavy work?"

Hosea nodded. "I believe it's the best way. Actually," Hosea placed Richard on his hip as the child took off Hosea's hat and put it on his own head. "It's the only way." He smiled at the boy as he took the hat away and put it back on his head. "This one's a handful. Is he not?"

Betsey laughed. "He's rarely content, like his sister. I should have named him Hosea Baker Swain."

Hosea eyed his daughter but changed the subject. "How about we take a walk down to Grammy's cabin to see her?"

The boy nodded his head. Julia scrambled to hold Hosea's hand. "Me, Bopa. Me go, too!"

"You need to ask your ma."

Betsey put her hands on her hips. "Pa. Ma's got enough things of her own to do. She doesn't need to be having to watch these two."

"Jillian and Etta are there to help. You have no one. I'll bring them back up the hill after dinner. That way, you can get some of your chores done, too. Besides, when this mill gets up and runnin', I won't have time to take these two on walks anymore."

Betsey smirked. "Well, you don't have to ask twice." She pointed to the excited children in the care of her pa. "You two be good for Bopa and Grammy, do you understand? You mind them."

Both children grinned as Julia jumped beside Hosea, still holding his hand. "Yes, Mama."

Hosea wasn't sure what made him happier—getting ready to start a new venture or just walking down the trail between his daughter's house and his own, with grandchildren in tow.

Jillian heard laughter coming from the trail headed up to Betsey's house. She could hear Julia's squeals as they approached the barn. Pa looked to have his hands full. He moved Richard onto his other hip and called to Jillian as Julia slipped out of his grasp and began running toward her.

"Jilly! Come help your pa."

Jillian stood just in time as Julia came at her faster than a runaway horse. "Julia! Slow down, honey. Why are you running so fast?"

"Me want to see Grammy."

Jillian picked up the child, who gave her a quick hug. "I want to go see her." Jillian attempted to correct Julia's grammar.

"Yes, me do!" The child laughed and clapped her hands.

Jillian shrugged, then smiled at her niece's excitement. She could hear Richard babbling something to her pa as they finally drew near. "Betsey needs a break to get her work done. Can you take a break to help Ma watch these two?"

Jillian was happy to quit mending the chicken fence to watch her niece and nephew. It had been a few days since she'd seen them. "Of course, Pa."

As Jillian and Pa walked toward the cabin, Jillian asked, "How's Betsey?"

"Busy. She's trying to get her laundry done, but this one—" Pa nudged Richard under the chin, "keeps running toward the fire."

"I don't know how Betsey does it. I'm glad we're close by to help her when she needs it." Jillian turned to find Julia already rounding the front of the cabin at a breakneck speed. "I think Ma had planned to scrub the floor today. Not sure how it will be with Julia running in with dirty feet."

Pa chuckled. "She won't be as upset as she was when you were little. Grandchildren seem to have a magical effect on grandparents. We don't mind near as much as we did when it was ours causing problems."

The father-daughter conversation ceased as they heard a horse approaching from the south. Jillian looked up to see Billie Black. He slowed down, jumped off the brown stallion, and led him to where they were standing.

Taking off his hat, he addressed Pa. "Mr. Baker." Then he turned to her. "Jillian."

"Hello, Billie. How are you?" Pa answered the young man with gusto.

Jillian had nothing to say. Each time she was in Billie's presence, it seemed her tongue wouldn't work. She could feel her face blush and turned away so Billie couldn't see it.

"What brings you here on such a gorgeous August afternoon?" Pa greeted the young man with a handshake.

Richard squealed at the horse, which lifted his nose to Pa. The child went from excitement to panic in a second as the horse approached the young boy. Richard shivered and turned his head away from the inquisitive horse.

"What's wrong, Richard? Don't you like Billie's horse?" Pa rubbed the nose of the horse as Richard reached out with hesitation to touch the animal. The bristles of horsehair must have poked Richard because he pulled his hand away quickly. "It's okay. Pet him."

"I've come for two reasons." Billie quickly changed the subject.

Pa continued to rub the neck of the horse beside him. "Well, let's hear them."

"I've come to tell you I'll be available to help you at the mill raising next week."

"Splendid, boy!" Hosea exclaimed. Richard jumped in response causing Hosea to smile.

"Also," Billie pulled out a piece of mail. "This came for you. Whitmore wanted to be sure you got it today. It's been at the post for a week now."

Jillian glanced over at the mail Pa took from Billie's hand. "Who is it from, Pa?"

"Looks to be someone from New York." Pa held up the letter against the sun. Jillian wasn't sure why he did that. Opening it would be a better way of seeing who it was from. "Let's take it to your Ma so she can read it to all of us. Why don't you come into the house, Billie? Fetch yourself some cool water from the barrel."

Billie took off his hat and nodded. "Thanks, Mr. Baker. It is hot."

Jillian felt tingles from the tips of her toes move up through her body as Billie led his horse to the barn to tie him to a post there. She tucked loose strands of hair back under her bonnet. Cringing, she looked down at her once-white apron, which was now speckled with dirt. All she wanted to do was to run to the cabin to change. But it was too late. Instead of following Pa to the cabin, she waited for Billie to tie up his horse so she could walk with him.

Billie smiled. "Thanks for waiting, Jillian. What have you been working on?"

"The chicken fence. It doesn't want to stay attached to the side of the barn. It's probably a 'coon fiddlin' with it during the night."

"After I get a drink, I can come out and help you. If you'd like."

Jillian waved off her recent job. "It will be here when I return. Seems it's fixed one day and broke the next." With a wave of sudden courage, she added, "It's good to see you."

Since Caroline had decided to marry Horace the year before, Billie had still been coming to the farm weekly. Often, he would help Pa with the crops or planting, but he also had become a useful farrier. Aaron had hired him to help with his horse so he could spend more time with Betsey and the children when he had time off, which was rare. He'd told Jillian often how valuable Billie had become in caring for the horse.

Jillian would soon turn fourteen in October. She couldn't wait for the day when Pa would allow her to have a beau. She knew, without a doubt, whom she'd love to have ask to court her. His smile gave her chills, despite the hot summer day. She hoped Billie would wait until she was old enough.

The couple walked in silence to the cabin. Jillian's nerves prevented her from speaking. She wondered if Billie had the same issue.

Sally Mae had Julia on her lap, her clean floor showing traces of tiny footprints, when Hosea came to the door with Richard. The little girl babbled on about what she'd been doing for the day.

Hosea paused at the door. "Oh, Sally Mae...sorry about the mess on your clean floor."

His wife, who was showing the weariness of being a farmer's wife in the deep woods of the Michigan Territory, shrugged. "It's okay. It will dry soon."

Hosea held up the paper. "We got a letter and even another visitor!"

Sally Mae kissed Julia on both cheeks and then motioned to Hosea. "You might as well come ahead. A letter and that baby you have are better than a clean floor any day."

Hosea took off his hat, placed Richard on the floor to walk to his grandmother, and scooped a ladle of water from the barrel by the front door. He slurped a long drink. "That walk from Betsey's seemed long today, or maybe it was because I had these two in tow."

"Where's Betsey?" Sally Mae gave him a quizzical look.

Hosea wiped his mouth off with the edge of his sleeve. "She needed a break. This one," Hosea pointed to Richard, who was climbing Sally Mae's lap to sit with his sister, "was givin' her fits. He wouldn't stay away from the fire."

"Oh, how I remember those days." Sally Mae pulled the boy firmly onto her lap and planted a kiss on his cheek as he snuggled down and put his head on his grandmother's shoulder. His thumb went instantly into his mouth. Sally Mae hugged him close. "Remember how it was with Ambrose and Betsey so young?"

"But they weren't as close as these two." Hosea went to the mantle for his spectacles. He'd found his need for them had grown stronger over the past year or two. Placing the spectacles on his face, he sat at the table to open the letter. "We don't get a letter very often."

Sally Mae rocked with the two children on her lap. Richard acted as though he'd rather fall asleep than scurry around anymore. Julia seemed content on Sally Mae's lap. "Who's it from, Hosea? And who's our visitor?"

"Let me get it open, dear wife, and I'll tell you."

Hosea opened the letter as Billie and Jillian came through the door.

"Billie!" Sally Mae motioned to the couple, "I'd stand up and welcome you, but as you can see—"

"No need. It's fine." Billie motioned for Sally Mae to stay seated.

Jillian dipped the scoop into the cold water by the door and handed it to Billie.

He smiled as he took a good long drink, as Hosea had just done. "Thank you."

Jillian came to the table and sat. As she did, Julia slipped off Sally Mae's lap and climbed up on Jillian's.

"Looks to be from New York." Hosea turned the letter over and adjusted his glasses better behind one ear. "Yes, sir. It's from Nicholas."

"Nicholas? Nicholas Harder?" Sally Mae cuddled her grandson closer as he fell asleep. "Read it to us."

Hosea cleared his throat and adjusted the glasses on his nose. "These things are such a problem."

"Oh, Hosea. Stop fussin' and read."

"Hold on to your horses, Sally Mae. Let's see here." Hosea held up the letter closer. "Dear Hosea—"

Jillian interrupted, "Pa, hold on a moment. I think Etta is down by the river. Let me holler for her. She'll want to hear what it says, too."

Hosea took off his glasses. "I'd hate to read a letter from New York twice!" He chuckled at his daughter. Whenever letters arrived, the family would often read them three or four times in one day. With letters costing twenty-five cents to send, communication from loved ones remained scarce. Each letter contained news from far-off states. Settlers never knew when another letter would arrive, and the paper would grow thin from being handled so much.

Jillian jumped up from the table and called to Etta from the door. As she did, Hosea couldn't help but read at least the first paragraph to himself.

Etta soon came in, putting more fresh and muddy footprints on Sally Mae's floor. Hosea glanced over at his wife for a reaction, but all he saw was a grandmother enjoying cuddles from the now droopy-eyed boy on her lap.

"Okay. We're all here now. Right?"

No one answered aloud, but everyone nodded.

"Dear Hosea—"

Sally Mae interrupted him. "Talk loud, Hosea. So we can all hear."

"Tarnation! Can I just read the letter?"

Sally Mae tucked her face behind her grandson's head. "Yes. Forgive me."

"Dear Hosea. I hope this finds you all well there in the Michigan Territory. I was very pleased to receive your letter the winter before last." Hosea sat back in his chair. "By golly! When did we send him that letter, Sally Mae?"

"I think it was before Richard was born."

Etta spoke up. "I think I helped you write it, didn't I Pa? I'm fairly sure it was around the time that Billie arrived. When he arrived sick."

Pa spread the letter onto the table. Perhaps it would also help his eyes adjust to see better. "I believe so, Etta."

"Just keep reading, Hosea." Sally Mae adjusted Richard so she could pat the toddler's back.

"I need to apologize for not writing back sooner. I've been very busy here as the dear Lord hasn't seen fit to heal the nation yet." Hosea laughed right out loud. "Sounds just like Nicholas."

"Keep reading, Pa." Jillian patted his hand.

"I've given your invitation to travel to the Michigan Territory significant consideration. My practice here is established, and people trust me. That's very

important for a doctor, yet I understand the need for medicinal care for those settling in a new territory."

"If only he knew how badly he's needed here." Sally Mae continued rocking.

"I hesitated to write you back until I gave the matter considerable thought and when I felt I had a specific answer to give to you. With that thought, I believe we'll make the journey soon." Hosea hollered right out loud. "Praise God!" He was so loud that baby Richard's eyes popped open. Sally patted his back, whispering to him to place his head back on her shoulder.

It was now Hosea who whispered apologies.

"It's not your fault. I told you to speak up." Sally Mae winked at him.

"We plan to leave this coming fall and may arrive shortly before harvest season. I'd like to get your advice on the best means of travel to your location, but I'm afraid we'll be leaving New York before a letter would have the chance to get back to me.

"You've made the trip into the territory. Perhaps you could write to us and advise the best way. I'd also appreciate you finding a place where we could stay until we could get a cabin erected. I will come with my wife Sallie and children. We have three daughters and four boys now. Our oldest daughter, Elizabeth, is twenty-two, followed by our twins Moses and Joseph, John Nelson, who is sixteen, and Hannah at age eleven. Our youngest daughter, Adaline, is six, followed by Nicholas who is just a year old."

"Hosea? Did that say "Sallie his wife?" What do you think happened to Margaret? And last we heard from Nicholas, he didn't have so many sons."

"I don't know, Sally Mae. Let me keep reading." Hosea turned the letter over. *"We thank you for the invitation to come to the country and the confidence to move to an unknown territory. I pray our journey will be quick and efficient as I'm eager to start up a practice there and join you in becoming a founding settler in your new village. Until we meet again, your friend, Dr. Nicholas P. Harder."*

"I vaguely remember the Harder family, Pa." Etta stood to wipe off her hands on a damp rag hanging off the table to dry.

Hosea took off his glasses, refolding the letter. "You were pretty little when we left New York, Etta. The Harders are a respectable family. You'll enjoy getting to know them again, I'm sure."

"I don't understand his letter. Do you think Margaret has passed?" Sally Mae seemed disturbed by the different name of the doctor's current wife.

"I'm sure we'll understand it once Nicholas arrives. I hope nothing has happened to Margaret."

Richard wiggled from Sally Mae's shoulder to her lap. "Oh, to have a doctor again. One we can trust and be assured is good." Sally Mae kissed the top of Richard's head. "Especially with our grandbabies needing one from time to time."

"It will be good. Blessed be the name of the Lord for providing for our every need. Let's pray they arrive soon and that we'll be able to find them a place to live and set up Nicholas's office."

"I've heard that John Swain wants to sell his little cabin. Didn't he say he wanted to head north of here after Abigail passed away?" Billie chimed in.

"That shack!" Etta shook her head. "I wouldn't let an oxen team use that place as a stable, let alone the new doctor coming to town."

"I wonder if Nicholas could have been a help to Abigail. She never quite got over the ague she had last winter. It is hard to see John now struggling to know what to do and where to live." Hosea felt awful that the first grave on the hill of his property had to be a relative of Betsey and Aaron.

"I still wonder why he brought that woman into the territory in the first place," Sally Mae fussed. "She wasn't comfortable here. Not for a minute."

"It's not our place to judge, Sally Mae." Hosea scolded his wife. But he also knew how hard it had been to deal with John's wife, Abigail. Her gossip about their family had been hurtful, particularly unkind. "She was just a troubled woman."

"Troubled? That woman was an enemy to everyone she met, Hosea. I'm sorry the illness took her life. She was young and could have improved herself. My heart hurts for John. Despite her attitude and personality, he loved his wife. He now seems so alone and lost. I've been praying he finds peace. Perhaps now, senseless deaths like Abigail's can be avoided."

The family murmured in agreement.

"Is John wanting to move north, Billie?" Sally Mae's rocking had taken on a faster rhythm at the mention of Abigail Swain.

"Yes, ma'am. I'm pretty sure. He's been asking Ambrose if he knows of anyone who would be interested in the cabin. I know it's not a very nice place, but we could get some settlers together to fix it up. Especially if they know a doctor is coming to town."

Hosea loved the thought of having a doctor close; he also grew excited at the prospect of seeing his long-time friend again after so many years. As he placed the letter on the mantle, he wondered about Nicholas and his wife Margaret. What had happened since he'd seen him last?

CHAPTER FOUR

Caroline placed another wet garment over the rope Horace had purchased for her on his last trip into Pontiac. Whenever she hung a freshly washed garment over the clothesline, it reminded her of Horace and his attempt at helping her to dry clothes after they'd first met. He'd gotten a severe case of poison oak the summer after using its vine to string up for her. She slipped a pair of his overalls over the line, giggling to herself at the memory.

It had been almost a year and a half since she'd married Horace. They'd had their share of troubles, but Caroline felt blessed to have a loving man to fall asleep beside each night. Horace didn't snore like Pa but breathed a soft whistle of sound while he slept. It would often soothe her to sleep instead of disrupting her night. Being a wife brought her joy. Being Horace's wife gave her life purpose and contentment. The only thing missing from their life was a child.

It hadn't taken Betsey long to conceive, and Caroline questioned her regarding any reasons she might know that would be preventing Caroline from the same experience.

Betsey would shake her head, "I don't know, Caroline. Look at me now." Betsey had her hands full with two young ones under the age of three. Julia would soon celebrate her third birthday in

October and Richard would turn two in December. Caroline's greatest desire was to make Horace a papa, but God hadn't seen fit to bless her yet.

Ma would scold her if she knew the impatience brewing in her heart. "All things work together for good," Pa would add. She knew without a doubt they were right, but it didn't take away from the monthly disappointment she endured. Thinking of waiting nine long months after conceiving made her heart even more anxious. It was all she could think about.

A new family had moved in next door. They were living in their wagon until they could erect a home close to Horace and Caroline's house. Three children were a part of the family, and they visited Caroline almost every afternoon to see if she'd baked anything fresh that day. Caroline didn't mind sharing what they had, and she adored the small ones and their daily requests. It comforted her, despite the hole in her heart left from not having children of her own.

She watched the three children as their mother washed a child in a large, galvanized tub beside the mounting timber walls being erected right beside them. They'd have a home before winter set in, but Caroline would miss watching the mother take care of her children in such a non-private way. Before she picked up her basket to head back inside, she waved. The only one to see her was the youngest, who waved back. The others caught sight of her and began jumping up and down, the water sloshing from the buckets they were carrying to help rinse off the child in the tub. Caroline thought it odd their baths were happening during the middle of the day. Most children got so dirty playing outside, baths were left for later.

As each child turned to wave, the mother scolded them for spilling water they'd probably had to retrieve from the river. She smiled at Caroline, but her expression seemed more frustrated than usual.

Walking back toward the house, Caroline desired nothing more than to rest until it was time to start supper, but she knew there were a few more of Horace's overalls to wash before it would be too late to hang them outside to dry. The day was warm, and a slight breeze blew. She needed to take advantage of this day to do as much washing as she could. They needed rain desperately; she needed to take advantage of the warm day to dry her laundry.

It was just a few more days before Caroline would turn nineteen. It would inevitably be only another day in the week, another day to hoe the garden, another day to sweep her constantly dirty floor, and unless her family remembered, no one would know she had turned older. Glancing around the cabin, Caroline felt gratified to know she was at least a wife. Etta pined away for an eligible man to come into the territory and find her. As much as Caroline longed for a child, Etta longed for someone to love.

As Caroline took a rag to wipe crumbs off the kitchen table from lunch, she thought of Billie and Jillian. There was a definite attraction there. Everyone could see it, but with Jillian so young—it would be a few years before Billie could ask for her hand.

Caroline placed another pair of overalls and one of her skirts into the copper kettle filled with hot water on the bar hanging parallel to her fireplace. After using a metal rod to push the clothes deeper into the water, she swung the bar back over the fire. It was warm inside to be doing this, but lately, the mosquitoes were such a torment that doing it outside brought red itchy welts down Caroline's arms. At least today's breeze gave a little relief from the critters.

A soft knock on the door caused Caroline to stir from her thoughts. Wiping her hands on her apron, she went to the door, knowing pretty much who would be there to greet her.

"Hey, Miz Knapp!" The spry oldest boy of the family next door greeted her with a toothless grin. "Ma was wonderin' if you'd be willing to come over for a while?"

Caroline looked back at the fire, now helping to clean the kettle's contents, and knew she could leave it for a few minutes. "Sure, Samuel. Tell her I'll be right along."

The child scooted away. "Thank ya!"

This family had ventured into the territory from Ohio. They had a distinct twang to their dialect, and Caroline loved to hear the children talk. The Bakers had once housed a family from Virginia in their home while back in Pennsylvania. The family talked like her new neighbors, with the same type of accent.

Caroline brushed back her hair with her damp hands and hoped she looked appropriate to go next door. She wasn't sure why it mattered, but Ma had taught her to always dress her best when calling on neighbors. Venturing outside, the cool breeze refreshed her face as she went next door. She tapped lightly on the outside of the wagon.

"Come in, Caroline!" A voice spoke from inside.

A flap of canvas opened at the back of the wagon and Caroline stepped up onto the wooden ledge, made as a step to get up into the home on wheels.

It took a while for Caroline's eyes to adjust to the darkness inside the covered wagon. She didn't dare step forward, knowing she might place a foot on something valuable. Once she could see figures, she held up her hand. "Hello."

"Caroline. Thank you for coming." Samuel's mother, Sarah, stood above a child that now Caroline could make out as the two-year-old child of the family. They called the child Belle. Caroline loved the name.

"What seems to be the problem?" Caroline could easily see the child was suffering the ill effects of something. Her body shivered despite the warm wagon. Sarah had wrapped the child up tightly in a blanket and was wiping off the droplets of water still in her hair from her bath.

"She seems to be burnin' up. She can't stop shiverin'. It's a fever. Like I've never seen before."

Caroline had seen this before. It had attacked every single member of her family at least two or three times since their arrival. Now she knew why the woman had been bathing the child in the middle of the day. "It's probably ague."

"Ague?" Sarah looked back at Caroline, fear etched on her face.

"We've all had it. We think it comes from the river water, but no one is certain."

"How bad does it get?" As soon as the words left her mouth, Sarah motioned for the two other children to leave the wagon. Samuel carried out his little brother.

Caroline bent down to feel Belle's forehead. "She's very warm."

"How long does it last? Is it bad?" Sarah shot off questions to Caroline. Caroline offered her best suggestions.

"It seems to not affect the children as bad as an older person. Can last days or weeks. It all depends on the health of each individual."

"What do I do for her?"

"Keep her cool as best as you can. She'll stop eating and become delirious. They're normal symptoms."

"She's awful small. She hasn't been eating at all well the past few days. Hate to see her hurtin' so. I wish our cabin was finished. We have to be cooped up in this hot wagon all day."

Caroline knew she should probably ask Horace first, but knew this mother needed some assurance that her child would be well soon. "Sarah, bring her to our house. We'll make a bed up for her in the corner. You can come in and out anytime, and I'll keep an eye on her, too."

Sarah pulled Caroline into a hug, "I thank ya. Truly, I do."

"I'll head home and get the corner swept up and ready for you. I have a small mat we can use until we can make her a proper bed. Bring some blankets you have. Might be best if the other children stay away for a time. I don't think it's contagious, but I don't know for sure."

Sarah nodded. Even in the dim wagon, Caroline could see tears rolling down her face.

"It will be okay. She's a strong, healthy little girl, Sarah." The disease seemed to take the stamina out of so many. Caroline prayed for confidence in assuring her friend that all things would be well, but in reality, it was all up to God's providence. For everyone.

"Where is this place you're talkin' about?" Frank Sergeant spit near the fire. The tobacco juice hit a hot ember and sizzled upon impact.

"North of Knagg's Place. Do you remember Peter Whitmore Knaggs?" James Ball didn't quite know how to point out to his friend exactly where Hosea Baker lived. The place didn't have an official name yet.

"I remember the name Knagg's. Just can't pinpoint exactly where 'tis."

"It's a few miles north of here. Places around that area are bustin' open almost as fast as John McGraw can draw a pistol."

James leaned back against a nearby tree. The two men had set up camp just outside of Pontiac and were heading north to meet with a man named Hosea Baker to talk about the specifics of a mill he was planning to build. They'd been hired to help him. James had helped put up a mill closer to Pontiac. He had some expertise regarding the building process but was always eager to learn more.

Frank, one of his neighbors, had wanted to travel with him. Frank had been pining to build a mill near Oakland County and wanted to be on hand to watch Ball at work, especially to see how it could be done with minimal workers. Riverbanks along the Shiawassee were steep. To complete it successfully, they'd have to be sure to have the timber ready and also enough men. James was curious to see how Baker would make it work.

"So how much is this Baker fellow paying you?"

James shook his head. "That's my business. I was just asked if I could find a few men to help. We'll meet up with others once we make it closer to the new Genesee County line. That's what they've been calling that area this past year."

"I'm hopin' this is a helpful incentive for me to tag along. Putting up a mill is a mighty daring venture. Is this Baker fellow up to such an endeavor?"

Shrugging, James stirred the fire. It came to life as flames licked through a large section of wood. "I've heard he's ambitious. One of the first settlers to head into Indian territory. He's farming the land, and they need a mill. From what I hear, the man only has a houseful of women with him."

James's eyes grew wide. "Women?"

"Young daughters!"

Frank guffawed and spit again. "Figures."

"Few settlers past Pontiac, but it must be filling up fast cause this Baker fellow is getting a head start on supplyin' all with lumber needed for new homes. Seems a smart, capitalizing feat to me."

Frank folded his arms. "I'll give that to him."

"I'm just skeptical of the entire ordeal. The logs needed to build these mills are heavy. Takes lots of men to lift them into place, especially up steep banks."

James knew the dangers. He'd watched men do it all along the riverbanks in the unfamiliar territory. "I know, but how else is there to do it?"

Frank shook his head. "Not a clue. Be interestin' to see it happen. Also, my nephew, Stephen will be meeting us there. He lives just south of Knagg's Place."

Rhoda had no clue why she hadn't thought of it sooner, but for the next few days on their way to Pontiac, she and the children got out of the wagon and walked behind it. The exercise and the views were much better than sitting in a wooden wagon being tossed about like a boat in a stormy sea. The children pranced, danced, and even skipped in excitement at finally getting closer to the Uncle Hosea that she had been talking about for weeks.

"Who are our cousins, again?" Rhoda Ann looked up in anticipation with her familiar bright smile lighting up her face.

Rhoda couldn't remember the last time she'd seen her seven-year-old grin. Before she could answer, Philinda answered for her, counting off cousins on her fingers.

"There's Betsey, who is now married."

"Who's her husband?" Martha stopped skipping long enough to listen intently.

Philinda shrugged. "Momma, do you know?"

"His name is Aaron. Aaron Swain. We haven't met him yet. Betsey got married in Pennsylvania after Uncle Hosea arrived there."

"They didn't always live in Pennsylvania?" Martha scratched at a welt on her neck. The mosquitoes had been tormenting them all along the way.

"Yes, Momma, why did Uncle Hosea and Aunt Sally leave New York?"

That was a long, in-depth story, and it wasn't something Rhoda wanted to talk about, especially to her children. She knew she needed to answer her children's questions, for if she didn't, they'd certainly embarrass her when they arrived at her brother's home. Rhoda sighed.

"Did they do something bad?" Philinda looked up at her with pleading eyes.

She was much too young to remember the scandal. How the church had humiliated her brother. How the only way to make peace with the situation was for Hosea and his family to leave New York. For good. But if that wasn't bad enough, the circulating rumors from those whom she believed were friends, fellow brethren, and even family members had also changed Rhoda's heart. In ways she never thought possible.

"Momma, you're making a frown!"

She'd never been able to keep her face from showing emotion. If Sidney didn't catch on that something was wrong, her children did.

Rhoda forced a smile. "It's okay, love. It's up to us now to make things work. Your momma will get us through." She picked up the small hand of her daughter. "And Daddy, too."

It had been one thing to change her own beliefs, but reprogramming her children had been quite the task. She was determined to give them personal strength. Perhaps, for now, her example would be how she'd venture into a place on her own. Coming to the wilderness in the Michigan Territory had been her idea. And she didn't need a god to help her do it. Quite the contrary, her family needed only one thing—each other.

CHAPTER FIVE

"Men will arrive from all around to help with my mill." Hosea scratched his head as he peered down the steep riverbank just south of the homestead. "I can't see it taking long once we have all the lumber ready and piled to put into place."

James, a man Hosea had hired to help build the mill, glanced down the slope. "It's a steep incline to the river."

Looking over at all the logs Hosea Baker had stacked up beside the shore, Frank wondered if it would be enough.

"This mill will be the first in these parts. I'm aiming to have it up and running before the others. Cut lumber is a need now. More and more new settlers comin' every day. This venture will secure my family for a generation or two by having another means of income besides crops."

"We've got men coming from nearly twenty miles away. Is there a place where they can stay until the work is finished? It's mighty primitive country up here."

Frank knew James needed to ask those questions. He was right. Without a hotel close by, where would the men stay? Also, who would feed them? His nephew, Stephen, had stayed behind to gather a few more men. They would arrive soon.

"Gotta get all those details worked out. I'm working on finding a suitable place for the men to sleep. I figure if everyone brings his pack to sleep, we'll have plenty of room. My wife, Sally Mae, will figure out the food provisions with the help of my daughters." Hosea placed his hat back on. "I appreciate the help. I'll give everyone ninety cents a day to help plus, of course, room and board. Hopefully, it should take just a day to finish the work."

"A long day!" James got out his ciphering paper and, with a pencil, scratched a few notes on it. "I'll let the men know about your accommodations. I think ninety cents a day is reasonable, Hosea." Reaching out his hand, he and Hosea shook on the deal.

"We've only done one mill in the southern portion of the territory, and none are on a bank as steep as this one. We'll need to inform the others of the dangers."

James looked back at his companion and nodded, stuffing the paper into his front pocket again. "I agree, but it is doable."

"Much obliged for your help, gentlemen. Cut lumber will be appreciated here in these parts."

As the men walked back up the bank of the river, Frank inquired of Hosea more. "Where will you get the blades for your mill? The men can bring them if it would help."

"Yes, bring the needed resources with you. Do you need money upfront to pay for them?" Hosea patted his front pant's pocket.

"No. You can pay me once we arrive to start work. I'd feel better not to have to cart your money with me through the woods to get home and back."

James tipped his hat. "Thanks for doing this for us. We both live close enough that we might be regular customers to use your mill just as much as the other settlers around these here parts."

"I hope my mill can be of service to many. Thanks for all your help." Hosea saluted the men.

"How many men?" Sally wiped off her forehead. A slight breeze of the August afternoon wasn't giving any kind of relief from the scorching heat of the day.

"Not exactly sure, Sally Mae. Could be ten, maybe twenty." Hosea had been sitting to chat with Sally about his conversation with the men in charge of helping him build the mill.

"Twenty?" Sally took a deep breath.

Hosea chimed right up. "Could be less. Probably not more than. Is the garden produce up to filling up a few hungry men's bellies for a day or two?"

Sally glanced over at the turnips now piled up to be stored. They'd gotten quite a few ears of corn in the last day or two. "I reckon we can manage. They might not leave full, but we should have enough to feed them for a day."

Hosea went for their money jar hidden in a barrel in their bedroom. As he came toward her, he held it up to show the coins. "I think I've saved enough from wolf pelts to pay the men. Let's get to counting gold pieces to see if we'll have enough for at least one day of work. I figure if we don't have enough, I'll offer them free cut lumber for a first visit to the mill. But soon, this mill should produce some good profit."

"Oh Hosea, I hope so. That's all the money we have in that jar of yours." Sally checked the boiling water she'd been heating at the fireplace. She hadn't seen Hosea this excited about anything after the Indians had taken Alexander back to live with them. His excitement gave her more determination to help him on this project.

"We have plenty of berries to make a few cobblers. Aaron just recently brought me a sack of flour. I can also do well with the eggs the chickens are laying. Do you think you could find a turkey or two? That would give us plenty of meat."

"That's the thinkin' woman! We can do this." Hosea poured out the coins on the table and began counting them. "I'll need at least twenty or thirty dollars to pay the men. I can use the winter's wolf pelt money, but I don't know how much is left after paying for seeds. I'm going to also need a bit for the saw blades." Hosea finished counting. "We'll have just enough. That mill will provide cut lumber soon after it's built." He sat back in his chair and stared at the money now piled in rows on the table.

"We've done well here, Hosea. Those pesky wolves aren't nearly as big a menace as we thought. They're actually helping us make our way here. I hate to go into winter without anything extra in our jar, though." Sally sat and fingered the coins.

"It's a risk we'll just have to take. I'll line up workers to help with the sawing, so as soon as the mill is ready, we'll be cutting timber." Hosea took her hand. "And that Sally Mae, will never run out in these parts."

"What's that?"

"Trees!"

Ambrose and his brother-in-law Horace had been working non-stop on the essentials needed to get Hosea's mill up and running. They would soon head to the river to begin the operation of creating a sluiceway for water to maneuver down to power the flutter wheel. The wheel would have the water flow over it, conducting enough power to work the vertical saw in the mill.

"We need to get busy and work on an arm to attach to the saw." Ambrose looked over at Horace. He seemed to not be able to get enough to drink for the day.

"I have a good board over here that might do the trick." Horace pointed to an extra-long board leaning against a wall of Ambrose's house.

"We'll need eight pieces of wood to make up the carriage. Let's use oak. It's the strongest we have."

"I believe this one is a piece of oak. Came from that large tree we cut down a while back for the mantle for my house." Horace placed his cup of water on the porch near him.

"Pa wants it all to be ready to insert into the mill as soon as the workmen have it finished." Ambrose put up a board to compare the strength of it to the piece that Horace had just shown him.

Horace sat for a moment to gulp down more water.

"You okay? Seems like you're as parched as a desert today."

"I don't know. Can't seem to get enough to drink." Horace took another swallow.

"It's warm. Let's take a break."

Lately, Ambrose had been noticing Horace dragging through each day. A tired, weary, old man seemed to have replaced his usual energetic brother-in-law. He'd welcomed breaks for the past two weeks.

"Do you think this idea of your pa's will work? I mean, I give Hosea credit for his ambition. He seems determined this will be a good venture for the community, but it's a risk."

Ambrose laughed. "My pa never takes an idea and sits on it for long. He's ambitious, and sometimes fool-hardy as well. But I guess, if all of us had ideas and never acted on them, where would we be?"

"You'd be back in Pennsylvania!" Horace laughed right out loud. "And I...wouldn't have the pleasure of being your beautiful sister's husband."

Ambrose took a long swig of water and wiped his mouth, "I wouldn't know about that," embarrassed to have a man talk about his sister in that way.

"Can we finish making this carriage today?"

Ambrose looked over at the lumber. "If we get the pieces cut today, we'll be lucky. We'll concentrate on putting it together tomorrow."

Horace nodded and placed two pieces of lumber about two feet apart on the grass. "I think these two sections will be strong enough to be the vertical sticks on each side of the saw. What do you think?"

Ambrose agreed with a nod.

Both men sat in silence, Ambrose contemplating their next move.

"Hey, Ambrose!"

"Yeah."

"Once we have all this finished, what do you want to do in the village?"

Ambrose had been thinking long and hard on this very thing. He'd been saving everything he made for some kind of venture. He was Hosea's son. "I've been thinking. I don't think I want to work at Pa's mill. I think maybe you or perhaps Billie would like to be a part of it, but I've been contemplating on starting up a store."

"A store?"

"General store. Once we get more people here, they're going to grow tired of heading to Pontiac for supplies."

"I agree."

"Maybe build furniture, too."

Horace smiled. "That's been a thought I've had as well. I was thinking, if Hosea allows, I'll work for a while at the mill, and then when more people get settled here, they'll need tables, chairs, bedsteads..."

"That makes sense." Something caught Ambrose's eye as he saw a figure come out of the forest near his home. "Well, here comes the boss. We better get back to work."

Both men laughed as Hosea walked toward them with a huge grin.

"I didn't hire you boys to sit on your hands all afternoon. Get that carriage made for the week after next. We're gonna have a mill raising party!" Hosea clapped over his head.

Ambrose just laughed. His pa knew good and well they were just taking a brief break. "You know, Pa, most carpenters are getting paid seventy-five cents an hour now. I haven't see'd hide nor hair of any of that money, have you, Horace?"

Horace stood to hold up the piece of lumber they were considering as part of the carriage, but he had a grin on his face to accompany Ambrose's remark.

"Don't be shy, Horace! Tell Pa that he's getting nothin' but cheap labor for this here project of his."

Again, Horace just grinned.

Hosea slapped his son-in-law on the shoulder. "He knows good and well not to be rude to the boss of this here project."

Ambrose could do nothing but shake his head. He hadn't seen his pa this happy in a long while.

CHAPTER SIX

Knowing only a tarp stretched over a flimsy wooden frame stood between Rhoda's family and the howling wolves outside caused Rhoda a queasy stomach. Tonight, the prowling creatures seemed closer than they'd been in nights past. As Rhoda tried to calm her legs from shaking, she heard a rustle at the far end of the wagon.

The flap lifted as Augustus stuck his head in. "Ma'am, those howls are getting way too close. I'm gonna sit here at the end of the wagon, if you don't mind."

Rhoda felt her modesty leave as the pudgy man positioned himself at the end of the wagon. Despite her shyness, it made her feel safe having him inside with the rest of her family. He'd been sleeping underneath the wagon since they'd left Detroit, but Rhoda didn't blame him for seeking higher ground on this night.

"Is this normal?" Rhoda reached for a blanket near her feet and threw it toward the man, who was keeping an eye out the back but also shimmying for a place to settle and to lay his head. Perhaps the blanket would do the trick. Rhoda called out to Philinda to snuggle closer to her sisters. The wagon was stifling from the warm August night.

"Might be best if we leave this flap down tonight. It's normal to have wolves out and about, but tonight they seem to want to be circling the wagon closer than usual." Augustus lifted the flap a little with the tip of his rifle. "Not had them roaming so close before. Maybe they can smell our dinner from tonight."

Rhoda didn't know what to say. Having a stranger so close didn't help her anxiety. She took a deep breath and tried hard to get comfortable despite the lack of air circulation in the makeshift shelter. Thankfully, the younger children stayed asleep when a howl made even Augustus jump.

"I believe—" Augustus whispered as he pointed the end of his rifle through a small hole in the canvas "—they're right close."

What was he going to do? Before Rhoda could think of potential scenarios, Augustus's gun went off.

The children woke with a start. Giles rubbed his eyes to see as each girl let out a squeal or scream. It was all Rhoda could do to keep herself from crying out. Four pairs of eyes stared at Augustus as he reloaded quickly.

Philinda crept closer to Rhoda. "Momma—?" Before she could finish her sentence, Augustus's gun went off again.

A yelp erupted loud and clear from just outside the wagon.

"I think I got 'em!" Augustus again reloaded and pushed the loaded gun barrel outside the hole.

The younger two girls were now crying, Philinda and Giles were covering their ears, and all were clawing toward Rhoda. Soon her arms were full of upset children.

Augustus held his finger to his mouth and whispered, "Try to keep the youngsters quiet."

How would Rhoda achieve such a task? She had four children, all crying and clamoring for comfort, all at once. Again, another shot filled the wagon. The smell of gunpowder reached Rhoda's nostrils. Giles sneezed after he hiccupped a whimper.

Augustus got onto his knees and loaded his gun again. As he did, the howls grew more distant. It appeared that Augustus had scared them off.

"Are they gone?" Despite the children clinging to her, their arms brought her comfort, too.

The man sat back, leaning against the side of the wagon. "I believe so. Never had 'em come so close before."

"Those logs over there—pull them closer!" Hosea's voice grew hoarse from shouting instructions to the men helping to arrange cut logs in place to build the sawmill. The lumber pile was now high beside the river bank's edge. The only beings not suffering from exhaustion seemed to be the oxen team who snorted as if they wanted to drag more. He muttered to himself, *"Much increase is by the strength of the ox."*

Ambrose came beside Hosea, laughing. "Too bad we aren't all made like an ox. They seem to relish the idea of working harder."

"If only they went faster." Hosea spit toward the pile of logs. "I'd give a million dollars for a good team of oxen over a horse or mule any day. They are worth their weight and—" Hosea jerked one ox from munching grass instead of moving toward the felled trees surrounding the border of the sawmill property. "They require only grass to sustain them. And we got plenty of that—and trees. Almost like getting our supplies and manpower for free."

Ambrose adjusted a suspender over his shoulder. "These two have earned a bucket of grain tonight. They've always been a strong team."

Hosea patted the rumps of the team. "They sure have."

"How many more logs, Pa?" Ambrose pulled his pants up higher after adjusting the strap.

"I think we're about done. I want to get a few extra onto the pile. Just in case we need them."

Ambrose grabbed the halter of the oxen team to turn them around to haul another log. He clicked his tongue to get them to move.

Hosea dug into his pockets for something to chew on. Once they got the last two logs in place, they'd head home for supper, and tonight—his appetite was ready for one of Sally Mae's finest. He prayed she didn't disappoint. With Ambrose and a few other men joining them for supper, Hosea was sure the meal would be extra special.

Henry Leach came out of the woods, entering the property on a horse. "Hosea!" He waved as Hosea returned the gesture.

"Henry! How many workers were you able to round up?"

"Twenty. I've found twenty men willing to help."

"Fine. That's just fine. Thank you for doing that for me."

Henry gazed at the stack of logs now piled in front of Hosea. "Looks like you've been busy today. Nice job."

"Pulled 'em all here all by myself." Hosea put his hands on his hips and didn't crack a smile.

Henry slapped his leg. "You beat all, Hosea. You must have the strength of an ox!"

"Two!" The corner of Hosea's mouth twitched. "You'd never know it by just lookin' at me."

Henry chuckled. "You're right about that."

Hosea broke into a chortle. "Henry! Shame on me for lying. Hope you know the difference."

"Of course, Hosea. You don't fool me near as much as you think you do!"

"Six days thou shalt do thy work, and on the seventh day thou shalt rest; that thine ox and thine ass may rest." Hosea now grinned. "Mine are both tired." Wiping off his forehead with his hat, Hosea motioned for Ambrose to put another log alongside the last one drug into place. "These trees are mighty. They will make a perfect foundation for the sawmill and soon we'll have the ability to churn out cut lumber for everyone." Hosea crossed his arms. "I plan on building a real frame house for Sally Mae soon. We'll have a massive fireplace in the center," Hosea spread out his hands to help Henry envision his dream. "And on winter evenings, we'll sit by the warmth and cuddle our grandbabies."

Henry's approval was obvious as he nodded. "Sounds like a splendid plan, Hosea. I wish I could do the same."

Hosea turned to his long-time neighbor. They'd become good friends. "Why can't you do the same?"

Henry dismounted from his horse. "We're movin' on, Hosea. Farther west. Come spring."

"Dakotas."

Henry smiled. "No, not that far. We'll stay in Michigan, but the ague has taken its toll on Claire and the children. Close to a good doctor. A reliable school. We can't wait two or three years for it to be organized. My young'uns need one now."

"I don't blame ya. We'll have those things soon."

"I know. But Claire feels strong about having them in school now before they get too old, and we need them more on the farm than in school during the day."

Hosea turned toward his friend. "We're sure gonna miss you."

Henry patted Hosea's shoulder. "We'll miss you as well, Hosea. It's been awful good to be around your company these past two years. We couldn't have done it without you."

"We all need to work together, but I hope you know—the sentiment is mutual."

Stephen was traveling north to meet up with his Uncle Frank. The trip to Knagg's Place had been fairly smooth. Getting through the territory here could be treacherous for travelers, but the men heading to Whitmore's post were riding horses, not dragging in teams of oxen with wagons.

Stephen had just arrived that spring with his family. They were like many other settlers in the New Territory, wanting to start new communities on the land offered to citizens for just a dollar and twenty-five cents an acre.

It was easy for Stephen to fall asleep despite the hard ground for a bed. He'd tucked his knapsack under his head as a pillow and was thankful his wife had insisted he take a blanket with him. Despite the heat of the night, it kept the mosquitoes at bay as he slipped the blanket over his head. He slept well until something else disturbed his night.

It was a cloud. A cloud of dust. It twirled, twisted, and engulfed Stephen in a flurry of billowing dirt. The dust took the form of animals he'd encountered in the Michigan Territory. One animal was an ox, the other a howling wolf. The next tiny swirl erupted into a squirrel scampering around in circles. Soon the squirrel turned into a chicken and then—a beaver. Each animal seemed to grow into a bigger one with each spin of the dust. The last animal stampeded toward Stephen. He'd never seen a buffalo, but this resembled much of what he'd heard about them. Stephen jumped out of the way just before the large animal trampled him.

Stephen choked. Every time he tried to take in a deep breath, another swirl of dust caught in his throat, causing him to suffocate. He struggled to take in a deep breath. Then he grasped for any kind of breath. He coughed, and each time, he spewed out more dust to mix with the swirls of dust surrounding him. He was choking, and there seemed to be no way to catch a breath of clean air.

Looking up, he could see a blue sky. If only he could grow wings to fly above the dirt. Looking down, he observed large rocks trapping his feet to the ground. The pain was excruciating, and he cried out in agony. He needed to free himself. Keeping his eyes on the sky, he kicked to loosen his feet from the crushing boulders, but the more he struggled, the more his feet felt trapped. Was he in quicksand? It couldn't be. His feet entangled in rocks, not mud.

Suddenly, the clouds of dust dissipated, and he could see clouds covering the sun. Relaxing, he realized the more he struggled to free himself, the deeper he sunk. When he stopped twisting, the rocks stopped falling on his feet. As the dust swirls gave way to the blue sky, the dirt disappeared. In front of him were piles and piles of logs. Each placed atop the other. It formed a formidable wall.

Men he knew and had worked with were climbing the logs. His Uncle Frank among them. Magically, the wall grew higher and higher as logs floated to the top, and the men nailed them into place.

A building took shape and looked nearly finished. One worker climbed high on the logs and upon reaching the top, he turned to the crowd of men now surrounding Stephen and removed his hat to wave. Just as he did, a log beneath him broke loose.

Stephen watched in horror as the man came tumbling down the large stack of logs. It was as if the finger of God began plucking out each log as it fell, one by one. The man became battered as the stack of logs bounced around him. Stephen gasped as he saw the man lose consciousness on the ground beside him. Bleeding from his mouth, his friend's eyes were fixed. He stared up at Stephen with a white face. Stephen knelt to feel for a pulse and, upon finding none, he yelled for help.

No one was around. The men who had been working on the wall were gone. Rocks no longer covered his feet, but only the body of the dead man and logs. Soon, the ground beneath both of them saturated and started to suck them down. Stephen attempted to scream, but the mud rose. Slowly, the muck swallowed the man's body and Stephen's feet. It crept to his knees. Struggling to free himself, he soon felt fingers clawing at his waist. It was the dead man.

Stephen reached down to peel the man's grasp from his waist, which pulled him even deeper into the mire of mud and logs. As his friend's face covered in sludge, Stephen felt the mud rise to his hips. He was sinking deep and fast. The only thing he could do was holler for help, but his mouth felt like a desert. His tongue stuck to the roof of his mouth. Unable to make a sound, the mud now encircled his belly. As it reached his shoulders, Stephen extended his hands above his head. The mud touched his chin.

When he could taste the mud on his lips, Stephen gave one last gasp. It covered his nose, and before it could penetrate his eyes, Stephen closed them.

A shriek pierced the air as Stephen sat up. His blanket, which must have been covering his face, fell to his side. Beads of sweat trickled down his cheeks. Stephen wiped his eyes with his sleeve.

"Who was that?"

"Who's screaming?"

Stephen opened his mouth to take in a deep breath. "Oh my!" The night air filled his lungs. He realized he'd been having a nightmare.

The man closest to him shook off his covering and crawled closer to Stephen. "Hey! You okay?"

Stephen attempted to slow his labored breathing. He uttered a few expletives and even took the Lord's name in vain. It had been one of the most vivid dreams he'd ever encountered.

The man who'd crawled to him patted him on the shoulder. "You must have had a bad one. You okay now?"

Stephen glanced at the man. "I think so." Stephen felt embarrassed around the other men now gazing at him with glassy eyes.

The man crawled back to his bed and covered himself. "I'd take heed of a dream like that. They often say the worse they are, the more they actually come true."

When his breathing returned to normal, Stephen lay back down on his bed and relaxed to control his shaky legs. He wiped his forehead with his blanket and reached for his canteen to cool his cottony mouth. His throat burned from the chili they'd fixed for supper. The cool water brought relief. It was a dream. Just a dream. But the thought of drowning in quicksand made him shiver despite the warmth of the August evening. Perhaps it was a warning or maybe a mere implication to lay off the strong whiskey before bed.

CHAPTER SEVEN

Stephen and the men he'd been traveling with met up with his Uncle Frank and the man who had hired them for the job, James Ball. They headed north from the designated meeting place.

"That's silly, Sergeant! Why would a dream make you so skittish?" James Ball reacted to the man telling him about his dream from the night before. "Sounds like the kind of dreams my children have from time to time. I'll tell you what I tell them—it's just your imagination playing tricks!"

"Sir, I don't mean to sound superstitious." Stephen reined in his horse, as all the animal seemed to want to do that day was gallop off their intended trail. "I dream. Quite often, actually. But this dream..."

"He woke with quite a scream." The man who'd awakened to Stephen's scream the night before added to the conversation. Several of the other men who'd spent the night with Stephen snickered about the incident.

"I am sorry I woke the rest of you with my hollerin'." Stephen felt embarrassed by his nightmare reaction. Sleep was hard to get while on the trail. As if the howling of the wolves and the incessant mosquitoes buzzing in ears weren't enough, even the normal wilderness nighttime sounds were loud enough to keep even the soundest sleeper awake.

"I'm sure it's nothing," announced James. "I've hired you to help build a sawmill. You'll be getting a good wage, some delicious meals, and a place to lay your head tomorrow night. But if any of you feel this dream that Sergeant had would deter you from giving me a full day's work, you better tell me now."

It was all Stephen could do to hold his tongue. The dream had scared him, that was for sure, but as with the other men, he needed the money to survive the coming cold. His family had arrived too late in the season to plant a crop to feed them through the winter. His family's livelihood depended on the money he'd earn helping build this man's sawmill.

The other ten or so men echoed their continued support and their commitments to help.

"Well, then, let's get a move on. The sun will set faster than the miles we'll have to put in to arrive at our destination." James clicked to his horse and snapped the horse's reins to continue down the Indian trail that would lead to the trading post of Whitmore Knaggs.

"We're about a day out," Augustus told Rhoda as the wagon moved through the thickest forest they'd seen since leaving Pontiac a few days before.

"Only one more day!" Philinda shouted to the children, who followed behind the wagon as it meandered and wound down another slope on the trail. The children all cheered their excitement.

Rhoda smiled back at them from her seat at the foot of the wagon. She'd walked as far as she could that morning and now just wanted to sit to regain enough strength to disembark and walk some more. The cheers from the children brought joy to her heart. The thought of being close to Hosea and Sally's home made her also sigh with relief. If only she were sure there'd be enough money to pay Augustus once she got there. She'd die of embarrassment if she had to ask Hosea for additional money to pay off the faithful driver.

She'd convinced Augustus to take them past Pontiac and beyond to Hosea's house with some bribing. While in Pontiac, she hated to think of having to hire another stranger to take them farther interior, so she'd told Augustus that a good meal and a fine place to stay would be at the end of their trail. She'd also given him nearly all the money she had left from their trip here. She was worried that if it took everything she had, what would they live off of until her husband, Sidney, could meet up with them? She was chagrined to think of living off Hosea and Sally for the next few months. She wouldn't do that to her brother.

"Momma, tell us again about Uncle Hosea," Martha asked as she picked a bunch of wildflowers from the side of the trail and handed them to her.

Rhoda put the tiny nosegay of blue and yellow flowers to her nose. They didn't have much of a smell, but they did make her nose tingle into a full-blown sneeze. Her children all laughed. She smiled back at them. What a joy her children were to her. She couldn't wait for Hosea to see how much they'd grown while they'd been apart from each other.

"Will he be happy to see us?" Rhoda Ann stopped her, skipping long enough for Rhoda to pick the child up and set her directly beside her on the wagon's edge.

Rhoda smoothed down the hair of her namesake. Shoots of errant hair poked out of her braids. Rhoda couldn't wait to give the children baths. It had been weeks since they'd left Detroit and the hotel there. She wished she could make them more presentable for their initial visit to their uncle. "He will indeed be thrilled and excited to see you. Don't you remember him when we visited his family in Pennsylvania?"

Rhoda Ann twirled her braid around a finger. "Not really. I remember playing with Jillian. She taught me how to play hopscotch."

"I remember that!" Martha hollered.

"Your Uncle Hosea loves you very much. He always enjoyed coming to our farm if only to see you. Don't you remember how he took you out into the woods and taught you the names of all the trees?"

Philinda and Martha nodded.

"He would snip a leaf off the tree and show us the shape and how beautiful God—" Philinda paused and looked at Rhoda in fright.

Rhoda felt her forehead scrunch, but she didn't scold her daughter for her slip. "It's okay. What else did he say about the leaves?" She wouldn't squelch her child's memory of her brother.

"It was fall, and we lined the leaves all up in color order. A cornstalk green, blood red, pumpkin orange—"

"He always loved to describe the colors with an object." Rhoda smiled. "Why don't you children find me an oak leaf and bring it to me?"

Like ants seeking food, Rhoda's girls took off in opposite directions, Giles close at their heels. Rhoda Ann took a flying leap off the back end of the moving wagon and began chasing the others as they searched for an oak leaf in the woods.

Soon, Martha produced a large one and held it up for Rhoda to pluck it from her outstretched fingers. The leaf was full and bright green. Rhoda then told the children to find a maple leaf, and again the children whirled in different directions to find a maple tree, which seemed more challenging than an oak leaf. A bump in the road bounced Rhoda on the back of the wagon. She rubbed her behind. There would be no missing this trip, nor the seats on the wagon made of unyielding wood.

Before long, the children lined up all their collected leaves along the edge of the wagon. They admired the veins in each one and how broad and whole the leaves appeared. Rhoda was sure it would please Hosea to know they remembered what he'd taught them just a few years before. After the gathering of the leaves, all the children scrambled onto the back of the wagon to take a break from their afternoon activity.

"What else can you tell us about Uncle Hosea?" Martha's curiosity always made Rhoda pause. She asked questions like a two-year-old.

Rhoda smiled. "I love my brother. He's a good man. As you remember, he loves trees and little girls."

"Not boys?" Giles looked up at her with his piercing blue eyes.

Rhoda rubbed the top of his head, causing his hair to stick up in places. "As well as little boys." She thought long and hard about what she could tell her children about her brother. Rhoda and Hosea had been inseparable as children, despite a ten-year age difference. He was her big brother and would often take her out on adventures while their mother cared for their younger brother and sisters. "We had one brother, and Hosea was nineteen when he was born. Before that little brother was born, Hosea gained five sisters." Rhoda smiled. "I think that's why Hosea loves little girls so much."

"So there was Uncle Hosea, five girls, and then Uncle—" Philinda stopped short at the name of Rhoda's youngest brother.

"Benjamin." Rhoda filled in.

The children clapped their hands together as they remembered all the family, but especially their Uncle Ben.

"Where does Aunt Sarah come in the line?" Martha asked as she gathered up their collected leaves and began going through them one by one.

"She's number four." The children knew their Uncle Ben and Aunt Sarah well, for they both lived in New York.

The children chatted about how they would miss playing with their cousins, but they were eager to get to meet their other cousins, the daughters of Uncle Hosea.

Rhoda couldn't help but wonder what Hosea would think once they arrived. She hadn't seen him in a few years and Rhoda hadn't had time before she and the children left, to warn him they would be arriving. She hoped Hosea's family would have accommodations for them, because if they were going to have to pay for a hotel or a place to stay when they arrived, Rhoda wasn't sure she'd have enough money left to do it.

Sally rushed to bake three more loaves of bread before she cooked the meat for the men's meal the next day. She hadn't baked these quantities since she'd been in New York. They'd had multiple church potlucks when all she did on a Saturday was bake bread.

Her thoughts drifted off to the church in New York. After traveling to Pennsylvania and then since their arrival here in the New Territory, she hadn't given that time in their life much thought. Hosea had been accused of such a heresy there; one that rocked his world, not only as a deacon in the church, but also as a man. His integrity, as a man who loved God, was put to the test. And unfortunately, many had believed the lies that spread through their church like a grassfire out of control.

Sally thought of all the people she'd once considered good friends. She'd trusted them with not only her friendship but also in caring for her young children. Many taught their children to believe in the same God whom Hosea and Sally worshipped. Often those families were a part of an impromptu prayer meeting at their home. Yet when the lie spread about Hosea, many of these same people took part in spreading the rumors. She chided herself for her trust in them.

As she added more broth to the meat now simmering over the fire, she thought about when they'd heard about the rumors filtering through the church. They held a meeting without Hosea being present. When he learned of it, he questioned everyone. Why? What were people saying? What was the accusation? No one would tell him anything, but the looks of disdain, disappointment, and disbelief led Hosea to know the accusation was serious.

Sally stirred the broth so none of the meat would scorch the bottom of the copper kettle she was using.

They left the church not knowing all the details of the scandal. Hosea felt it better to leave before the situation grew worse, despite Sally's pleas for him to stay and prove his innocence. It was as if he could see what would happen if the truth came out. The church would take sides. Probably split. Right down the middle. And Hosea knew he couldn't stop any of it. Yet despite his best intentions, the church dissolved anyway. His sister Rhoda and her husband, Sidney, were the first to leave. Following them was his younger brother, Benjamin. Those and many others left angry and upset. Many had their faith shaken.

As Sally again stirred the boiling pot, she mulled over who the perpetrator might have been. Several women in the church found that spreading rumors satisfied them. She grimaced at the thought. Why would anyone want to spread false rumors about people? As Hosea and she conversed about it, she knew it was mainly because of jealousy.

After leaving New York, Hosea had taken a job at a local hotel in Pennsylvania where he'd worked hard until he had earned enough money to travel again. That's when the family left for the New Territory. That got them far enough away from the accusers.

Far enough away that no one could point a finger or challenge the issue any further.

Sally dumped the contents of two loaf tins of fresh bread out on a towel on the table. She separated the dough for two more loaves, filling the still-warm pans so they'd rise in time to bake before nightfall.

Thinking back on the scandal in New York some more, Sally could now see some good had come out of the situation. Her husband's faith had not grown cold, but much stronger. He knew the accusations were false, and because God knew the truth, that was all that mattered to Hosea. He felt his integrity was still intact and solid if he had the chance to ask God. Because of that, it didn't matter what those left behind believed. It had been a wonderful example to Ambrose and Betsey. They knew, without a doubt, they could not only trust their father but also God, their spiritual Father. Sally's faith had grown, too. She knew who to trust and how to test people before jumping into new relationships.

She knew others hadn't come out as well. Hosea's family suffered and his sister, Rhoda, still had issues with what had happened. Sally prayed for her as she whipped up some eggs to put into a cake she was making. Perhaps someday, they too could see the truth of what happened. That God had meant it for good and not evil.

All because of jealousy. Jealousy over Hosea's close relationships with many in the church. One man prided himself on being the godliest and hated the fact Hosea's faith was stronger and more confident than his own. Sally wondered what had become of the man who needed those accolades much more than a solid church body.

And at that moment, she thought back to the promptings God had made to get them to the Michigan Territory, she smiled. They'd had their share of sorrow, sickness, and tragedy, but starting again in a new land had brought additional challenges. Tomorrow, they would add a major business to this new community. One that would allow settlers coming into the territory to have framed houses before winter could hit. The going had been rough, but they had so much to show for their few short years here. It was all good in God's eyes and in her husband's, whom she loved with her whole heart. She couldn't imagine their lives being any different. And as God had taught her to do, she prayed for the one who might have started the rumor. Whomever he or she might be.

CHAPTER EIGHT

A loud yell woke Etta out of sound sleep. She sat up straight in bed.

"Whoo-hoo!" Her pa let out another yell.

"Hosea!"

Ma scolded him. "Everyone is sleeping."

"Not anymore. Get up, girls! Sally Mae! Today is a big day and the sun will soon be up. We need to be ready to start a new endeavor. We're lumber men now!"

Etta wiped the sleep from her eyes and peered in vain through the dark cabin at the disturbance her pa was making in the room.

Jillian took her pillow and placed it over her head. "It's too early to be up!"

Etta pulled the covers off her legs and pushed against her sister's back. "Get up. We have lots of work to do. Ma will need us."

Jillian groaned. "Just a few more minutes."

Etta could hear Pa rummaging near the fire.

"Need a good log to get this fire started this morning. Today is the *day* the Lord has made!"

Etta giggled at how excited her pa was to begin a new day as she pulled up her skirt and snapped the back. Bending over, she tugged her shoes on. Before leaving the bedside, she pulled back the covers to reveal Jillian's bare legs. "Get up, sleepyhead. It's a new day!"

"Etta! Why do you have to be so much like Pa?" Her sister whined as she tried to pull the covers back over herself. "Stop it."

"Girls, girls," Pa scolded. "Today is not the day to be cross with one another. It will be a good day. A new beginning. Today will be the start of our new business. And if you're both good girls and help your ma, I'll be sure to give you wonderful cut lumber to build your own houses someday."

Etta smirked as she went toward the door to gather up the buckets to fetch water. "By that time, you'll have forgotten a promise made on a morning like this."

Pa snapped his suspenders. "No, I won't, Etta girl! I promise you."

Etta opened the door to the cool air and scurried down toward the water's edge to gather water for Ma. Ma had asked her to not get spring water first thing this morning, but to fill the washtubs first with river water. She would heat the water in them to wash dinner plates. That way, there'd be plenty of plates washed for the next crowd. Ma had organized the day so they would have ample food and clean dishes to feed the men who would come for lunch and supper. After they ate tonight, the men would head to Betsey's house to sleep the night away in her loft and living area. Betsey had more space than at the small Baker cabin.

The spring birds had disappeared, giving way to the sounds of frogs chirping and locust buzzing. A few squirrels scampered away and into the tall grasses as Etta made her way down to the river to gather water. She dipped a bucket into the water to scoop up a full load before bending to do it again with the other bucket. Walking away from the river, droplets of water landed on her skirts from the overfilled containers. The smell of the ragweed made Etta sneeze three times.

They hadn't had this many men ever come onto their property. Their summer gatherings and even Caroline's wedding hadn't brought so many visitors. Perhaps there would be some young men who lived nearby and who might be looking for a good woman. There was always that possibility. The idea made her smile. Etta wouldn't tell a single soul about her thoughts of today. It had absolutely nothing to do with building a new sawmill.

Coming back into the cabin, Etta found Jillian struggling to get her clothes on by the bed while Pa did nothing but chatter on about the sawmill raising today.

"The way I have it figured, we'll have this all done by nightfall. But if not, we'll feed the men in the morning after they sleep and get the rest done tomorrow. What do you think, Sally Mae?"

Ma just nodded and started slicing up bread for their breakfast. "Whatever you say, Hosea. I'm sure God will provide men to get the job done."

"Yes, He will." Hosea slapped the table with his hand. "Now, what can I do to make your job easier?"

Ma rattled off a few ideas about how best to feed so many men in such a short time, and as always, Pa agreed to the plans. "Sounds good, Sally Mae. Sounds good."

Etta hadn't seen Pa this excited in a long time. She never really thought about the magnitude of getting a sawmill built and working in less than twenty-four hours. But if anyone could make that become reality, it was Pa.

Jillian made her way to the fire to warm her hands. It was Jillian's morning ritual. She hadn't done it long before Ma told her to fill the tubs with Etta's water, and then she sent Etta for two more bucketsful.

As Etta again made her way to the river, the sun brightened up the sky toward the east. Crickets jumped out of her way as she made her way down the trail to the river's edge. Standing at the side for a moment, she looked both ways to see if any deer were attempting to get a drink this morning. As more and more people came into the area to settle, the deer had not been as prevalent as they'd been when they first moved here. Pa often had to hunt a whole day to even find one to kill. They'd been watching to see if the bucks they saw had rubbed the velvet off their antlers yet. Once that happened, fall was soon to follow.

Etta knelt to scoop more water. A frog hopped at her feet, causing her to jump. She giggled at being afraid of a frog as she turned to make her way back to the cabin. Whenever she had to do this chore so early, she'd hum to herself so she'd not be afraid of the dark. Often the humming would lead to singing so it would scare off anything on the path near the cabin.

Glancing back up toward the cabin, she thought Pa's newest idea of moving from their property and closer to town. Also, what would it be like to have a framed house? Pa wanted to be closer to the sawmill. She'd grown accustomed to the cabin near the river and to think of moving from this home made her sad. As intimate as it was to have a one-room home, she wasn't sure she wanted to give up hearing Pa's loud snores or hearing Ma clanging pots at the hearth to start their day. Pa had promised both her and Jillian that soon he'd build them a big enough house so they could each have a room. Etta wasn't sure that's what she wanted. Pa had yet to tell Ma.

When she entered the house again, Pa was busy sorting through some food to take with him to the worksite. "I want to head there soon. Perhaps some men will begin showing up this morning and I want to get them working as soon as they arrive."

Ma kissed his cheek. "Then get a move on. I have enough things to do around here without having you underfoot." She grinned at him as he returned her kiss.

Gathering up the items for his breakfast, Pa bit into a slice of bread as he headed for the door. "I'll be back for lunch. Wish me well."

Ma raised her hand in greeting. As the door closed behind him she commented, "Mercy me. You'd think it was Christmas morning and your pa was only five."

Both Etta and Jillian laughed.

"Are the babies and Betsey coming to spend the night?" Jillian took a few cloths and wrapped the sliced bread to keep it from drying out.

"Yes. Pa thought it more appropriate for Betsey and the babies to stay here with us tonight; that way the men can have Betsey's entire house. That will prevent the babies from waking the men during the night. I hope I'm not too tired to enjoy their visit with us."

"We'll do our best to help, Ma."

Ma looked up at Etta. "Thank you, sweet girl. You girls are always such good helpers."

Ambrose and his pa met at the river's edge almost at the same time. They both sat on a nearby log to have the picnic-like breakfast food Ma had prepared for both of them.

"When do you think they'll arrive, Pa?" Ambrose took a large bite of bread.

"Soon. It will take them time to get here from Whitmore's place. That was the plan, to stay there last night and venture their way north this morning."

Ambrose swallowed. "Are you sure this will work?"

"Positive." Pa took a long swig of water. Once he swallowed and let out a burp, he added, "I hope."

Ambrose shook his head and smiled. Pa's excitement never seemed to curb his appetite.

Just as they were finishing up their meal, a few neighbors began making their way toward them from all sides of the property. Henry Leach accompanied Jacob Wilkerson. Coming in from the south were Josiah Pierce, Isaac Banks, Samuel Whitcomb, and David VanWormer.

Pa reached his hand out to each man to thank them for helping him. He offered them the first bundles of lumber to be cut at his mill. These men were hard-working and courageous. They each had homesteads nearby and had settled in the territory just as the Baker family had done. Each had skills to offer. They all knew the significance and benefits a sawmill would have for their families and the future of their village, and each wanted to take part in getting it started.

The sun now rose bright over the river, reflecting iridescent sparkles on the stream. Light illuminated everything around him. The air was quiet. A slight breeze contained a cool bite to it, despite it still being August. The men would be grateful for the coolness as the day progressed. Ambrose stripped off his coat and hung it on a nearby tree branch.

Two wagons approached from the south. Each wagon contained several men. As the wagons drew close, men jumped off the back to walk the rest of the way to the work area. The oxen drawing the wagons would help lower and raise the logs to be stacked one on top of the other to build a deck where most of the sawmill's working parts could be stored.

One man in particular reached out his hand to Pa as he approached.

"Good morning, Hosea. Nice to see you again."

"James. Nice to see you as well. How many men did you find available to help us today?"

"Twenty-two. I also see you have neighbors on hand."

Pa took James around and introduced him to all the men now standing in a circle near the river bank's edge.

James stood in the middle of the crowd so everyone could hear him. "You men are here to help put up the first sawmill in these parts."

Most of the men cheered or clapped.

"Today we'll be raising these logs in position to get the base and floor of the mill started. I need the strongest workers to wield the axes. Once we get notches made at the ends of the logs, we'll begin hoisting them up into place. That's where we'll need men with agility. If you've ever climbed logs, this is when we'll need you." Most of the men shook their heads at this comment, for it was probably the most dangerous of jobs. "I'll only need about four good men for this. Once we get them stacked high enough, we'll start on the mill's wall. More men can form a dam to route water into the sluiceway. This way, the greatest amount of current can power the mill. For this job, I'll need vigorous men who aren't afraid to lift rocks and dirt all day." James wiped the sweat off his brow. "That's about it, so let's get started."

Most wandered down to the edge of the river to shovel dirt for the sluiceway. Some hiked up their trousers to their knees, while others just went into the water with their boots on. Some waded into the river to pile rocks to stop the water flow. A few others brought out axes to chop notches at the ends of the logs Pa and Ambrose had piled near the work area. They raised the axes in the air and began chipping away at the logs, one by one.

James and his head men, Frank and Stephen, stood off to one side to evaluate the best place for them to get started. Ambrose hoped the day went smoothly, for his pa's sake.

"Why don't you men follow me out to the river's edge, and we can figure out the best position to place the oxen for the maximum amount of pull?" James called the order out to Stephen and Frank.

Frank stopped short and pointed to Stephen. "He's got something to say."

James stepped back and folded his arms. "Go ahead. Is there a problem?"

Stephen took a deep breath and took off his hat. "I don't mean to put a damper on this entire event here, but I don't think I'm going to be climbing any logs today."

James relaxed his arms. "What do you mean?"

"I just can't seem to shake that dream on the way here. I have young'uns at home who need me. A wife. This day might end badly."

James turned and spit. "So, you're gonna let a silly dream stop you from helping me today?"

Stephen looked at the ground. "Yes. That's what I'm saying."

James cursed.

"I'm sorry, boss. I know you counted on me being a man to help raise these logs, but I just can't. Not today."

"Fine! Are you okay to keep working, Frank?"

Frank nodded and picked up the reins of the oxen team nearest him. "Yes sir."

"Stephen, I'd love to say you're a fool, but I respect you too much. You head out into the river and direct those men on where to put the rocks for the best benefit of a strong current for the sluiceway."

Stephen began slipping off his boots to wade into the water.

James overheard him mumble.

"I hope quicksand isn't an issue in this part of the Shiawassee River."

As Stephen walked toward the river, James shook his head in disgust. "All over a silly dream."

Rhoda took the hands of her children and led them toward the cabin by the river. Indians approached her and made faces. Her children crowded around her close, their hands tucking into hers or grabbing an edge of her skirt. It seemed none of them wanted to confront one of the dark-skinned men on the trail leading to the fur-trading post.

Rhoda stepped inside the dark cabin. Once in the building, she had to wait a few moments for her eyes to adjust. Once they did, she saw a man dressed from head to toe in buckskin, standing off to one side. He looked to be in charge, and his eyes twinkled upon seeing her walk through his door. Rhoda felt her cheeks grow warm.

"Ma'am. Can I help you?" After nodding to her, he offered his hand.

Rhoda shook the rough hand. "Hello. My name is Rhoda Seymour, and I'm here to see my brother."

"Your brother? Who is?"

"Hosea. Hosea Baker."

Whitmore took off his hat and rubbed his chin. "He's your brother?"

Rhoda watched the man's eyes closely. Had this man heard the rumor about her brother? Surely not! Why would anyone from this area be skeptical of Hosea? For a moment, Rhoda felt the guilt that had followed her for years reopen.

The man replaced his hat and grinned. "Sure. I know him well. You're his sister?"

Relief filled Rhoda's heart. The man seemed to be teasing her. "Yes. He will probably not be expecting us. Is his homestead far from here?"

"Well, ma'am, funny you should come lookin' for Hosea today. He's raising a sawmill on his property just north of here, a way. The entire community is there helping him today. I was going to finish a few things here and then head up to help. Would you care to join me?"

"My driver here, Augustus Drake, would like to head back to Pontiac today. Could you guide us the rest of the way to Hosea's house?"

Whitmore adjusted his fur hat. "I'd be happy to. Might be a bit of a walk. Perhaps an hour or so. Is that okay?"

Rhoda smiled. "We're used to walking." Rhoda looked around the room. "Could we get a bite to eat first?"

"Of course! I have some squash with venison simmerin' over the fire. Care to join me?"

A meal like that sounded delightful compared to the meals the family had been having on their trip here. Even Giles grinned when he heard what they might have to eat. "We'd love to join you. Let me get out to Augustus and settle up with him. We'll be back soon."

Before Rhoda walked back out to the wagon, she gathered their satchels and began handing them to Philinda and Martha. She encouraged the children to carry them to the post. The satchel containing her funds she held back. Digging inside a side pocket, she walked to Augustus. "We thank you, sir, for getting us this far. I think we have finished with your services. Thank you for agreeing to go with us past Pontiac. You've been a trustworthy driver. How much do I owe you?" Rhoda's throat tightened, and she held her breath. The coins, now in her moist hand, were all she had left. Would it suffice for payment to the kind man who had gone out of his way to get her and the children this far?

"The way I figure it, I'd say ten dollars would be enough."

Rhoda counted through the last of her coins. Having acquired change from a purchase in Pontiac, she'd thrown the loose coins into the satchel pocket without counting them. She fished and fished to find the ten coins and then realized there was just one coin left. She handed the money to Augustus. "Thank you, sir. You were indeed a great help."

"Thank you, ma'am. May God guide the rest of your journey."

At the mention of God, Rhoda squirmed. "I don't need Him to do that but thank you."

For the first time, Augustus's expression seemed to question her words, but he shrugged and left her standing by the side of the road as he pulled his oxen in the opposite direction to head down the trail from where they'd just come. Rhoda reluctantly watched him go. After what they'd experienced together on the trail here, he'd become a trustworthy companion.

When he was finally down the road, Rhoda turned to head inside. Her children had only gone a few feet from her. Each child seeming to size up the Indians staring back at them.

Giles was the first to speak. "Momma, do we have enough money left to eat here?"

Rhoda opened her palm to look at the coin's denomination. It was twenty-five cents. "Let's go see. I'm hungry, aren't you?" She wrapped her arm around her oldest daughter and led the children back into the post.

CHAPTER NINE

It amazed Hosea and many of the village residents how all the equipment they needed to make a sawmill function was being constructed along the side of the Shiawassee River. They spread out the jobs of making that happen among those wanting to help. Some worked at making a gate to be used to direct the water past the dam and into the sluiceway to power the mill. Others piled notched logs near the shore where soon they would be hoisted into place by ropes and oxen power. Rocks formed a dam that led to the sluiceway between the sawmill and the riverbank. The only thing missing was the equipment that Ambrose and Horace had made and Hosea was still waiting on saw blades to arrive from Pontiac.

Walking back to his cabin at noon, Hosea found his wife and daughters placing steaming hot plates of food on the kitchen table, which was set up outside. Each man sat or removed their hat as Hosea said a blessing. They appeared eager to get some nourishment, but also to head back to the river to finish their designated job.

Jillian and Etta worked hard to keep everyone's thirst at bay with a bucket and ladle. Each man scooped out what he needed as the girls held the bucket for them. Hosea patted his daughters on the head as they worked their way around the table.

As each man took a drink of water, others dug into their plates of food provided for them. Sally Mae had outdone herself, and plates were full of cut potatoes, turkey, a bit of venison, and turnips from the garden. Once a man had eaten his fill, he left to give other men the opportunity to eat. Sally Mae took the plate to a washtub, washed and dried it quickly, and loaded it with food for the next worker. There were only so many plates to be used at a time.

Hosea noticed two men sitting side by side who looked alike. He asked if they were brothers. The men laughed and nodded.

"Our name is Chalker. Charles, and this here's my brother, Chandler."

"Nice to meet you, boys. Where you from?"

"Born in Vermont, raised in New York."

Typically the territory had filled up with many New Yorkers, it was surprising to find these two from as far as Vermont.

"Where have you homesteaded?"

"East of here."

"It's near my place, Hosea." Henry Leach waved at Hosea and announced from the opposite end of the table. "I invited them."

"You boys look mighty young to be homesteaders." Hosea had to comment. As he did, he noticed Etta was attentively keeping the young boys filled with more water than the rest of the table. He smirked at the revelation. He thought about mentioning it to her, but then kept quiet. It would only embarrass her to point it out.

"Our father is Nathaniel Chalker. He should arrive sometime next year. He'll be bringing with him our younger brother, Calvin, and our sister, Eliza."

"Nice to have your help, boys." Hosea patted them both on the back.

Hosea greeted all of his neighbors and thanked them for their help. Some men who'd arrived with James Ball lived much farther south, so he introduced himself to them. "Once this mill is up and running, I'd appreciate your business."

Everyone nodded as they continued to eat the food offered to them.

When everyone had finished, the entire crew set off to walk the distance to the rising sawmill. Hosea encouraged Sally Mae and the girls to stop by that afternoon to see their progress. The girls agreed to try, but Sally Mae assured Hosea she had enough work to keep them busy all afternoon. The job of feeding the working men later would come soon.

Hosea stood on the riverbank to observe the work completed so far. Piled logs sat beside the river to be hoisted into place next. Water filtered through the sluiceway running directly beside the bank. The power from this water would give the saw the energy it needed to cut wood. Hosea marveled at the design made by Ball and his men. He knew how a sawmill worked and the layout, but seeing it all working in the way it was being constructed, marveled him. This project, if it proved profitable, would keep him out of the crop-planting business, bringing his tired and weary body relief.

Before long, the last log fell into place. It didn't stay in place for long after being dropped and James mentioned it might need to be adjusted later.

Hosea watched in wonder as James shimmied up the logs with ease. It was his job to position the next log into place as the oxen teams lifted it with connecting ropes. Other ropes held him fast to the wall of wood. Safety was a priority for James, and he had assigned men to the job. Men who had finished their assigned task stood along the shore covering their eyes from the sun to watch the wall being assembled for a snug fit.

Nearly to supper, Hosea looked up to see Whitmore with some children and a woman headed in his direction from the south. Hosea had wondered why Whitmore hadn't arrived to help. He'd been surprised by that. Who could the family be? Before he could greet Whitmore and his guests, Ambrose was calling for him to lead one team of oxen back to graze before needing them again.

While he walked the team back toward some high grass, Whitmore called to him. "Hosea! I have a surprise for you. Do you have a minute?"

Hosea raised his hand in greeting. "Just a minute." As he turned to head toward Whitmore, he focused on the woman coming toward him. Within seconds, Hosea recognized his younger sister. "Rhoda?"

Rhoda picked up her skirt and began running toward him. Following her were four children, seeming to be as excited to see Hosea as his sister.

"Hosea!" She called out with a big smile and a wave.

"Rhoda! I don't believe it."

When she reached him, she jumped into his arms. "Hosea. You don't know how happy I am to see you."

Hosea hugged his sister tight. "How? When? What are you doing here?"

"We've come to stay."

After hugging his sister, he pulled her away for a moment to look her in the face and then back into another hug. "Where's Sidney?"

"He's not here. It's just me and the younger ones. He's selling the store in Sodus and will join us soon."

Rhoda introduced the children one by one. "You remember Philinda?"

Hosea pulled the girl toward him. "Of course. You've gotten big, child."

"Then we have Martha, Rhoda Ann, and Giles."

Hosea got down on one knee and took all three of the younger children into his arms. "Children. I'm your Uncle Hosea. Do you remember me?"

"Nope!" Giles spoke first, which made Hosea laugh right out loud.

"Where'd you find this wonderful family, Whitmore?" Hosea stood and put his arm around Rhoda's shoulders.

"Came in a wagon from Pontiac this morning. Thought I'd do a special delivery and check out how the mill is shapin' up." Whitmore added, "Think I'll head down to the river now to take a look."

Hosea was astounded to have his sister standing right beside him. It had been a long time since he'd seen her. He'd never met Giles, but he recognized her daughters and how much they'd grown.

"Why didn't you write? Tell us you were coming?"

"I tried, but you didn't leave a forwarding address." Rhoda laughed. "Hard to find a brother in the wilderness. If you give me a few minutes, I'll tell you how much."

Hosea roared with laughter. "When did you leave Sodus?"

"About a month ago, and I have to be completely honest with you, I'm broke. I just fished into my satchel, and after buying some food from Whitmore, I only have a ten-cent piece left to my name."

Hosea's heart dropped. More mouths to feed. After today's endeavor, it would be hard to find enough food to fill up his own family's bellies, but he knew, without a doubt, God would provide.

"Why don't you make your way to the farm and greet Sally Mae? She's a might busy today with having to feed all the men, but she'd probably welcome your help. Just follow this path here, and soon you'll be at my farm. It's down close to the river."

Rhoda kissed his cheek. "It's so nice being close to you again. Once Sidney gets here, we'll find another place to build a store. We'll be sure people here have all they need and more."

"Sounds like a good plan. Head off this way and you'll find a wonderful place to stay for tonight."

Rhoda took the hands of Giles and Rhoda Ann and headed down the trail toward Hosea's cabin. He shook his head. As delightful as it was to see her, he wondered why she'd come all this way alone. It wasn't unusual to have Rhoda trying to be independent. She'd always been that way, but this arrival stunned him. He couldn't help but think the reason was much larger than bringing a new store to the village.

Hosea watched in relief when the last peg was pounded into place, and the building of his new endeavor took shape. They tested the sluiceway for workability and most of the men were now taking a break along the riverbank. It had been a long, hard day.

Hosea hoped Sally Mae and the girls were ready for the next meal and motioned to the men to head toward Hosea's home. There were a few things to do to finish the project, but some men could eat while others continued to work and then shift when the first wave of men had finished eating. He'd have to give Sally Mae his best attention when this was all over. She'd been fabulous at getting meals ready for the men.

Twelve men broke away from the work area and headed to Hosea's cabin down the path toward the cabin. Hosea didn't have to direct them for this meal. Standing on the bank with Ambrose, the men looked over the project. Hosea couldn't stop smiling. It had been a beneficial day not only for Hosea but for the community.

James rappelled off the last log and onto the ground, examining his work as he stood off to one side. He hollered to one of his men nearby. "I don't like the look of that." He pointed to the last log they'd put into place. "It's not set right."

Frank and Stephen, who'd refused to climb the logs, gazed up at the log to which James was pointing. They both nodded and agreed that something wasn't quite right.

James moved toward Hosea and sat on a log nearby. "I'm worried. That last log twisted a bit when we hoisted it up and into place. I'm wondering if I should shimmy up there again and adjust it. I'll need the oxen to support it while I maneuver it into place."

Hosea nodded. "I'll head over for the team."

James shook his head. "No. Let's wait. I'm famished and need to eat before I do it."

"Well then, let's get back to my place and grab a bite to eat." Hosea pointed down the path where the other men had gone.

The rest of the working crew gathered and left down the path toward the Baker cabin. As they walked, James voiced his plans to fix the log. All the men agreed his plan should work. "Once we adjust that log, I'm sure the other logs will settle in as well. They just seem to be off a tad. In fact—" James stopped. "I'm gonna head back and take one more look."

"I'll go back with you," Stephen added. "I hate waiting in line for my food."

"Thank you. I'd appreciate the company."

"Are you sure you don't want the rest of us back there to help you?" Ambrose turned to ask.

"No. I'm just gonna take one last look. Go to the cabin. We'll be there shortly." James and Stephen returned from the way they'd come.

Sally couldn't wait to finish feeding all the men and clean up. That would mean her day was over. She'd been working constantly. She didn't have a clue how many men still needed to eat. Jillian, Etta, and now Philinda and Rhoda were there to help. She just kept mixing and cooking food. Hosea came into the cabin with the widest grin she'd seen in a long time.

"It's up, Sally Mae!" He took his hat off and rubbed his forehead with his sleeve. "It's mighty pretty."

Sally just laughed at him. "I've never heard a sawmill described in quite that way before."

Hosea laughed, too. "Isn't it great to have Rhoda arrive today?"

Sally drew close to her husband. "To be honest, I could hardly believe the providence of her arrival, today of all days. I don't know how we would have managed without her."

"Will there be enough room to bed them down here tonight with you women?"

Sally took a stick and stirred the fire up. "Yes, we'll manage. It sure is a blessing to see her and the children."

A shout from outside interrupted their conversation. Hosea headed to the doorway to see what it was all about. Sally wiped off her hands and went to him as a frantic call could be heard from the south.

Hosea took off toward the voice and as Sally looked out, she saw a man struggling to make his way to the other men. She wondered if he'd been hurt. Some of the other men, who were eating, stopped and ran toward the man, who fell to his knees as if he was in pain or distraught.

"Ma, what's happening?" Etta came close to the doorway and nearly spilled the bucket of water she was carrying.

"Be careful, child." Sally wiped droplets of water off her apron. She squinted to see what was happening with Hosea and the other men as they drew near to the distraught man's shouting.

"He's shouting for help. Something's wrong." Jillian scooted past Sally as she came into the cabin.

Sally watched the group of men surrounding the man now kneeling on the ground. Two or three of them started running back down the path leading to the sawmill. Hosea and Ambrose were close on their heels.

"Something's wrong!" Sally instructed the girls to keep a close watch on the stew bubbling up in the kettle over the fire and yelled to Rhoda. "Rhoda, come with me. Etta, watch Rhoda's children."

"What do you think is wrong?" Rhoda asked breathlessly.

"We'll find out soon enough."

The two women scurried across the yard and made their way to the man, now sobbing into his hands on his knees.

Sally knelt beside the man, putting her hand on his shoulder. "Sir, what's happening? What's wrong?"

He stopped sobbing long enough to swallow. Sally had never seen such a pained look on a man's face. "It happened. Just like my dream. James fell off the building. I didn't think he'd try to do it alone."

Sally and Rhoda exchanged glances. What was he talking about?

"Is someone hurt?" Sally rubbed the man's shoulder.

"No, ma'am. He's dead."

CHAPTER TEN

"We mean to take him back to his family, sir. Us and the rest of the men. He has a wife and young ones back home. We appreciate your kindness." Stephen and several other men had the body of James Ball in the back of one wagon, wrapped in blankets. The only thing visible was the man's boots.

Hearing about the accident, Aaron arrived around noon the next day. "I'll go along with them, Hosea, to be sure they get home safely and I'll let the family know nothing out of line happened. That it was just an accident." Before mounting his horse, he kissed Betsey and their children.

An awkward few moments passed until Pa spoke. "Tell them we're sorry for their loss." He gulped, as if trying to maintain his composure. "Let us know if there is anything we can do."

Betsey felt bad for her pa. He'd been ecstatic to get this mill built. They were nearly ready to declare the project complete. The worker's death brought agony instead of joy. You can't put a price on a man's life. She'd found out about it when she'd arrived at the cabin to spend the night with her sisters, Ma, and also her Aunt Rhoda and cousins. She drew close to her pa, giving him a sideways hug. "Pa, it's not your fault."

Hosea shook his head as if wanting to believe it, but knowing it wasn't true. He walked away from everyone standing near the wagon and went toward the barn.

Ma whispered. "He's taking this real hard."

Ambrose started to follow his pa, but Ma pulled him back. "Let him be."

Everyone stood silent as the wagon, carrying the body of the worker, made its way off the Baker family property. There was nothing anyone could do to make this moment easier for Pa or anyone else. A self-imposed obligation fell over the family.

"What more could we do?" Ma wiped the tears off her face with the end of her apron. Rhoda drew her close.

"We need to heat leftovers from yesterday and feed this crew." Rhoda motioned to her daughters to follow her into the cabin.

Betsey grasped Julia's hand, leading her and carrying Richard back inside. She had no clue how long Aaron would be gone, but she knew she needed to get the children fed and ready for afternoon naps. Perhaps she needed to pack their overnight belongings and go home. Last night had been such a difficult evening. Pa had been unusually solemn and silent. The air was thick with sorrow. No one felt able to say how they were feeling for fear of making the tragedy worse for Pa.

Betsey's children were too little to understand their sorrowful grandparents, who only held them tight and wouldn't play or laugh with them. Betsey did her best, during their visit, to distract Julia from asking her usual assortment of questions, but the inquisitive child made that impossible. Thankfully, Julia had grown tired of trying and went to Jillian for entertainment. Jillian had obliged and distracted her until bedtime.

As she neared the cabin, Ma turned and took Richard from her. "Let me carry this boy for you."

Betsey thanked her as Julia begged to be held as well. Betsey picked up her long-legged daughter. It wouldn't be long before carrying her, as she did Richard, would be impossible. The hours needed to care for her children almost made Betsey feel it was impossible to help others as she'd like. They took up so much of her time. She felt more of a burden to her family than any help.

"Will Pa be okay, Ma?" Jillian asked in a voice sounding like she was ready to burst into tears. They all looked to Ma for an answer.

Ma gave them all a pained smile. "He will need some time with God. Just as he was when the Indians took Alexander, he needs to be alone."

Betsey knew how hard it had been on her pa to have Alexander taken from them. Pa needed months to recover from it. Even after all this time, he still couldn't talk about the child without tears. Now, this.

Ambrose sat at the table. "This whole incident is scary. The man who told us about James falling had said over and over, to all of us, he didn't want any part of climbing up that structure while it was being made. He told everyone that he'd had a premonition or what did he call it...?" Ambrose snapped his fingers. "A dream. He dreamed something bad was going to happen. He refused to even take part in securing the structure."

Ma sat beside Ambrose. "I've heard of people having premonitions, but never so specific."

"Me, either." Ambrose sighed. "It's so sad. Pa was so looking forward to having the mill here. If he can't get over this, I wonder if he'll give it all up."

Rhoda drew a chair close to the table. "Is there any way we can help him?"

Ma placed Richard back in Betsey's arms. She went for the kettle by the hearth and filled some cups. "I don't know. He'll work it out with God and then move forward. He always does."

Rhoda turned her back to the group, muttering, "I wish that's all it would take."

Betsey looked at Ma, who seemed not to have heard what Rhoda said. "What did you say, Aunt Rhoda?"

Rhoda turned around abruptly. "God doesn't care. He doesn't care that this was something special to Hosea. He doesn't care that it will kill him to move ahead with the project. It feels like God has a vendetta against Hosea. Or maybe, He doesn't care at all!"

Everyone was taken aback by Rhoda's angry tone and thoughts.

Ma chimed in. "Rhoda, you know that isn't true."

"What do you mean? It *is* true. When has God done anything good for Hosea? He's tormented him his whole life!"

Betsey glanced around the table at the other faces. They exchanged questioning looks.

"Aunt Rhoda, why would you say that?" Betsey wanted to cover Julia's ears from the woman's rant.

"Because it's true. The sooner all of you hear it, the better. Resign yourself to the fact that if there was a God, He wouldn't be treating someone as faithful as Hosea like He does."

Betsey looked to Etta, who scooped up Richard from off her lap and also took Julia's hand and led them back outside.

What had caused Aunt Rhoda's outburst? She'd never heard her talk so defensively about Hosea and so angrily about God. Betsey felt bad for her cousins, who seemed oblivious to their mother's words. How could Aunt Rhoda talk like this in front of her children?

The group was either too stunned to speak or didn't have a clue about what to say. Betsey knew she needed to leave. "I need to head home. My babies need their naps." Betsey quickly grabbed their belongings and moved toward the door. "We'll come back tomorrow, Ma."

Ma escorted her to the door and, as soon as she left the cabin, she shut the door behind her.

"I'll help you, Betsey," Etta spoke up as she lifted Julia to her feet. The child fussed as she'd been trying to pick one of Ma's flowers.

Betsey scolded Julia. "You leave Grandma's flowers alone. Come on. Let's head for home." She took Julia's hand and tugged her to walk with her. Etta carried Richard.

As they made their way to the path leading to Betsey's cabin, Etta spoke. "Betsey, is Aunt Rhoda not a woman of faith?"

Betsey didn't know what to tell her sister, other than what she knew to be true. "She's been bitter since Pa's problem in New York. Perhaps she's more angry than any of us imagined."

Horace came into the cabin in a flurry. "Have you heard the news?"

Caroline placed a shirt she'd been scrubbing over the edge of a water barrel. "News?"

"Someone died while helping your pa at the sawmill."

Caroline gasped. "Who?"

"One of the workmen in charge of putting it up. He fell from the top when he was trying to adjust a log. He'd done something in a hurry and didn't put a safety rope on."

Caroline sat. "Oh no. Did we know him?"

"His name was James Ball. I didn't know him. Your pa said the workers were coming from as far away as Pontiac to help. Perhaps it was one of those men."

"I need to go to my family. Pa will be devastated."

Horace raked his hair with his hand. "I'm sure. Do you want me to come along?"

Caroline took off her apron and hung it on the line beside her. "I'll finish this laundry when I come back." She smiled up at Horace. "You stay here. Try to rest."

Horace nodded. It was one reason he'd not gone to help that day. He felt quite ill.

"I'm changing. I'll be out shortly."

Horace felt awful. He couldn't have been any help to Hosea and the work crew, but now he almost felt relieved he wasn't there to see something happen. He hated to think of a man dying on the job. It was a tragedy that might haunt anyone, but for Hosea, it was personal.

Caroline came out with a clean, dry dress on and swooped her hair up in a bun behind her head before she adjusted her bonnet. "I won't stay long. Do you think you could mind the fire while I'm gone?"

Horace picked up a stick and threw it into the fire under the kettle filled with wet clothes. "Do you want me to keep washing these?"

Caroline smiled, but shook her head. "No, you rest. I'll get to them later."

Horace plopped down on a nearby stump and watched his beautiful wife head down the trail toward the Baker cabin. As he watched her leave, he thought about how much he loved Caroline. She was strong. It had been almost a whole year since they'd been married. There wasn't a day he didn't thank God for his new wife.

They had been shy newlyweds. They loved nothing better than their own company rather than trying to go out and visit other folks. Caroline had fixed up Horace's new home to make it comfortable and welcoming. Betsey and the babies would come over often, but it was usually just him and Caroline on most days. But now this. Would Caroline's family need her more than he needed her? He felt selfish as a new thought filled his head. What if he never got better?

Horace hadn't been feeling well for almost a month now. Doing any kind of exertion with the simplest of chores left him exhausted. He'd lost weight. So much so that Caroline was constantly taking a tuck in the waistband of his trousers. His ribs were showing, but he was eating as much as he could. It's just that food seemed to not stick to his bones anymore. It was as if he was merely wasting away. Horace stood up and went to the nearby bucket to get a long drink of the cool water. Why was he always so thirsty? Within minutes, he'd want to go for more.

Horace wanted to finish the laundry for Caroline. Have it all on the line, so when she returned, it wouldn't be another worry for her. Putting a wooden paddle into the hot water, Horace stirred the clothing once and then twice. It took all the energy he had, but he was determined to help.

How could a sick husband care for a wife? And do it well? Who would bring in an income? Why had God allowed him to get sick?

After rinsing out two of his shirts and twisting them free of excess water, Horace hung the two shirts on the line outside their house. The effort exhausted him. He sat on their cabin's threshold and leaned his back against the door. If only he could shut his eyes for a moment, then he'd get back to finishing up the laundry for Caroline. But his thoughts tormented him. He wanted to be the provider. The hero in Caroline's life. But his exhaustion made him realize he couldn't do any of that. An inadequate feeling flushed through his soul. He shut his eyes.

Caroline rushed to the Baker cabin. She'd stayed away too long, but with Horace not feeling well, it seemed her duties had grown larger. She wished she knew what was ailing him. As she scurried down the trail, she said a prayer for her husband. She prayed for

God to heal him. She prayed that a doctor would arrive soon who could examine him and see what might have caused his exhaustion and weight loss.

As she neared her former home, Caroline found her pa leaning against the chicken coop, his head down. He seemed absorbed in thought. Her problems disappeared at the sight of him.

Not sure if she should approach, for he looked to be praying, Caroline stood off to the side for a moment to see if he would stop to look her way. As she waited, she saw his shoulders shaking. She gently placed her hand on his shoulder. He pivoted. She'd startled him.

Her pa's face took her breath away. Tears filled his eyes and his face was damp. He attempted to wipe them away with his sleeve, but it did no good. Caroline pulled him into her arms, and he sobbed on her shoulder. It was one thing to watch her pa cry, but another to have to soothe him. Within a few seconds, he stepped back, embarrassed. How could a daughter possibly know how to commiserate with a parent? She quickly decided, just as she would any other person.

Caroline reached for his hand and held it between hers. "Oh, Pa. I'm so sorry."

"I never meant—" Her pa wiped his mouth off with his hand. "I never meant for this to happen."

Seeing her pa so heartbroken left Caroline weak in the knees and fighting back tears. "Everyone knows, Pa. Everyone."

He looked up at her. "I'm sorry, child. I don't mean to be such a blubbery mess."

Caroline patted his hand. "It's okay, Pa. I'd be more worried if this hadn't affected you as it has. I'm sure everyone knows how sorry you are."

Pa's facial expression showed fear. "What if they don't? What if I'm accused again of something I could have prevented? Perhaps this time they'd find me guilty."

"Pa, what do you mean?"

Pa looked up. "This has happened to me before. Men and women began repeating something about me that wasn't true."

"When?" Caroline didn't remember.

"New York. Before we moved to Pennsylvania. It split the church. Caused a major upheaval in the community. Some believed me and some didn't. When the rumor came out, I ran. I ran because I didn't want to cause any further issues. But before I could leave, I'd caused friends and family to choose a side. I don't think—" More tears followed, and Pa couldn't answer.

Caroline waited.

"I don't think I could survive something like that again."

"Pa. Listen to me."

Her pa stepped back, wiping his eyes.

"No one would believe you caused this. No one around here, anyway. You know that. Were you there when it happened?"

Pa shook his head and sighed.

"Then why would the blame fall on you?"

"It's my mill!" Pa shouted. He pointed to himself. "It was something I had to have."

"Yes, the project was yours, but the entire community needs this mill. You, as well as everyone around here, knows that. We need a place to cut up all this lumber," Caroline swept her hand over the back of Pa's property, "and get it processed to make homes, businesses, and even a school." Caroline sighed. "Right?"

Pa sighed as if trying to fight back more tears.

"We need a mill here. If it hadn't been you who started it, it would have been someone else. Would you be blaming that person now, if it had happened to them?"

It seemed as if Pa understood Caroline's words as he looked at her. He shook his head.

"Then why do you think anyone would hold you personally responsible? Many love you, Pa. If I've heard one praise, I've heard a million more. No one will assume you or consider this accident to be your fault. If they do," Caroline stood taller, squaring her shoulders. "They'll have to deal with me!"

Caroline saw Pa's face react to her comment.

"See. I'm right. You know I'm right. Now come on, let's get up to the house and get you a cup of coffee. Let's sit down as a family and work this out. Perhaps we can send some money to the family. Does the man have a family?"

"I don't know. Oh God, I hope not little ones."

"Even if he does, you'll make it right. Won't you?"

Pa wiped the remaining moisture off his cheeks. "I'll try."

"Of course, you will." Caroline took her pa's hand. "Now, come on. We'll handle this together. Just as we have always done. I'm here to help."

Pa gripped her hand. Caroline could see him age ten years right then. For the first time, Caroline felt like an official adult. She knew Pa would come around. She needed him to. Despite her age, Caroline didn't want to be in charge of the Baker family or even her own. But she felt her pa needed someone to lean on for just a moment.

She looped her arm into Pa's as they walked together back toward the Baker cabin.

CHAPTER ELEVEN

Rhoda stood off to the side, her arms crossed, as she listened to the Baker family make plans on how to comfort the family of the dead man. Hosea hadn't changed. He was still loyal and gentle. He was determined to care for the dead man's family until they could manage on their own.

She overheard Hosea.

"I don't have much left to give them. I've spent nearly all the money I have in getting this mill up and running."

Sally fidgeted with the hem of her skirt. "We'll need to sell a few things. Perhaps?"

"What, Sally Mae? We need everything we have to keep going."

"What about the oxen?"

Hosea nodded. "Yes. We could do without at least one of them with little trouble."

"But Pa, how would you get the ground ready for planting next spring?"

"We'll have a smaller crop next year. If this sawmill does its job, we'll have money from that."

Ambrose tipped his chair back. "I hate for you to sell any of the animals. I have lumber left over from building my house. I was going to start a store soon, but—"

Sally chimed in, "No. We will not take your money, Ambrose."

Caroline offered a suggestion. "Why don't we ask the community for help? If all of us give just a little, we might come up with enough to give the family."

Rhoda knew Caroline and her new husband probably didn't have a lot to give either, but it sounded like a good idea. She wanted to comment but knew this was a decision she should best leave up to Hosea and his family. For in doing something, Hosea might gain back his will to keep going.

Hosea took a sip of his coffee. "That might be true, but I still feel it's my responsibility."

"This mill is for everyone," Caroline interjected. "The entire community needs it. I'm sure if some can give a portion, we will soon have more than enough."

"Almost feels like we're paying off the family. No amount of money will take away their pain," Sally added.

Hosea patted his wife's hand. "I know Sally Mae. I agree, but I just can't allow the family to go without—with winter at hand—without us trying to help."

Sally brushed Hosea's cheek with the back of her fingers. "Okay. Let's ask. Hopefully, others will understand our intentions."

Rhoda felt the tiny piece of money in her pocket. It was the change for the twenty-five-cent piece leftover from their meal at the trading post. She needed every cent to feed her family. She couldn't expect Hosea to care for her or her children. They were her responsibility. But how would she manage it with a mere ten cents? The feel of the small coin made her truly understand the plight now facing the widow of James Ball.

"It was good of Betsey to invite Rhoda and the children to stay in her loft." Sally Mae lifted her nightgown over her head and shimmied as the gown fell over her slight frame.

Hosea didn't say anything as he crawled under the blanket on their bed.

"I can't believe she brought those children here. All by herself." Sitting on the edge of the bed now, Sally took a brush to her hair.

"It was a risk. That's for sure." Hosea placed his hand under his head as he lay back.

Sally loved feeling the brush smooth her hair. If she didn't take time to get the snarls out each night, she'd have a mess on her hands come morning. "The children sure have grown."

"That little Giles is a sprite little fella." Hosea's face grimaced. "Reminds me of—" Hosea swallowed.

Sally turned to see tears brimming his eyes. She wanted to say Alexander, but knowing her husband's already pained heart, she couldn't voice the name out loud. She didn't have to, as Hosea continued to speak.

"I hope the boy is healthy and well."

The pain on Hosea's face made Sally wince. She turned back to the wall. She hated to see Hosea in anguish over the boy who'd brought him so much joy. And now, after today, Hosea would have to shoulder the sorrow of a man losing his life to build the mill. How much pain could one man hold without bursting?

She shared with Hosea how Rhoda reacted during their conversation that afternoon.

"Doesn't appear that Rhoda has come to grips with her hardened heart. I can't understand it. That woman knows the truth. Anguish comes to us all. But the issue with the church has long been over. We left so others wouldn't lose their faith over it. Now look...my sister has more pent-up bitterness than anyone else. Even me."

Sally placed her brush on the stump beside her bed and pulled back on her side of the blanket. As she snuggled close to Hosea, he reached around and grasped her shoulders. He hugged her and placed a kiss on her temple. "Perhaps that's why she's here."

Hosea lay back again. "Here?"

"Yes. Why has she followed you here? Her soul is upset, still concerned after all these years with something that just made *you* look bad in the eyes of others. Why else would she come?"

"There's a myriad of reasons why she's come: cheap property, a new place to live, her children can be close to their cousins as they grow up...I don't think it has anything to do with what happened to me in New York."

"How can you be sure?"

"Well, for one thing, Sidney isn't frivolous, nor does he decide things based on Rhoda's feelings. We both know that about him. And why would he allow Rhoda to come first? Why didn't Rhoda wait until they could all come together?"

Sally had been having many of the same questions arise in her own thoughts. It seemed odd. "Perhaps she was just missing you too much." Yet as the words left her mouth, she knew this couldn't be true. Rhoda was a strong, independent woman. She didn't need Hosea in her life to help her.

"I think something has happened between Sidney and Rhoda."

Sally turned her face to Hosea. "Like what?"

"Who knows? Even you and I don't know why situations turn us against each other. Perhaps it was just a disagreement, and she turned on her heel and left town to prove something to her husband."

"She would do that." Sally nuzzled her face into Hosea's neck and giggled. "I might even do that."

Hosea pulled her closer. He didn't laugh with her. As suspicious as they were about Rhoda's arrival, the events of the day were far greater.

"Was it bad?" Sally knew she didn't have to explain her question. She knew whatever state Hosea had found the dead man in, she'd never be privy to the details, but she asked anyway.

"Nothing prepares you to view the body of a dead man. Nothing. From what I can tell, his neck broke instantly. He never knew what hit him." Hosea sighed then pulled Sally closer.

She knew not to ask anymore.

"What do you think about asking the community for donations for his widow?"

"I think it would be appropriate. I've got some egg money tucked away for a rainy day. You may have it." It was less than a dollar, but she felt a need to give from what she had.

"I'll head out tomorrow. Once we gather a collection, perhaps Ambrose will accompany me to take it to the widow and her young ones."

"It's the least we can do." She closed her eyes. Exhaustion was the only reason for her silence. But even as she did, she knew it wouldn't be the same for Hosea. Despite his fatigue and heavy heart, Sally would be the only one who would sleep this night.

Hosea had forwent his breakfast. It wasn't like he didn't have things to keep him busy and his mind occupied for a few days, but he just couldn't force himself to go down to the mill to finish assembling the parts to get it up and running. Not yet. He found a part of the chicken fence that needed mending and worked on that as the chickens clucked and pecked for food at his feet. The heat of the day made the chicken coop smell worse than usual.

He'd often talk to the small creatures when he came out to feed them, but today, he had more things on his mind. Even as his hands did multiple chores throughout the day, his mind kept envisioning the man falling off the logs at the mill. He prayed fervently for the man's family and the other man who'd watched him fall. Seeing a man die could haunt another for years. He prayed this wouldn't be the case for Stephen.

He remembered the warnings Stephen had tried to communicate the day the men arrived to work. Who would have thought a dream could predict something like that? Hosea knew God sometimes worked in mysterious ways, and He had spoken to men through dreams or visions in the Bible. That, he knew. But what kept Hosea's mind mulling over everything again and again was his responsibility for the accident. Of course, it was Hosea's mill and his idea to build it with the help of the community. What if he could have prevented it? What if he'd been there? Could he have stopped James from climbing to the top to adjust that last log?

"Hosea!"

Startled from his thoughts, Hosea looked up to see Rhoda making her way to him from across the yard. He wondered how she'd gotten so close without him realizing it.

He called back a greeting and raised his hand.

She came, winded, holding Giles's hand.

His young nephew looked up at Hosea as if he were begging for some attention. Hosea had never met this child before yesterday. He'd been born after he'd last seen his sister. He knelt on one knee. "Giles, my boy, how'd you sleep?"

"Good."

Hosea attempted to get the boy to give him a firm handshake. The tiny hand felt warm and soft in Hosea's rough one. The warmth made him think of Alexander and the same feeling he always got when the young boy reached for his hand. Tears welled again. "That's good. It is good to have you here young man." Hosea stood. "What do you know about chickens, Giles?"

Giles looked up and grinned. "I like them."

Hosea handed him the bucket of scraps from the kitchen that Sally Mae had given him. "Why don't you feed them for me? Would you?"

Giles took the bucket and began taking handfuls of apple and potato peelings and tossed them over the now repaired fencing. "Here chick, chick, chickies!"

Rhoda smiled. "He wanted to come with me today. Sometimes a small boy can help repair a man's heart."

"That's what Pa used to say." Hosea smiled back and watched as the chickens pecked at the scraps. "I miss Pa."

Rhoda helped Giles with the last few scraps in the bucket that needed dumped over the fence. "Me, too, Hosea. We had a good childhood, didn't we?"

"Yes, we did. Pa and Ma were wonderful parents to us." Hosea took the now-empty bucket from Giles. "What are your plans today?"

"I need to know if there is an empty cabin close by. A place where I and the children may live until Sidney can join us."

Hosea scratched his chin. "I'll have to think about that for a bit."

"Betsey said her brother-in-law had a place not too far away that he isn't using. Is it still available?"

"John's place? It might be. But Rhoda, you don't need to—"

Before Hosea could say anything more, Rhoda interrupted. "No. I do. You have more than enough mouths and people to care for here, and we didn't come to be a burden to you."

"Family is never a burden."

"Of course it isn't, but right now the less you have to be concerned about, the better. Please let me do this. I have money. Not much, but enough to figure out what to do next. And our ma and pa gave me enough training in how best to care for a family. I just need a place to settle."

"When is Sidney planning to arrive?"

"Before winter. So if I can find a place and get it ready for his arrival with the children's help, we'll be fine."

Hosea walked into the barn and placed his tools on a ledge there. He came back out to find a few horses approaching them from the south side of the property. "Let me think on it, Rhoda. We'll figure something out."

Three of Hosea's neighbors came close, reined in their mounts, and jumped off. "Hosea." They took off their hats and tipped their heads to Rhoda. "Ma'am."

Hosea introduced them all. "Not sure if you men met my sister. This here is Rhoda. My younger sister."

The men all nodded.

"Nice to meet you." Henry Leach held out his hand.

Rhoda smiled and shook Henry's hand. She hesitated for a moment before adding, "I'm going to scurry up to the house and see if I can do anything to help Sally today. It was nice meeting you gentlemen." Rhoda took Giles's hand and left them.

"Hosea. We're here to let you know that several people in the community have taken up an offering they'd like to donate to your fund for Widow Ball." Henry held out his palm, which held a few coins. "It isn't much, but we all feel indebted to her. This mill might be your project and idea, but we all need it. We hope you'll accept it and give the money to her."

Hosea didn't know what to say. He could only stare at the warm coins in his palm. He was a blessed man. This would prevent him from having to humble himself to ask for money from his neighbors. "Thank you, men. Thank you so much."

"What now, Hosea?" Josiah Pierce curled the reins of his horse around his hand.

"I hope you all understand. I need some days to ponder the accident and misfortune."

Josiah held up his hand. "No apologies needed. We all feel terrible about what happened. But out here—you know more than any of us that these kinds of things happen daily. Some people die from disease. Others pass away because of starvation. Accidents happen, Hosea. This was nothing more than that. Please don't feel guilty about something out of your control."

"I'm not sure why God allowed it to happen. I just need time to think over it all."

"Understood." Henry acknowledged with a nod. "Let us know when you're ready to assemble the carriage and saw. We'll all come to help. Just have Ambrose come fetch us."

Hosea dropped the coins into a pocket. "Thank you, friends. You indeed bring me more comfort than you can ever imagine."

The men mounted their horses, but before they could make their way home, Hosea mentioned Rhoda's housing needs.

"There is the Swain cabin. John left it to move north to Big Rapids. Don't think he wanted to stay there any longer without Abigail. She's more than welcome to live there."

The other men agreed with Henry's statement.

"Thank you. I'll let her know." Hosea waved to the men as they left his property.

Reaching into his pocket, he fingered the coins. In God's way, He'd handled the situation for Hosea. Now if only Hosea could allow his mind to stop feeling guilt and continue the mill project. Perhaps thankfulness for his friends would encourage his heart to follow.

CHAPTER TWELVE

Rhoda labored to get her and the children settled in the former Swain cabin. It had taken all she had to make it a suitable place to reside. Despite a dirt floor and no furniture, her family had constructed two beds, swept out the small one-room shack, and fixed the stones around the fireplace to make it livable. Ambrose had come one day and helped Rhoda repair the roof with Giles's help.

She'd had to do most of the work herself, as Hosea and his family had finally finished work at the mill. It had now been a functioning mill for a week. Hosea had hired two men to help him. They were new to the area and needed quick work to make a few dollars before winter hit. Rhoda didn't have that luxury. She didn't have the strength of a man to get hired anywhere. Hosea and Sally had been gracious enough to share much of their garden produce with her to get by. It was still summer, but soon it would be fall. From what Hosea and Sally had told her, she didn't want to be caught without provisions and good shelter. What if something prevented Sidney from coming? Could she manage to live without him?

She'd thought and thought for days about what she could do. Fiddling with the ten-cent piece in a handkerchief in her pocket, she knew it was time to do something with it. If she bought food, it wouldn't last them long at all. If she purchased even the supplies she needed, the same would be true. What would a copper kettle do if she had nothing to cook in it? She needed to work. Earn her keep. But what would that be?

One Saturday morning she gathered the children and set out for Whitmore's post to ask if anyone in the area might hire her. She had the stamina to take care of another family, as well as her own, but was there anyone around who could afford to hire her? Of all the neighbors she'd met so far, each had money problems of their own.

As she made her way close to the river, she noticed two mill workers down by the water. They were bachelors who had come to the Michigan Territory to get settled. Hosea had hired them, almost immediately, to help with the work at the mill. As she approached them, she could smell fresh-cut lumber, which was now being processed by the new mill.

The men must have heard her approach, for they both put down dripping shirts to greet her and the children. "Ma'am."

A younger man added, "Good morning."

"Good morning, gentlemen. Perfect morning for you to be by the water."

The men were doing their laundry. A mound of wet clothes sat beside each of them.

"Doin' our laundry. It's what bachelors do on a bright and early Saturday morning here." Both men laughed.

"Quite resourceful." Rhoda smiled, noticing neither man had a bar of soap. "What are you using to clean them?"

"Just water, ma'am. That will have to do for now."

"Well, enjoy your morning."

Both men nodded and got back to their job of washing their clothes.

"Momma, how can those men get anything clean without soap?" Philinda exclaimed.

Rhoda hushed her daughter and hoped the men hadn't heard her, but she was thinking the same thing.

"Momma, I'm hungry again."

Rhoda had heard this from her children so much during the past week that she didn't know how much more she could take. Last night they'd used the last of the potatoes that Sally had given to them on their last visit to Hosea's farm. She couldn't humble herself any longer to ask for more. She had two more yellow squash to eat. Hosea said they'd had an abundance. Rhoda wanted nothing more than to use her ten cents to buy some flour, even cornmeal. Hosea's chickens laid plenty of eggs for all of them, but a variety at a meal would be such a treat for her and the children.

"No whining now. That isn't necessary. We'll eat as soon as we arrive back home. Is that understood?"

Her children nodded, but she knew their hunger would linger. She needed a job. She needed to feed them. They were her responsibility. If only she knew how.

The idea hit her fast. She stopped walking. The children looked up at her with questioning expressions. Instead of walking farther, she felt an irresistible urge to turn back to check with the men still down by the stream. She had to try. This could be her only option, but she had to know for sure before she went to the post today.

She took Giles's little hand and held it out to Philinda. "You children go on ahead. I need to speak to those men. I'll be along shortly."

Philinda nodded. "Yes, Momma." She picked up the hands of Rhoda Ann and Giles and motioned for Martha to follow her.

Rhoda rushed back to the mill workers.

"Hello."

Billie turned so abruptly that he dropped a log on his foot. His face contorted with pain. "Ma'am."

"We're here to see Whitmore. Is he available?"

Billie slipped the log he was holding directly onto the fire. It sent shoots of sparks up the chimney. The fire blazed in response.

"He's gone to Pontiac for a week. May I help you?"

"I need soap. A bar. Do you have it?"

Billie wasn't sure, but he rummaged through the post contents to see if he could find a bar of soap. It was unusual to see a family entering the trading post. They didn't have many provisions for the town folk, but as the year had gone by, Whitmore had been trying to stock more than just his usual gunpowder, furs, and copper kettles. Billie looked on many of the shelves containing the essentials and at the very back of one shelf, he found an entire bar of soap, still wrapped in paper.

Bringing the bar to Rhoda, he held it out to her. "Is this what you're looking for?"

Rhoda smiled. "How much?"

Billie didn't usually make the trades for Whitmore, but he knew that whatever money he took in would be adequate for his boss. "How about ten cents?"

The woman sighed and handed him her ten-cent piece. "Thank you, young man. You've made it possible for me to feed my children."

Billie scratched his head as he watched the woman, followed by her four children, traipse out of the post door. He felt sorry for the children. The only time he'd had to eat soap was when he'd told his pa a lie.

CHAPTER THIRTEEN

"Jillian!"

Jillian stopped singing to wipe her bangs from off her eyes as she saw Billie approaching her from the south end of the property. Her hands were dirty from digging potatoes all morning. The sweat from the unusually warm day had cemented the bangs to her forehead, and they were down in her eyes, making it impossible for her to see well. She'd enticed Etta to cut them a few weeks before. Ma had scolded her at breakfast for doing something so drastic, but she loved how they made her feel like a grown-up. After just a few weeks, she now realized she'd need to trim them more often.

Billie must have walked from the trading post. He'd been there for most of the summer, helping Whitmore with many of the post's building projects. More and more settlers lived in the vacant rooms until they could get their own homes built. Billie had replaced John Swain to finish the project after Abigail's untimely death.

"What are you doing here?" Jillian used her sleeve to wipe off her forehead. She was embarrassed to have Billie find her in such disarray. She stood up to greet him.

"How's my favorite Baker?"

Jillian felt only joy at the compliment. He often said that to her. Despite what he probably meant by the endearing words, every time he said it, it made Jillian quiver with happiness. She wondered if Pa would allow a boy to court her yet. Since Caroline's marriage to Horace, she'd wanted no one else but Billie to find her attractive, and she was ready to have a suitor.

Billie looked at her for a moment and then smiled. "Did you do something different to your hair?"

Jillian looked away for fear Billie would see her blush.

"I like it. You look older."

Jillian's heart soared. "What did you come all this way for? On a Tuesday?"

"Whitmore wanted your pa to know he'd be needing his services soon." It was Billie who looked down at his shoe now. Before he could say what type of services Whitmore needed from Pa, he added, "I heard you singing. It sounded like a sad song."

"You heard me?" Jillian looked away. She loved singing but was often embarrassed when people told her they could hear her and liked it.

"Don't be upset. I love hearing you sing."

"I was actually praying." Jillian looked up again to see Billie's response.

His eyebrows arched and his forehead wrinkled. "You sing your prayers?"

Jillian nodded. "Sometimes."

"That's beautiful. So, it isn't one particular song?"

"I make up tunes as I work. Keeps me working and also praying at the same time."

Billie smiled.

"Pa's in the house. He just finished up fixing the barn roof. A few patches were showing daylight after last week's storm, and he wanted to get them fixed before the weather turns cold again."

"If today is an example of the fall we'll have, I'm sure he will have plenty of time."

Jillian picked up the discarded potato plants.

"Let me help you with those."

"I can get them. They aren't heavy or anything." Jillian picked up the heap and threw them into the compost pile near the back of the house.

Billie picked up one of the potato plants. "Isn't it odd that a potato plant has such deep roots and at the end of those roots is the bounty of not one but several large potatoes?"

"I love digging up potatoes." Jillian stooped to pick out two of the large potatoes near the surface. "It's like finding a wonderful treasure below the plants. The roots of the potato plant run deep. Sometimes I worry I haven't dug down deep enough and have left potatoes in their dark spots under the ground."

"That would be a shame not to find them."

"Exactly!" Jillian looked up with a smile. "Not to sound like my pa, but he often comments that we find good things under roots that grow deep. Pa says that if a good Christian has deep roots in their beliefs, they'll rarely have moments when they don't trust in what they believe. Corn roots aren't as deep. A strong wind comes along, like trials in life, and blows the corn stalks right out of the ground. If that happens, a stalk won't produce any corn. Trees are the same. They have strong, deep roots. When heavy winds blow, a tree can withstand much more than even a potato plant. As believers, our deep roots can't be grounded here on earth, but affixed to God.

"I love nature and thinking about how it can correlate to our lives. I want to have deep roots, so that's what I've been praying," Jillian sighed, "Or singing, that I'd always have deep roots and have them attached to God. It kinda makes sense, don't you think?"

"Pretty and smart!"

Jillian jerked her head toward him. "What did you say?"

"Oh, nothing. I need to see your pa."

"I'll go in with you. I need something to drink."

As the two entered the house, Ma and Pa looked up.

"Billie." Pa stood up from sitting at the table. He stretched out to take Billie's hand. "What are you here for on this fine day?"

"I've brought you a message from Whitmore."

Hosea put his hands on his hips. "What message?"

"There have been sights of Indians off to the west. He thought it might be the tribe who took Alexander. He's seen the chief from time to time in that area."

Hosea sat back down. He grew pensive, but added, "Thanks for letting me know, Billie."

"Can you stay for supper, Billie?" Jillian's ma flashed a smile at her.

"No ma'am. I wish I could, but I need to be gettin' back. It gets darker earlier each night. I didn't have a horse to get me here. I just walked."

Ma went to the tin by the stove. "Well, here, how about a biscuit or two to eat on the road?"

"Thank you. I'd like that."

Ma wrapped two biscuits in a cloth and handed them over to the young man.

"I'll be going now." Billie placed his hat back on. "You have a good evening."

Jillian wished for an excuse to hold the boy there. She longed for him to stay for supper, but she also knew the dangers he might encounter if he waited too long. The darkness and Michigan Territory were too wild to chance walking home later.

She went to the door with Billie and as he walked away, he looked back for a moment. When he did, he winked.

"Bear grease?" Rhoda picked up the small jar that Sally had handed her and took a large whiff. Her expression sent her nieces into hysterical laughter.

Sally laughed, too. "It has a horrible odor to it, but you get used to it. Rub it into your hands. It will take away the raw feeling and help heal them."

Rhoda took another small sniff and her eyes watered. "How will this help my chapped hands?"

"I don't know how, but it heals things." Sally patted her shoulder. "Trust me."

Rhoda took her finger and dipped it into the thick salve. She carefully spread it over the back of her right hand. As she did, the redness of her hands and the cracks around her nails filled in and she found instant relief.

"We use it for mosquito repellant, too. It doesn't smell very nice, but it sure does wonders for medicinal purposes." Sally took the jar and placed it back on the mantle. "Now put your hands in these gloves."

"I'll ruin the gloves!" Rhoda pulled her hands away.

Sally held out the opening of the right glove. "Go ahead. We use them normally for just this purpose. Sleep with them on. By morning, your raw, worn-out hands will be almost like a newborn's skin."

Rhoda put on the glove, and then Sally helped her pull up the other. "Believe me, sister. You will come back for more in about a week."

Sally wiped the residue of ointment down her apron. "You're working too hard, Rhoda."

Rhoda sat and placed her gloved hands on her lap. "I have to."

"No, you don't. We have food. We can share with you without you having to pay us for it."

"I can't do that. You have enough mouths to feed without adding me or the children to the hardship. Please, just take my coins. They are a pittance to what I owe you for eggs, extra portions of the deer Hosea hunts, and even for this bear grease." Rhoda couldn't help but grimace at the smell now emanating from her lap. She must have made another scowl, because Caroline laughed right out loud.

Caroline set down her knitting. "It's okay, Aunt Rhoda. We've all had to get used to the smell. After all this time of applying and using it, none of us seems to mind the smell anymore."

Rhoda didn't know what else to say. Hosea's family had been so kind to her since her arrival. She had to trust them. She had no choice.

The door swung open, and Hosea stamped his feet outside before entering with a flourish. "Gettin' chilly out there!" He shivered and slapped his hands together. "It won't be long before winter will be full on us. Probably sooner than we think."

Rhoda's mouth grew dry. She'd been working so hard the last few weeks that she hadn't even noticed the days were getting much shorter and the evenings cooler. It made her wonder if Sidney would appear yet this year. He'd promised her to not be far behind, but she'd been here for almost two full months now. There had been no letter. The only thing she knew to do was to ask, "Hosea? Do you have a letter for me?"

Hosea placed his coat on a peg by the door and turned to her. "Rhoda. I told you it takes a long time for letters to get through. Didn't I?"

Asking nothing more, Rhoda sighed. Hosea had left early that morning to make it to the trading post. Everyone was eager to hear any news. Whitmore seemed to always know just what was happening in this part of the country and farther away. Men traveling through always had some news to share, and he was happy to keep others informed.

"We need a newspaper started here. Don't you think?" Caroline went back to her knitting. She'd told everyone she wanted to make a sweater for Horace for the upcoming holiday season. She wanted it to be a surprise, thus why she'd been working on it at her parents' home.

"That's why God's given us Whitmore. He knows all. He also—" Hosea pulled a dingy, very wrinkled letter out of his shirt, "Makes sure we get our mail on time." He handed the letter to Rhoda.

Before she could raise her hand to take the letter, Sally came to her aid. "You keep those hands in those gloves." She took the paper from Hosea. "I'll place the letter here, near your coat. You can take it home to read in private."

"What is that smell?" Hosea grinned at his sister. She blushed, knowing it emanated from the bear grease now seeping into her cracked, chapped hands.

"You know good and well what that smell is. Rhoda's hands are a mess." Sally looked at Rhoda. "Unless, of course, you want to read it now."

Everyone looked at Rhoda in anticipation. Letters of any kind were precious and scarce.

Rhoda smiled. "Open it, Sally. I don't think I can wait any longer to hear when my husband will arrive."

Everyone cheered. Sally sat opposite Rhoda and next to Hosea. She unfolded the letter as Jillian ceased stirring a pot over the fire and Etta neared the table after sweeping the floor beside the beds to join them at the table.

"Go ahead and read. If things get too personal—" Rhoda frowned, "I'd be pleased if you stopped when I ask."

Sally unfolded the letter and read. "*Dear Rhoda and my children. I pray this finds you well. I wish there was a way for me to know if you've made it to Hosea or not. I'm praying the good Lord kept you safe until you arrived in the New Territory.*" Sally looked up.

Rhoda sighed. She didn't need God to help her. She'd done very well on her own. Hosea gave her a look of concern. She ignored it. "Go ahead. Keep reading."

"We have had a successful time selling the store. We will leave for Michigan Territory on the 'morrow."

"What's the date on the letter, Sally?"

Sally glanced up to see if there was a date. She shook her head. "There isn't one."

Rhoda put a gloved hand to her forehead and began rubbing it. "Of course, there isn't. Oh, Sidney. Keep reading."

"We will bring as many things along as we can. I want to keep our main inventory to bring with us, but not sure if it wouldn't be wiser to sell all here and just bring money to resupply us when we arrive."

It was Hosea's time to reply, "I hope to goodness he doesn't do that. We could use some tools here."

"We talked about that before I left. But keep reading, Sally."

"I've brought as much as I can pack in barrels. The children have been helpful. Even more so, knowing that soon we'll all be together again if they work hard. They miss you and the younger ones."

Giles leaned against Rhoda. If any of his children missed their father, it was Giles. She put her arm around the small child.

"Momma, please don't get near me." Giles turned up his nose in a wrinkled smirk and inched away from Rhoda, pointing to her hands. He leaned his head against Jillian's shoulder instead. Everyone laughed.

"We will begin tomorrow and if all goes well, making it to you around the first of October. That's my guess."

"But it doesn't say when he left. I hope this means it was in September."

Sally turned the letter over and shrugged. "I don't see a date." She continued reading. *"I've asked a few men who have been to the Michigan Territory and back about the prospects of getting supplies once we are there. They are all telling me I should pick them up in Detroit before heading inland—"*

"Either Detroit or Pontiac," added Hosea.

Sally placed the letter on the table. "It would be in his best interest." She pointed to the line where she'd left off. *"I will do that if I can't pay the shipping fees for the items I thought we'd bring with us. Other than that, the store is now under new ownership. Our bags and barrels are packed and ready. We set out tomorrow for the long trip. I'm so eager to see you, my dear."*

"That's good. The rest is probably for my eyes only." Rhoda announced.

Sally refolded the letter.

"Put it near my coat, please, Sally."

Sally did as she was told.

"He should be here any day now. Right, Hosea?"

Hosea held up his coffee cup to Jillian, who stood to fill it for him. "I would imagine so. If he had good weather and all went well." Jillian returned with a steaming mug and handed it to her Pa.

"It will be good to see the rest of your family soon. Especially before we celebrate Christmas."

Rhoda smiled at Giles, who gave her a big smile back. "It will be nice to have your father here soon."

The rest of the family went back to their chores.

Caroline thanked Rhoda for allowing them to read her private letter. "It will be good to have him here."

Rhoda had been working herself to the bone and had lost weight from the lifting and washing of clothes from the men at the mill. There were three employees now and every Monday they brought her their belongings to be washed, mended, and folded. They'd return on Wednesday to pick up their clothing. She didn't mind the work, and she'd even been able to save some of her money for when the rest of the family arrived.

"There is other news." Hosea took a small sip from the steamy cup.

Everyone turned to listen.

"There are two men who have come into the territory by Knagg's Place. Their names are A.L. and B.O. Williams."

"I've heard Horace talking about those brothers. They've been building a large building near the post." Caroline lifted her knitting, as if to get better light from the nearby lamp to see her work.

"Yes. They've been there since spring. The building will soon be completed. It's two stories high now. It's quite the place. Paned glassed windows with three fireplaces—on the main floor alone.

The ends of the building have maple gables with fine leaves carved into them."

"That sounds almost too elaborate to have somewhere like Knagg's Place." Jillian sat to listen.

"But the best news about it is—they are making rooms for many to live. Large rooms upstairs, so when travelers come through, they'll have a place to spend the night or a few days. Someone mentioned there will be a main stagecoach line traveling right past the place. The men are thinking of turning it into not only a hotel but also a meeting place of sorts."

'*Oh, my!*' Gasps echoed around the table.

"They plan on even starting a bank soon."

"A bank?" Sally's expression made the whole family laugh. "What do we need a bank for?"

"Their business is in furs. They will be traders for the Jacob Astor Fur Trading Company. They're a big trading company and will probably put Whitmore right out of business."

Rhoda couldn't hold back any longer. "How much will it be to rent the rooms, Hosea?"

"I'm not sure. I don't think they have it ready to rent out yet, but it'll be soon. Billie and Ambrose have both been helping them as much as they can. They pay well. But what I was thinking about was—" Hosea looked directly at Rhoda. "Perhaps that's where you'll be able to put your store. Maybe they'll rent out a portion of the building to Sidney."

Rhoda couldn't believe the timing. If this were true, they wouldn't have to build a store and that would put them in business sooner.

"They're naming the building The Exchange. It will be a modern building for these parts. But before they separate the rooms upstairs, they plan to hold a large dance when finished. Perhaps just after the new year."

That got all the women in the room smiling.

"A dance?" Jillian stood, picked up the edges of her skirt, and began swirling around the table. "I hope so. I love dancing." She began humming a tune.

"What about Whitmore? Will we lose him?" Sally pulled on Jillian's arm and pointed to the boiling pot over the fire. Jillian stopped twirling and went back to stirring the evening meal over the fire.

"I don't know. There aren't many Indians left here. Most have all gone farther inland. I think it will make his business obsolete. But more than anything, we'll have a place closer than Pontiac to get supplies. We'll soon be much more civilized." Hosea put his fingers behind his suspenders and stood tall.

Rhoda couldn't wait for Sidney to arrive. She knew when he did, he'd be excited about The Exchange. This could be the start of something beneficial for her family. If nothing else, the news and Sidney's letter had taken the attention away from the powerful smell still emanating from her hands.

Caroline wrapped up the yarn she'd been using for Horace's sweater and put it in the basket by the fireplace. She had gotten lots done, but she'd wanted to talk to her ma about Horace's health. They'd been so busy all day she hadn't had a second to pull her aside. As she tucked in the stray yarn, she asked her ma, "Ma, can I chat with you outside?"

Everyone went back to their chores. Aunt Rhoda had left with Giles and Pa had gone outside to finish the evening chores. She had just enough daylight left to return home.

"Just for a few minutes. I need to get dinner on the table." Ma pulled her apron off, reached for her shawl, and wrapped it tightly around her shoulders. "Let's go."

Caroline pulled on her coat and followed.

"What's wrong, Caroline?"

"I'm worried about Horace, Ma. He's not getting any better. He's losing weight." She made an effort to swallow the tears that wanted to fall; she knew if they started, she'd never be able to get them stopped before heading home.

"What are all of his symptoms?"

"He eats well but it doesn't seem to help. I even keep encouraging him to eat two helpings of dessert. Nothing is helping, and he seems to be thirsty all the time. I've heard him go to the water barrel in the middle of the night and gulp down water. All he keeps saying is 'I'm so thirsty.'"

"Doesn't sound right, does it? Are you sure it's not the ague?"

"He has no fever. I keep checking him for that. After he eats at night, I often find him sitting in his chair by the fire, sound asleep. It's the oddest thing. I don't think he's working all that hard every day to be so tired. Once I finish the dishes and sit down, it startles him awake and then when we go to bed, he quickly falls asleep again. He sleeps so soundly. I can't imagine him not being able to stay awake that late at night. He appears sluggish after his breakfast, too. It seems he's most tired after he eats."

"Hmm, I don't know Caroline. I'm no doctor. I wish Dr. Harder would hurry and arrive. I thought he'd be here by now."

"Me, as well. I just thought maybe you'd know. I've seen nothing quite like it."

Her ma wrapped her shawl tighter. "What about you?"

"I'm feeling fine." Caroline grew skeptical. "Why?"

"Well, you've been married now over a year and a half. Has there not been any signs of a child yet?"

This time, tears did spring to Caroline's eyes. She blinked. "Nothing. Do you think it has anything to do with Horace and his health concerns?"

"I don't know. Maybe. Our family doesn't have any female issues I know of. Once we've been married for a short time, children just seem to come easily and naturally. It could be."

Her response surprised Caroline. Now that she'd said it, she wondered if it could be true. Until now, she had blamed her own body, not Horace's.

"Well." Ma smiled and pulled her close. "It will happen. In God's time. I'll talk to Hosea about the symptoms. Maybe even Betsey. She's been able to diagnose more people than me. As long as it's okay with you?"

Caroline nodded.

"Perhaps we can put our heads together and come up with something."

Caroline buttoned her coat up higher. The chill in the air made her realize she needed to get home before darkness took away her ability to arrive safely. She hugged her ma and thanked her for the pleasant afternoon. The talk with her ma hadn't alleviated any of Caroline's fears. It had only heightened them.

Hosea trudged through the evening chores. What used to bring him joy now brought more aches and pains than satisfaction. He loved going to the mill and watching the men work. He'd often lend a helping hand, despite the pang of gnawing guilt still in his heart. His good fortune had come at a high price. A man had lost his life in helping him fulfill his dreams. As gloom crept in, he tried to remember a verse. *My soul melteth for heaviness; strengthen thou me according unto thy word.*

From those thoughts, Hosea also took it upon himself to shoulder Rhoda's burdens. He loved his sister. She'd always been the one to protect and listen to him when they were youngsters. Rhoda was the closest younger sister in age. They did most everything together until Hosea took Sally Mae as his wife and moved away. He adored her, but he now worried about her faith. If there was anything left of it. It appeared non-existent in her actions since coming to live near them. What had happened? Was Hosea responsible for her falling away?

Hosea filled the oxen mangers with grain. It would be wonderful to have a store closer than Pontiac. He wondered what Ambrose thought. Ambrose had wanted to start a store of his own. He'd even scouted out the land nearby on which to build. What would he do now? This put Hosea in a quandary. If Sidney and Rhoda proceeded with a store of their own, Ambrose might have to change his mind about his future.

In Hosea's thoughts about his son, *pride* didn't describe his feelings well enough. Whatever the project, Ambrose was helpful to everyone. He'd even taken on delivering the lumber for the mill.

Hosea knew that if Sidney pushed for a store, Ambrose would back away from his plans. That was the type of man he was.

Placing his shovel near the door, Hosea left the barn to go check on the last bit of crops remaining in the field. Summer was over, but harvesting would stop once they had a hard frost. He placed his hands on his hips and gazed at the field. Should he plant more or less next year? They could always use more food to store for winter. There never seemed to be enough at winter's end. The dismal sense of winter shortages filled his heart. He had to walk away, but something at the edge of his property caught his attention. Hosea stood still to watch a doe grazing on some grass near his field.

Every time something grabbed his attention near the edge of his land, Alexander sprung into his thoughts. Oh, how he missed the boy. He'd be such a help to him now that the girls were growing older and would soon leave home to start their own families. The only consolation for his lost son was his grandson, Richard, though even he didn't take away the agony of missing Alexander. Hosea often prayed for the boy who supposedly lived among the Indians. They'd escaped with him almost two years ago.

Whitmore often talked in detail about how the Indian population was dying away. Smallpox and cholera had taken its toll on the tribes surrounding Knagg's Place. Would Alexander ever return? Would Hosea ever see his face again?

Hosea gazed at the small deer as she ripped grass from the ground to eat. He knew that when he turned to head to the barn, she'd skitter off into the woods. God's beauty in creating such an amazing animal filled Hosea's heart with praise, replacing his anxious heart with joy. The deer had supplied needed food almost year-round for his family. It was like a message from God, letting Hosea know He was still near and ready to help the family through another winter.

Dried herbs filled the rafters of the lean-to. Sally Mae had been diligent to plant medicinal and cooking herbs throughout the summer months. Hosea had to duck his head as he made his way into their cabin. The warmth from the fire took the chill out of his soul. In all of his years, Hosea only knew one thing that could fill in the empty, sorrowful fears for the future, the aches that penetrated his soul. He would read tonight. Nothing could fill his grievous thoughts but the words of the One who created his heart. If He had created Hosea for this purpose in life, He had the verses to fill his heart with comfort. A comfort which filled even the depth of his longing soul.

As Hosea fingered the roots of the plants his wife had hung from the walls, Hosea envisioned his spiritual roots. Were they deep enough? Would they allow him to endure more in this new land and survive? He prayed that soon Rhoda would allow her spiritual roots to grow deeper. There was usually only one way to do that.

Unfortunately, it didn't always bring days without trials, but rather storms that covered the skies in dark, threatening clouds.

Hosea's family looked up as soon as they heard the galloping horse come near the front door of the cabin. Hosea wiped off his mouth and went to the front door just as a knock interrupted their breakfast.

It was Billie, grinning at the front door. "Good morning, sir. Whitmore has sent me to alert you to the fact that there's a visitor in town."

Hosea motioned for Billie to come in. "Come join us, Billie. Have you eaten your breakfast?"

Billie took off his hat and went for the closest chair. "I haven't."

Sally Mae rose and dished some of the fresh eggs and some bread on a plate, just as Jillian jumped up from her chair and rushed to her bedside. As Sally Mae handed the young man his portion, he gave her a big grin. "Thank you, Mrs. Baker. I'm starving!"

Everyone grinned at the young man's eagerness to eat. Hosea pushed back his empty plate as he sat to hear who Billie knew to be in town. The thought made Hosea smile. They had been having more and more people join them in this part of the Michigan

Territory. Inevitably, a town would soon develop, and that thought made Hosea grin even more. "Who's here?"

Billie took a large bite from a slice of bread just before Hosea asked the question. He looked up with eyes wide. His full mouth wasn't allowing him to answer.

Jillian came back to the table with a pale pink ribbon, pulling back her freshly combed hair. As she sat again, Billie smiled.

"It's your friend. From New York." Billie murmured between mouthfuls of food. "The doctor."

"Nicholas? Is Nicholas Harder here?" Hosea slapped his knee. "By Job, he said he'd be here this fall."

Billie picked up the cloth Sally had placed beside his plate and wiped his mouth. "He arrived last night. They were still sleeping when I left to come here. Whitmore wanted to be sure you knew he had arrived.

Hosea stood up. "Why, thank you, boy. I wanted to be one of the first to welcome Nicholas and his family to our community." Hosea handed Sally his plate. "I need to get a move on. I want to show Nicholas around. Can you do without me today, Sally Mae?"

His wife smirked. "I think we can manage, Hosea. Go. I'll prepare an enjoyable meal for tonight. Bring Nicholas and the family here. We can put them all up at Betsey's house for the evening. I'll send one of the girls up the ridge to tell her."

"Will be mighty good to have Nicholas here now. We need a good doctor."

Hosea went to the peg by the door to grab his coat. While putting it on, he asked Sally to pack him something to eat before he left. "You finish up, Billie. I'm gonna feed the oxen before we head south."

Billie nodded as he shoved another forkful of eggs into his mouth.

To Jillian, it seemed the only thing Billie noticed was that his slice of bread had fresh jam on it.

CHAPTER FOURTEEN

Hosea heard Nicholas and Whitmore exchanging trading information as he approached. He could spot Nicholas from several yards away, because he stood a foot taller than Hosea. Whitmore was translating a conversation between Nicholas and a well-known Indian medicine man. It didn't surprise Hosea that his doctor friend was already assessing how to best serve the people of the community. That was his style. He never thought his ideas were the only way to treat a patient.

"Have him tell me again how his tribe designated him as a medicine man." Nicholas seemed enamored with the Algonquin conversation between Whitmore and the Chippewa medicine man. With his arms folded, he was listened intently as Whitmore translated what the Indian was telling him.

Hosea waited a moment, so as not to interrupt the conversation.

"Good gracious, man! That seems like a torturous way to become a doctor." At that statement, Nicholas paused and turned. His face brightened as he glimpsed Hosea standing just a few feet away. "Hosea!" He held up a hand for Whitmore to stop and rushed to embrace Hosea.

Hosea welcomed him with open arms, but because of Nicholas's height, he found himself encircled in a hug, lifting him off his feet. "My friend, my friend. How are you?"

Hosea grimaced as Nicholas lowered him back to the ground. Looking past Nicholas's shoulder, Hosea saw Whitmore chuckling behind them.

"I am well, Nicholas." Hosea stepped back, so he wasn't displaced off his feet a second time. "It's good to see you again."

Nicholas grabbed his forearms and looked into his eyes. "Are you feeling well, chap? You look as though you've whittled away to nothing out here in the wilderness. You're light as a feather!"

Hosea had to admit he probably had aged since last seeing Nicholas. Perhaps Sally Mae's attempts at putting a stitch in the waist of his pants wasn't for naught, but to hear someone notice a change made him feel timid, despite knowing clearly that Nicholas didn't mean to make him feel that way. All he could do was give his friend the truth. "It's not easy getting settled in a new territory. It's just that you're used to all that rich food in New York and your high life as a doctor. We eat more like Daniel around here than King Nebuchadnezzar."

Nicholas's questioning face soon gave way to a full-blown guffaw. Hosea joined in.

"It's clear that the Bible is still of paramount consideration to you, Hosea."

"As it will always be." Hosea was sure Nicholas didn't take any of his words as an insult, just as he hadn't taken it personally to be told he looked old and worn-out. It was their way of continuing to cement a solid and noble friendship.

In actuality, they adored each other. Making that fact abundantly clear, Nicholas pulled him close again, slapping him on the back instead of lifting him off his foundation. "It *is* so good to see you, my friend."

"I see you've met Whitmore." Hosea motioned for them to join Whitmore, who seemed entertained by the men's interaction. "As you can see, Whitmore can keep our Indian-settler relationships intact. He's been a valuable interpreter, judge, and friend since we arrived here. We wouldn't have lasted as long as we have without his help and, of course, God's provision."

Whitmore smiled. "Thank you, Hosea. It's good to have a doctor here."

"We've been chatting with this Chippewa medicine man. I'm interested in the natural ways of the natives in treating themselves. But I need to tell you...if you want to be a medicine man in a tribe, it's a brutal test of fortitude." Nicholas leaned forward, cupping his hand over his mouth. "They literally torture you first." Nicholas flinched. "To see if they can disgrace you before honoring you with the title. And I thought finals at Kinderhook Institute would test a man beyond what he was able. I'm thankful I'm not a Chippewa medicine man."

Hosea hadn't heard what the method was to distinguish a medicine man, but their practices were far from lenient and often tortuous, to define prominent levels of hierarchy in a tribe. And a medicine man was in a high and distinguished position. "You'll have to share that with me someday."

As they were speaking, out the door came an elegantly dressed woman. She was followed by another beautiful, young woman who appeared to be near Betsey's age. Her dress was as fashionable and elegant as the woman she followed.

"Ahh, my dears. This is Hosea. Hosea Baker. I'm so happy to introduce you." Nicholas took the arm of the woman who came out first and presented her to Hosea. "This is my wife, Sallie."

Sallie extended her hand to Hosea. "It is nice to meet you, Hosea."

Hosea removed his hat and shook the woman's hand. She was strikingly handsome. He wanted to inquire about Margaret, but knew it wasn't the proper thing to do after just being introduced to another wife. He knew Sally Mae would want to know what had happened to Nicholas's first wife.

The younger woman also held out her hand. "Hello, Hosea. Do you remember me?"

Hosea surmised and took a guess. "Elizabeth?"

"You're correct. It is nice to see you again." Elizabeth resembled her mother, Margaret. If Nicholas hadn't introduced them both, Hosea would have addressed Elizabeth as Margaret. A young child clung to her skirt.

"And this—" Elizabeth pulled the child out and stood him in front of her skirts. "Is my little brother, Nicholas Junior."

Hosea stooped to the level of the small boy. The resemblance to his friend Nicholas was remarkable, but his hair was blonde. Nothing like Nicholas's jet-black hair. "Hello, young man."

The boy blushed and turned again to bury his face in his older sister's skirts.

Nicholas picked up the child. "No hiding, young man. This man is our friend. You will show respect." He placed the boy back on his feet.

Obeying, the child stood between his father and mother but held tight to Sallie's hand.

Nicholas introduced his other children. Four young men who appeared to range in their teens. John Nelson and Henry, Hosea remembered, but there were two more boys introduced as Sallie's boys. Their names were Moses and Joseph. More children followed, ten-year-old Hannah and six-year-old Adaline. Hosea winked at Nicholas. "That's quite a crew. You've nearly caught up to me, except with boys instead of girls."

At the mention of girls, Nicholas's boys seemed more attentive to the men's conversation.

"We have an assortment."

A refined Sallie only smiled. "I'm sure you're wondering why I'm here and not Margaret."

Hosea wouldn't deny his questioning. "Well, ma'am, yes."

Nicholas took over the conversation after placing the younger Nicholas back into his sister's care. The children all scampered off in different directions. "Sallie and I married three years ago. Moses and Joseph are hers from her first marriage. We both lost spouses and soon realized we didn't want to spend our lives in sorrow." At this pronouncement, Nicholas shrugged. "We found each other at a church social and combined both our families into one. This noisy brood is the result."

Sallie added, "But we wouldn't have it any other way."

Nicholas smiled at Sallie, who took hold of his hand.

"We are happy again. Losing a spouse is not for the faint of heart." Sallie glanced up at Nicholas with adoration.

Nicholas agreed with a squeeze of his new wife's hand.

Hosea couldn't imagine living without Sally Mae. He treasured her.

"Well, Whitmore. I think we will take leave of you now and head to Hosea's home if that's agreeable to him?" Nicholas looked to Hosea, who nodded emphatically. "It's been a long trip and we are eager to reach a final destination." Nicholas turned. "We thank you for your hospitality, Whitmore, at such a late hour last evening. We appreciate the food and accommodations. If you'll excuse us,

Hosea, let's go into the post and I'll settle up with how much I owe you."

"You owe me medical care when I need it," Whitmore acknowledged with a smile. "There will come a time, I'm sure."

"Done! Send for me in any emergency. I will do what I can." Nicholas released Sallie's hand and motioned for his children to get to the wagons. "It will take a few minutes to harness up the team, but we'll be ready to move in short order."

Sallie Harder left her husband, calling to the children to gather up their belongings. She shooed a few Indian squaws away from barrels hanging off the first wagon that the women had been trying to open. "There is nothing here for you. Be off!" It made Hosea smile even more. This woman matched Nicholas's temperament.

"Will Sally Mae be okay to have us drop in tonight?"

Hosea grinned. "She wants nothing else."

Nicholas rocked on his heels. "Good. Good. I'm eager to see her. It's been too long."

"I'm a grandfather, you know. Perhaps I'll let you see them."

"That's why you look so old."

"Or maybe not!"

Both men roared with laughter.

Hosea knew having a doctor near would bring the community even further in establishing itself. And for that, Hosea was thankful.

"We decided to not go the route of the Erie canal, but forged ahead with our teams through Canada to arrive here. Quite the journey for a man but with a family..." Nicholas sighed, "we struggled to make it before winter. For getting this far, we are grateful to God."

Nicholas seemed comfortable visiting the Bakers. The houseful of children made for cramped quarters, especially trying to feed them all, but soon the adults could sit and talk.

Sally gathered what they had left from a pot of stew she'd made a few days earlier and added another chunk of venison. Potatoes and some turnips made for a hearty enough stew to give everyone a full belly. From the satisfaction on everyone's faces, she felt grateful they had enough to share. Nicholas's boys seemed nourished enough. They encouraged the Baker sisters to show them Hosea's property along the river.

As the young ones headed out for an evening of fun, the adults discussed how best to get Nicholas and his family settled. Ambrose had stopped in for dinner, and Sally loved seeing him fit so well into the conversation. She admired the thoughtful, intelligent man her son had become.

"We need a good place to settle for the winter. Is there a house close by or will we have to build our own?" Nicholas placed his fork down after finishing up some of the apple cobbler Sally prepared that afternoon. "This is a mighty good cobbler, Sally."

"I've given your home considerable thought, Nicholas. I have a few ideas." Hosea placed his empty plate on top of Nicholas's.

"Good. Thank you, Hosea." Nicholas nodded to his wife, who hadn't said much of anything throughout the meal. "Now, how in the world will we keep you two ladies apart when we speak of you?"

Before Hosea could give Nicholas his housing ideas, the doctor changed the topic. It only made Hosea laugh. "I call mine Sally Mae. That might distinguish them for everyone."

Nicholas's Sallie remarked, "I'm honored to share a name with your wife, Hosea. If only—" She blushed before adding, "—I could bake as well."

"I've had much more practice, Sallie." Sally smiled at the young woman. "Are you sure you've had plenty to eat?"

Sallie leaned toward her. "I want you to know that my lack of eating tonight was not because of your cooking abilities. I'm with child, and within the last few weeks, nothing has tasted or sounded good to eat."

Relieved, Sally patted the hand of the younger woman. "Oh, how I understand those difficulties. Our Betsey has had two children in less than two years, and she has had her rounds of sickness, too."

Sally loved the quiet spirit of Nicholas's wife. Although she also presented considerable strength in her character, too. Instead of scolding a child for not using their manners throughout dinner, she would deliver just a glance in their direction. As a child caught sight of the look, they would immediately cease their antics or adjust their manners, impressing Sally. She could say much about children who behave with just a look.

"How long do you have?" Sally Mae whispered.

"Too new to know for sure. I'm also suffering from extreme exhaustion. At first I thought it was the trip, but I don't believe that's the entire reason now. I don't believe I was expecting when we left New York."

"Let me know if I can get you anything more."

"Thank you. You've already been very kind."

"Tomorrow I'll take you down to show you the mill. That's where you'll be purchasing the lumber for your house." Hosea wiped off the last of his dinner with one of the cloth napkins. Sally Mae was thankful he'd not used his shirt sleeve, as was his normal practice.

"You know," Ambrose spoke up. "I know Pa has a few ideas about where you can stay, but I have a fine house built just north of here. I had planned to move in this winter, but if you'd like to live there until you can finishing building a home, perhaps we can work something out."

Nicholas's eyes sparkled. "Ambrose, that's a mighty kind offer."

"How many bedrooms does your home have, Ambrose? As you can see, we have many children to accommodate." Sallie took a sip of tea.

"There are three bedrooms, but I can add more with a wall or two. I made it big, so perhaps a family, such as yours, could use it for the time being. Until, of course, I can fill it with a family of my own."

Hosea slapped the wooden table. Sallie's cup clattered, and she grabbed for the handle.

"Hosea! Calm down. What was that for?" Sally Mae steadied the table with her hands.

"It's the first time I've heard of Ambrose here wanting a family!" Hosea smirked.

"Oh, Pa, stop. When you head down to the mill tomorrow, stop by and see the place on your way. Pa will know how to get there." Ambrose stepped back from the table. "Speaking of that, I need to head home. It's getting darker sooner rather than later out there now." He reached for his coat on the peg near the door. "There is no pressure for you to accept my offer, but if you'd like the place, there is no reason we couldn't come up with a favorable agreement. I will look forward to seeing you tomorrow."

Nicholas stood to shake Ambrose's hand before he stepped out into the soon-to-be night. Children's laughter drifted into the cabin once the door opened.

"Sounds like the children are making the best of the warm fall night." Nicholas patted Hosea on the back. "It's so good to be here with you. Please sit and tell me about the area. What can I expect? Will folks be receptive to a doctor?"

As Hosea enlightened Nicholas on the community, Sally Mae offered her rocking chair to Sallie Harder. "Come. Sit by the fire. It's warmer there."

Sally Mae picked up her crocheting and showed Sallie what she'd been working on, as of late. "I like to start a new project as soon as harvest is complete. I don't get much time during the summer months to make a blanket or shawl. All the time I need for darning things takes up much of my summer knitting. One of the new neighbors brought a few sheep with them. It's been nice to have yarn again."

"I understand that. How have you managed here? From what we could tell as we maneuvered the wagons north, the woods here are quite desolate." Sallie leaned closer to Sally Mae and whispered. "What about the Indians? Are they dangerous? Should I be worried?"

Sally Mae looked up from her work. "Dangerous? No. We've had many encounters. Just after we moved here, we had our share of frustrations with them, but we soon learned they weren't a threat. Mostly, they've been helpful. During the summer months, our biggest worry wasn't the Indians but the mosquitoes. Now that fall has arrived, the mosquitoes are less of a problem. The Indians brought us a special salve which has helped to keep them at bay. I find many of their medicinal suggestions of great use."

"A salve?"

"It's a stinky sort of ointment that we also put on chapped and cracked skin, but we use it when we need to ward off mosquitoes."

"That bad?"

"They've crawled into our baking, give us excruciating misery from bites, and unless the snow is flying outside, endless torment." Sally Mae used her knitting needle to slip around to finish a row of stitches. "Once you get used to them, it doesn't make it any better, but the salve eases the pain and misery they cause."

"What are some of the medical needs in a community of this size, Hosea?" Nicholas placed his elbows on the table and leaned on them.

"We have some type of ague that is awful during the summer months. It doesn't seem to affect many during the winter."

"What are the symptoms?" Nicholas spoke in a hushed tone. "I need to be prepared to face whatever this wilderness will bring for patient issues." The doctor glanced over at his wife. "She's worried about the sicknesses here more than at home. Might as well lay it out for me now, then I can let Sallie know."

"The ague comes with a high fever. Delirium. Each of us seems to struggle with it from time to time."

"So, you catch it more than once?"

Hosea nodded. "Usually once or twice a summer."

"It seems to cause excessive thirst. I've probably had it five or six times since we've arrived. It brings not only a high fever but a thirst that can't be quenched no matter how much water the patient gets."

"What's the mortality rate?"

"Seems to strike the elderly harder. Betsey had it just before giving birth to her first child. Saps the strength right out of a person. We weren't sure if she'd be strong enough to give birth." Hosea thought back to the day when they worried about baby Julia. "If it weren't for herbal remedies of a local squaw, I'm not sure she or the baby would have survived."

"Medicines of an Indian?"

Hosea crossed his arms. "I believe she saved Betsey and our granddaughter."

Nicholas tapped the table with a finger. "Funny you should bring that up. I've heard tale after tale of the Indians and their herbal remedies doing wonders for others." He leaned back. "You know me, Hosea. Specific medicines and higher education are the best of all healing, but there has to be some kind of natural remedies that have cured things down through the years before all of us highly educated people came on the scene. Many doctors addressing the ailments of settlers have said that Indians have cured them of more diseases than some book learned doctors. I'm not one to disagree."

"It's true. I've seen how even Sally Mae can put a few things together like peppermint leaves or the roots of a specific plant, which inevitably cured things like an upset stomach or even my aching joints. Ginger tea always settles my stomach."

"I think we can all learn from what the Indians have used in the past. I'm sure I can learn more about the plant world and how it can be of help to all of us."

"I wish Waussinoodae was still here. She'd help you with those kinds of studies."

Nicholas leaned forward. "Who?"

Hosea smiled, thinking of the dear Indian woman. "I believe it was some kind of cholera that took her life." Hosea told his friend all about what had happened when the Indian woman arrived for Sally Mae to cure her. "It was a hard time for our family." Hosea briefly told his friend about Alexander. "I hope you can help us here, Nicholas. We need a doctor."

"I'm happy to be of help. This will be new territory for me in more ways than just a newly established village. I've never been out here in the wilds like this, but as Whitmore already assured me, I'll have plenty of business." Nicholas chuckled. "Kind of ironic that something people never wish on anyone, sickness, is what drives my profession. Almost doesn't seem right, does it?"

"You'll bring us assurance that at least if we get sick, we have someone to call on for help. We'll pray that just your presence will be enough, and we won't need you very often."

Nicholas smiled. "That's the hope of every country doctor."

Hosea leaned closer now and whispered, "What happened to Margaret, Nicholas? If you don't mind me asking."

"Even a doctor can't always save the ones we love." Nicholas sighed. "It was a cancer of some sort. She was ill for over a year. Slowly but surely, it took over her body, and before I could help her through it, she lost the battle."

"I'm sorry."

"It wasn't pleasant. Adeline was just six. I didn't worry about the boys, but with three girls—I needed a woman in their life. That's when Sallie came along. She's a widow and had the two boys, Joseph and Moses. It's been rough merging two families. Sallie has done it well. Very well. It's still not perfect, but we keep striving forward. I miss Margaret every day, but I know she's not suffering anymore, and more than anything, I want to raise our children to be good, law-abiding citizens. Sallie is helping me with that, as I help her with her two boys."

"I pray your life here will be good. It hasn't been easy, but I pray we have forged the path for others to join us here in the community."

"Do you miss New York?"

Hosea sat up straight. "I have to be honest. No. Our temporary stay in Pennsylvania helped me to heal from all that happened in New York. I don't know how things got so out of control there. I've gone over and over it in my head a thousand times. I hope you and all who were near us, during that time, believe me when I say I didn't steal from the church."

"I never believed it. Even then."

"I've also had more family from home arrive." Hosea wasn't sure how much he should share about Rhoda and her continued frustrations with the scandal in New York. Nicholas knew all about it. "Rhoda's here, too."

Nicholas's eyes grew wide. "Rhoda and Sidney are here?"

"Just Rhoda. Sidney's on his way. He's closed his store in Sodus and, for some odd reason, Rhoda came ahead of him. I'm still trying to figure out why."

"My! That's a brave thing for a woman to do." Nicholas took a sip from his mug.

"Yes. She brought the four youngest children with her."

"Amazing! When is Sidney due to arrive?"

"Any day now. We've just gotten word."

"The trip here is not for the faint of heart. I don't think I could have done it alone. Especially as a woman with four children. She must have a stronger faith in God than even you."

Hosea smirked. "If only that were true."

CHAPTER FIFTEEN

"Hosea?" Sally knew Hosea seemed deep in thought over his Bible.

"One moment." Hosea put a finger over the passage he was reading. "What do you need?"

Sally sat in the chair beside him. "Could we add another room? Perhaps separate this main room from the bedrooms. Build real walls instead of merely curtains?" Sally stumbled over her words. She rarely asked for anything as extravagant as this, but now that the mill was running well and producing lumber, she'd been dreaming of adding more room to their small cabin.

Hosea seemed to go back to his reading but answered. "Do you really think that's needed?"

"Needed? No." Sally stood. "But wouldn't it be nice to have a little more room? We could add on to the kitchen area. Or how 'bout—a new table? With real chairs? We've had so much company...as of late."

Hosea placed his finger back onto the passage he was reading. "What's gotten into you? We've lived just fine like this for the past few years. What's wrong with what we have?"

Sighing, Sally sat back down. "Of course. I apologize. I don't mean to sound ungrateful for what we have."

Hosea's eyes twinkled at her. "You're never one to ask for things, but I have been envisioning something for you. I just didn't want to tell you yet."

Anxiously, Sally waited to speak. After being married for so long, she knew now was the time to allow Hosea an opportunity to tell her his idea.

"Once we get through this winter and spring comes, let me build you a new house. Closer to neighbors. Up on the hill, across from the mill. That way, you'd still be close to the river and Betsey and the children could still walk to our home whenever they'd like." Hosea sat back in his chair. "When winter sets in, I'll use the mill in the late evenings to cut us up some lumber. Ambrose will help. We'll build you a fine new house."

Sally nearly dropped the cup she'd been holding. "But what will happen to the cabin?"

"There'll be plenty of newcomers who can use it. Perhaps Etta will find herself a husband and she'll have this place for her own. I won't finish the new house right away. Might take me a year or two to build it, but with the money from the mill now able to sustain us financially, I need something to look forward to. What do you say?"

Sally could only smile as she picked up where she'd left off knitting. It was the crown of a new baby's bonnet. "I won't begrudge you something to look forward to."

Etta and Jillian had gone to bed early. A gust of wind outside whistled around the cabin like winter despite it only being October. The fire snapped. Continual movement. Much like Hosea's mind, continually thinking up extravagant, seemingly impossible ideas. Sally loved Hosea the most when he seized the opportunity to make an idea grow from a small seed into something unbelievable.

"We've done well here, Hosea. Moving was hard. But our family is growing with grandchildren, husbands for the girls. I think the opportunities here have given us heartache but also a hopeful future. Don't you agree?"

Hosea looked into the fire. It was as if he wanted to agree. Yet Sally could tell that something deep inside him wouldn't let him.

Etta made her way up the path to Betsey's cabin. Ma had made bread and wanted to be sure Betsey got a fresh loaf. Betsey's children kept her so busy these days that baking took more time than Betsey had to give. As she approached the cabin, she admired the trees now shedding some leaves along her path. Fall in Michigan Territory proved as beautiful as all the other months. The maple trees were bright red with color. Yellow leaves made an oak tree gleam like a fresh chunk of butter.

Meandering off the path, Etta discovered a large walnut tree now bearing the round, green balls of nuts. One fell from the tree and landed right in front of her. She bent to pick it up. A gust of wind stirred the leaves as another green ball hit the ground with a thud. She'd have to scurry to get out of the way of the dropping hulls. As she scurried along the path, she wanted to remember where she'd seen the tree. Walnuts would taste wonderful this winter. She'd have to remember to tell Ma where to find them. They could use the hulls for medicine and dye.

Once at the cabin, Etta knocked with hesitation. She was always worried she'd wake sleeping children and send Betsey into a frenzy with little ones underfoot. Betsey opened the door, holding her finger to her lips. "Shhh, I just got the babies down."

Etta whispered, "I brought you some bread. From Ma."

Betsey broke out in a grin, scooted outside, and gently shut the door.

"I'm sorry to be a nuisance, Betsey. Ma just thought you'd like some for your supper tonight."

Betsey smelled the loaf and smiled. She whispered back, "You are not a bother. Tell her thank you. I just got them both children asleep. At the same time. It doesn't happen very often."

Etta laughed. "I'm sure. Is Aaron home?"

"He will be soon. Someone came for him this morning. A disturbance call of some sort. As more settlers move to Big Rapids, it seems he's needed more."

Etta set down her basket. "Perhaps John Swain suggests they call Aaron."

"Yes. I have a feeling it is. He just gets settled for the evening and another rider comes to ask him to help with another issue. I should be grateful he has good work, but it makes for long, lonesome days and nights without him around."

"Did you know about the walnut tree just off the path?" Etta pointed in the tree's direction. "I just about got hit by a hull."

"Aaron mentioned something about them the other day. I should take the time while the children are sleeping to go gather up some. They'll be mighty tasty this winter in a cake or pie."

"I'm sure they would."

"I'll have to get Julia to help me. We could peel them open by the fire each night."

As Etta pointed out the tree off the path, a horse and rider approached them from the south. "Who's that?"

"I don't know. Probably someone coming for Aaron."

The man reined his horse in and jumped off. "Good morning, ladies. I'm looking for Aaron Swain."

"I'm Mrs. Swain. Aaron isn't here right now. He's north of here settling a dispute. Can I give him a message?"

Etta recognized the man as a worker she'd fed at the cabin. "You look familiar."

"Charles Chalker, Miss."

"Charles. You were at our home to eat with your brother?"

"That's right. You're one of Hosea's daughters?"

Etta felt her face blush. "I am. This is my sister, Betsey."

"Yes. We were at the mill raising. My brother and I felt badly about the accident. I see it hasn't stopped your pa from continuing to get the mill up and running. We need a reliable sawmill close by. And yes, I was with my brother at the meal your family served the men. We live just east of here."

"It's nice to meet you, Mr. Chalker. My husband should be back around supper. Can he help you with your issue later?"

"Yes. There is no urgency. Somewhat of a property disagreement. It's no emergency."

Etta tried not to stare at the man before her, but as he was chatting with Betsey, she couldn't help herself. He appeared to be the same age or younger than Ambrose. He stood taller than most, and his clothes showed that farming couldn't be his only occupation. His eyes were warm brown and matched his tweed overcoat. To Etta, he was strikingly handsome.

He continued telling Betsey something about where Aaron could find him and where the dispute was, but Etta—even though she was paying attention to him—wasn't hearing a thing, until she heard Betsey say, "It's been nice to meet you, Mr. Chalker. I'll ask Aaron to stop by come morning."

"That would be fine. We live on the farm just east of here. John Swain told us to find Aaron. He is the closest lawman, is he not?"

"Yes."

"Well then, thank you for delivering the message to him for me." Mr. Chalker mounted his horse and tipped his hat to Etta. "Nice to see you again, Miss." And as quickly as he'd come, he was gone down the path.

Etta couldn't take her eyes off the horse and rider.

"Etta?"

Suddenly, Etta heard her sister. "Hmm?"

"Are you coming?"

"Yes."

Betsey giggled.

"What's so funny?"

"I've never seen you so attracted to a man before."

Etta felt her cheeks grow warm. "It's hard not to notice that one!"

Betsey laughed more. "He isn't sore on the eyes."

Rhoda found out the Harder family had arrived just the week before. Instead of bringing her joy like it brought to Hosea and the family; Rhoda felt intimidated and reluctant about the family's arrival. Would the scandal which haunted her brother in New York follow the Harder family here? If it did, she'd have to stop the rumors from penetrating the new community. She'd arrived in the territory, just in time.

Rhoda knew Nicholas and Hosea were close, but Nicholas's wife, Margaret, had seemed to fuel the rumors circulating about Hosea. She could never prove her guilt, but Rhoda knew how prominent Margaret was in the community. It seemed the affluent people in New York were all part of the scandal's circulation. Rhoda had lost friends just like Hosea. During the scandal, she didn't know whom to trust, but who was she to question any of them?

She asked Betsey about it when she visited one day. Betsey told Rhoda she needed to get out of the house for the day. The weather had turned colder in the last week, but today the sun shone brightly, causing the temperatures to hover at a much milder level. Betsey told her she'd needed to take advantage of it, for she knew it wouldn't be long before the snow would trap them all inside.

Betsey brought food with her. Her ma made extra that day, which was Betsey's explanation for the two warm loaves sitting on Rhoda's makeshift table now.

"Tell Sally thank you for these."

Betsey sat with Richard on her lap. Julia had scampered off with the younger Seymour children and they were now playing outside in the sunshine.

"I wish we could do more to help you."

Rhoda sat beside her niece. "Help me? You've done more than enough. You know that."

"Still. Here you are. All alone. I think you are a brave woman for coming all this way by yourself." Richard squirmed a little on her lap, put his thumb in his mouth, and leaned against Betsey. "This little guy is missing his normal nap."

Rhoda stroked the little boy's soft hair. "They keep you busy, don't they?"

"They do." Betsey kissed the top of Richard's head as his eyes fought to stay open. "I will probably be much busier come spring."

Rhoda smiled as the reality of what Betsey was saying became apparent. "Are you expecting again?"

"I am. It's early yet and my usual morning sickness hasn't quite hit yet. But it will soon. At least, it did with the other two."

"At least there's a doctor here now."

Betsey smoothed down the hair of the boy. She probably needed to cut his hair, but she hated to do it. She loved Richard's soft locks. "Hard to believe we'll have three soon."

"Even harder for me to believe. My little Betsey isn't so young anymore. Remember how you used to follow me around and help with my little ones when you were younger?"

Betsey smiled. "I do. I can't wait to see Harriet, Lucinda, and George. Do you think they'll remember me?"

"Of course. I don't think you're as anxious as I am. Perhaps Harriet can be of help to you, as you were to me."

"How is the laundry business going? Your hands don't look as red as they did the last time I saw you."

Rhoda held up her hands. "Your ma's bear grease did the trick. My, that stuff smells almost as bad as my husband's socks!"

Betsey's nose twitched. "It's worse than wet, dirty socks. I had gotten over the worst of the morning sickness before Julia was born when the Indians introduced it to us. I went right back to losing my supper every single time Ambrose came through the door lathered in it. Thankfully, you get used to it."

"I'm not so sure." Rhoda wrinkled her nose.

Betsey laughed. "I hope Uncle Sidney arrives soon. This Indian summer won't last forever, and once winter arrives...the amount of snow and cold can be shocking. Especially your first year here."

Rhoda shuddered to think of the heavy snow. A heavy rain always made her roof sag. What would several inches of snow do to it? "I hope Sidney is content to live here for the winter. It's so small, I can't imagine having to share it with four more family members."

"Perhaps we can help. The younger children can come live with us. We have a fairly large loft now. Aaron has even separated the space into two rooms. You know you're always welcome."

"I don't want to be separated any more than we have already. Once Sidney arrives, we'll figure something out."

"If only it were sooner rather than later."

"How's Margaret Harder?"

"Margaret?"

"The doctor's wife?"

"Pa said that Margaret passed away a few years ago. Nicholas has remarried. Her name is Sallie."

"He has?" Rhoda felt relief seep into her thoughts. "I didn't know."

"Neither did Pa. His new wife is much younger than Nicholas. She has two boys and from what Ma said, she's expecting again."

"Expecting? How young is she?"

"I don't know. She has boys seventeen and fifteen, but she's been a widow for quite some time."

Rhoda tried to remember if she'd heard of her before. "It's surprising they are having their own child now, especially at Nicholas's age."

"She told Ma that she and Nicholas wanted more children. From what I can surmise, it happened much faster than they would have thought. This is their second child together."

"If nothing else, it's good to have a doctor amongst us now. Adds more to the community."

"As children do." Betsey smiled. "Yes!"

Both women laughed now.

"Speaking of them, I was wondering if you'd be interested in schooling for your younger ones? I would love to start up a school. It will give Julia and Richard some interaction with other children and also get them started on their education, too."

"That would be wonderful, Betsey. Thank you for thinking of our children."

"The only thing hampering us from getting it started soon is the upcoming winter. There will be some days when the snow is too deep and the winter conditions too severe for the children to reach our house. But I plan to get some things started before winter officially sets in. Would Tuesdays and Thursdays work for you?"

Rhoda clapped her hands. Education was important to her and Sidney. "I think that will work. How many children do you think will take part?"

Betsey shrugged. "I don't know. You're the first family I have told."

"A school." Rhoda patted Betsey's hand. "Soon this place, out in the middle of nowhere, will be as civilized as Sodus. Sidney will be so pleased."

Hosea spent most of his Saturday morning doing a thorough check of the mill's operating equipment. If a saw needed sharpening, he wanted to be sure they did it correctly. Saw blades were scarce. "Hand me that rag, Ambrose." He pointed to the damp rag he'd been using to wipe off the blade.

"Are there customers coming for lumber today?"

Carefully wiping off the saw blade, Hosea answered. "There are a couple of brothers coming from the East. They're building a barn."

"With cut lumber?" Ambrose folded his arms.

"Yes, sirree!" Hosea grinned as he handed the rag back to Ambrose. "We're in a whole new way of living now. Cut lumber barns are the latest and greatest."

"Aww, Pa. They are not!" Ambrose grinned.

"Let's not let that rumor die. Okay, son." Hosea felt the sharpened blade as he and Ambrose heard what sounded like a wagon approaching the mill. "Sounds like customers."

Hosea wiped off his hands on the apron that hung from his waist. He took it off so the customers would know he wasn't a worker, but the owner. He needed to meet his customers—proper like.

Two white horses came into the mill yard, pulling a wagon, and on the buckboard's bench were two men. They looked familiar as Hosea and Ambrose walked toward them.

"Mr. Baker." One man approached.

"Oh, Mr. Chalker." Hosea held out his hand to the man. "Nice to see you again."

"Do you remember my brother from the mill raising. We both ate at your home with the men for lunch. Please call me Charles, and this is my younger brother, Calvin."

"Nice to see you again." Ambrose held out his hand. Charles's tall frame made Ambrose look small. Even the younger brother stood inches taller than Ambrose. "Where are you fellas from?"

"We live in Vernon Township, born in Vermont, but arrived here from New York." Charles slid off his horse. "So good to see this mill finally operating. We need good cut lumber 'round these parts."

Hosea crossed his arms. "There are plenty of trees to go around." Snickering, he added, "Don't think we'll run out."

Everyone laughed.

"Do you have my order ready?"

"I believe we do. Come on in. Take a look." Hosea escorted the men to a stack of lumber piled near the mill's entrance. He acknowledged the younger brother. "How are you, son?"

The young man nodded. "Fine, sir. Thank you."

As Charles looked over the lumber, piece by piece, Ambrose struck up a conversation with the younger Chalker brother. "Do people ever get your names mixed up?"

The grin from Calvin answered the question. "Every day, sir." Then he added, "What's even worse is, we have an older brother by the name of Chandler."

Hosea took off his hat. "Let me get this straight. You're Calvin. This here's Charles and you have another brother named Chandler and your last name is Chalker?"

"That's right, sir. My mother did it on purpose, so she tells us. She thought it memorable to name us Chandler, Charles, and Calvin Chalker. It gets confusing for some."

Charles paid little attention to the chatter. He'd heard the name confusion discussed more than once in his life.

"Are you satisfied with the lumber? Uh..." Hosea knew he'd never be able to keep these boys and their names straight.

"Charles, sir, and yes, looks nicely cut. I think we ordered this oak, and you quoted fifty-six cents per slab."

Hosea put his hands on his hips. "Sounds right."

Charles pulled out a change purse and handed coins to Hosea. "Thank you, sir. I'm sure we'll need more before the snow flies. Can I place another order while I'm here?"

"I'll make a record. Follow me into the mill."

As the four men entered the building, they answered Ambrose's questions about their farm in Vernon. "We've lived there just a year. Our goal is to make it a cattle farm."

Hosea liked to hear that kind of news. "What do you say about any additional orders of lumber you need to be traded for a milk cow? If you have any available?"

Charles had taken off his hat to check the lumber. As he entered the barn, he put his hat back on. "I think we could work something out, Mr. Baker."

"My Sally Mae will be ecstatic to hear." Hosea grinned.

The men shook hands before they left.

Ambrose stood to leave the mill. "Let me help you get that lumber loaded, gentlemen."

As the young men left, Hosea couldn't wait to tell Sally Mae about the deal. If only he could keep these boys' names straight.

After the Chalker brothers left, Ambrose stayed to help Hosea with cutting a few more logs.

"Pa, have you kept up with the building of The Exchange down by Whitmore's post?"

Hosea picked up a small log that needed to be cut one more time. "Yes. Have you seen it yet?"

Ambrose lifted the other end of the log. "It's magnificent. The brothers building it hauled in a log that is nearly the length of the entire building. They plan on it being the mantle to the fireplaces on the first floor."

"Fireplaces?"

"Three of them. One in each room."

"My!" Hosea took off his hat and scratched his head.

"Whitmore told me that supplies are coming every day to finish the building. We won't have anything else like it in these parts."

"Where do these men get their money to build such a building?"

"They are traders for the Jacob Astor Fur Trading Company."

Hosea slapped his knee with his hat. "We're in the wrong business, son."

"Do you think so, Pa?"

"Naw." Hosea laughed. "Course not. We have enough fur traders. We need farmers who can supply our neighbors with food. They're the ones to keep the community growing."

"Will you stop farming, Pa? Now that you have the mill?"

Hosea looked up at his son. "What do you think?"

"I'd hate for you to give up on it. I can see Ma coming alongside of you, or the girls, and keeping up with the garden, but growing crops?"

"I don't think we'd do well without a few crops on the property. I can tinker away at it. I still enjoy planting a field and watching it grow, but your sisters won't be around much longer. With men like the Chalker brothers coming into town, there will surely be one of them wanting to steal your sisters away from me."

Ambrose smirked. "They'll be gone before you can twist your whiskers in a knot."

"That is so!" Hosea grinned. "What about you? Have you found a young lady that might help to uphold the family name?"

Ambrose picked up the end of another log. "Not yet. Perhaps some of these young men coming in will have a sister or two."

Hosea picked up the other end of the log. "That's so, son. I'll keep my eye out for a pretty one. Just for you!"

CHAPTER SIXTEEN

Hosea marveled at the swiftness of the mill workers loading a large log into the mount to cut it into slabs of lumber. He loved watching the saw blade dig into the log, cutting it clean and easy. Smiling, he asked his employees, "How many have you been cutting in a day?" The men seemed unable to hear him. One cupped his ear and shook his head. Hosea just waved off his question and went outside.

The crisp air had replaced the fall's warmer temperatures. Winter was fast approaching. His bones could feel it. Looking to the east, dark clouds hovered on the horizon. Moisture in the air penetrated Hosea's body, making it ache even more. It wouldn't be long before the snow would make maneuvering logs toward the mill harder. The river would soon freeze hard. That's why Hosea had to keep the men busier over the past few weeks.

Looking up the trail, Hosea caught sight of Rhoda making her way toward him. She had a stack of clothes neatly folded and ready to deliver to the men working at the mill.

Hosea rushed to greet her so he could lighten her load. "Rhoda. Good morning."

Hosea was never tired of seeing his sister in the community. She reminded him of his mother and all the good things about his childhood. His mother had worked as hard, if not harder, than Rhoda. Raising seven children amid the struggles life gave as a farmer's wife. Hosea remembered her with great fondness. Rhoda's personality did not resemble their mother, but many who knew Hosea's mother told him that she did.

Despite being thankful Rhoda had traveled to be near him, the gesture didn't temper his misgivings about not hearing anything more from Sidney. Hosea knew there had to be more to Rhoda's story. This made Hosea feel even more responsible for his sister's welfare. If Rhoda's husband didn't arrive before winter set in, she'd have to move in with someone. It wouldn't be the first time that Hosea's cabin would burst at the seams with occupants.

"Hello, Hosea." Rhoda placed the stack of clothing into his arms. "Thank you."

"You sure keep these men clean and well-dressed these days. We appreciate all you do for them. Any word from Sidney?"

Worry lines etched his sister's eyes. "He has to arrive soon, doesn't he? It can't take him any longer than it did me. I came with four children."

Hosea sensed anger in his sister's response. "It's hard being here and waiting, but I'm sure it isn't any easier for him knowing you are here alone." Hosea turned to take the clothes into the mill for the men. "Is there anything I can do to help you?"

"You've already given us so much. Sally brings me loaves of bread, Betsey comes regularly to check on us. If he doesn't come before winter hits–" Rhoda took a deep breath.

"Rhoda. That house isn't properly roofed. You can't stay there. I kept thinking Sidney would show up, and he could do the job for you."

"I know."

"Come stay with us. You know we would manage."

"No! I will not place another burden on your lap."

"Even Betsey would open her home for you. You know that."

"I may have to ask Aaron and Betsey. I don't know what else to do. I don't make enough to rent out a room in the new Exchange, especially for the entire winter."

"We'll just have to pray harder that Sidney arrives."

Rhoda snapped, "Hosea! You know praying doesn't do anything to get Sidney on a boat and here in time."

As the words flowed out, Rhoda appeared to hesitate to say anything further, like she wasn't happy about what she'd said. Hosea knew that abruptly spoken words often reveal a person's heart.

"Rhoda. Sit down. It's too noisy to go into the mill right now. We need to talk."

As they sat, Rhoda burst out quick words. "Hosea. You might as well know. I don't believe in God anymore. He isn't here to help or rescue us. He has no place in my life any longer. And praying for anything is a waste of time." Rhoda exhaled like she'd been holding her tongue for far too long.

Hosea lowered his head at her words. "Rhoda, what has caused you to turn your back on God?"

"Life! Our parents. You. You've lived a life of goodness and love for all men. As a husband, father, brother...we could ask for nothing that you wouldn't go beyond even your own means to provide. Yet look how God has treated you!" The words spit out of his sister like venom.

"Treated me? Where is all of this coming from?"

"I've stood beside you long enough to know that you don't deserve for others to treat you as they do. From Indians who take your adopted son to now everyone blaming you for the death of the man here at the mill. All God has given you is heartache. Trial after trial. Give up on Him, Hosea. He has given you nothing in return."

Hosea balanced the clothes so they wouldn't fall off his lap and onto the dusty ground at his feet. "Your words are far from true."

"What do you mean? Ever since New York's scandal, all you've done is endure suffering. I've watched. Why serve a God who does nothing but bring you heartache after heartache?"

"Because He's worth it!"

"How can you say that?"

"Because it's true. He's given me far more than I deserve."

"You're wrong!" Rhoda stood up and took back the clothes from Hosea's lap. Clasping the bundle into her arms again, she walked away. "For once in your life, Hosea, give up on this God of yours! Trust me, you'd be better off."

Hosea buried his face in his hands. The venom and hate of Rhoda's words hurt worse than any trial Hosea had endured, including the scandal in New York, losing Alexander to the Indians, or the man perishing at his mill. Hosea's grief through all of those circumstances wasn't as bad as the sorrow he now felt for his sister's soul.

Squash of assorted colors and shapes dotted the field behind the Baker house. Hosea, Etta, and Jillian were hauling large, orange pumpkins from the field.

"It's sad to bring these squash to the barn. I love looking out at the field with the tiny dots of color among the dying plants." Jillian hefted a large one up into her arms to carry to the barn.

"It also means that winter is soon to be here." Hosea lifted the last of the acorn squash into a bundle to carry toward their barn's storage section. There, they'd piled layers and layers of straw to help the produce through the harsh cold of winter. "It seemed a few months ago we planted the seeds from last year's crop. And now...it's time to gather more seeds to plant for next year. *'Now He that ministereth seed to the sower both minister bread for your food, and multiply your seed sown, and increase the fruits of your righteousness; Being enriched in every thing to all bountifulness, which causeth through us thanksgiving to God.'"*

Hosea watched his hard-working daughters lift as many squash as their arms could hold and take them to the barn. What would he do without these two girls? Watching them took his thoughts back to the conversation he'd had with Rhoda. How he prayed that circumstances and trials would not hinder his daughters and their love for the Savior.

Life was hard out here in the wilderness, away from an established church and the fellowship of believers. The isolation often could change a man's heart to thoughts only of himself. He'd watched many solid Bible-believing Christians turn inward and not manifest the fruit of the Spirit to those around them. He prayed this untamed land wouldn't tarnish their desires to always follow God.

Once inside, Hosea slapped his hands together near the fire as Sally Mae hung up his coat and urged everyone to sit down for dinner. The cooler air sent steam rising from the warm dishes she'd placed on the table.

"Hurry and sit down. All of you. The food will grow cold." Sally Mae tapped Hosea's shoulder, so he'd sit down.

"Let me add a few more logs to the fire, Sally Mae." Hosea chided his wife. "We'll be warm and toasty in no time."

As the family sat to eat, and after saying grace, Hosea asked the family about his premonitions regarding Rhoda's children. He had to be discreet without slandering his sister at the same time.

"Jillian? Have you been to Aunt Rhoda's house this week?"

Jillian had just taken a bite of the potato chunks on her plate. Chewing, she motioned to her pa to wait a moment and then answered. "Yes, Pa. We've been helping Betsey decide what subjects to teach when she schools us this winter. I can't wait. Perhaps some of the other settlers have girls my age. It's been fun having Philinda close, even though she's younger."

Hosea poured gravy into the white potatoes on his plate. He thought he'd never tire of having fresh garden potatoes at each meal. Savoring every bite wasn't hard in the fall months. "How about you, Etta?"

"They're too young for me, but I do like having other girls my age around. Although I've been so busy helping Ma lately, I haven't had much time to socialize."

"Have you heard them talk much about their pa? Are they eager for him to arrive?"

Jillian wiped off her mouth before speaking. "Oh, yes. Philinda is excited. She brings Uncle Sidney up quite a lot. She misses him. Will he be here soon, Pa? Do you think?"

"I hope so, Jilly. They need their pa, especially before winter sets in."

"Do you think he'll arrive in time?" Sally Mae dished out a few more green beans onto Hosea's plate. Hosea never had to worry that there wasn't enough on his plate, thanks to his wife.

"I'm hoping he arrives before the snow. Rhoda can't stay in that small cabin once winter sets in. The roof isn't stable. I was hoping Sidney would arrive soon and he could fix it properly." Hosea sighed. "I just hope it's soon. If he isn't here before the end of next week, I think Ambrose and I will have to move Rhoda and the children to another location."

"But where, Pa? There isn't any place else to go, is there?"

"Perhaps Aaron and Betsey's. I know Rhoda will be upset to do that, but I can't imagine her living in that cabin all winter." Hosea dipped a small potato into the gravy left on his plate. "This gravy you've concocted is delicious, Sally Mae."

"I used some of the chicken broth I had leftover. It seems to give the mixture a bit more flavor."

"I agree. Keep up the good work." Hosea winked at his wife, who blushed and slapped his arm playfully. "Have you noticed a change in Rhoda, Sally Mae?"

"Change?"

"We had a chat today at the mill. She was delivering clean clothes to the men."

"I'm so proud of her." Sally Mae sat to eat. "Since taking on the men's laundry at the mill, she's been able to support her and the children. Her hands are a dreadful mess. All chapped and red. But as far as change..." Sally Mae stopped, seeming to think about Hosea's question. She glanced at the girls and then at Hosea. "I have noticed one thing."

"What's that?" Hosea asked.

"I'm sorry to interrupt, Pa, but I *have* seen something different about the cousins." Etta looked up with skepticism in her eyes. "I noticed it soon after they'd been here a few weeks."

Hosea motioned to Etta with his fork. "Go ahead. Tell us."

Etta set down her napkin. "I thought it odd, but the more and more it happens, it bothers me. Whenever I hum or sing a hymn while out working—Philinda doesn't join in singing with me anymore, like she used to. Sometimes she'll start to—but then quickly stops, especially when Aunt Rhoda is nearby. I feel like it isn't something Aunt Rhoda wants for her to do, so then I stop."

"Oh, that!" Jillian nodded, affirming Etta's statement. "I've noticed it, too. The younger children don't even seem to know any of the tunes."

"Have you tried to teach it to them, girls? Perhaps you know different hymns than they know." Sally Mae shrugged.

Jillian shook her head. "I've never tried."

Etta nodded. "I did, but once they heard God or Jesus mentioned, they immediately stopped singing with me."

Hosea gave Sally Mae a look. She glanced back. Hosea knew they needed to drop the subject now before the girls caught on that he was fishing for clues.

That night, before going to sleep, Hosea brought up the conversation he'd had with Rhoda to Sally Mae. Tears filled his wife's eyes. "Hosea, what has happened? Surely what happened to you in New York wouldn't cause her to give up on her faith, would it?"

"That's what she's claiming."

"Oh, my!" Sally Mae snuggled closer to Hosea. "What can we do?"

"I don't think *we* can do anything. God needs to work in her heart. I'm also worried about Sidney not arriving yet. You don't suppose they are having marital issues, do you?"

Sally Mae backed away to look into Hosea's eyes. "Oh Hosea! Let's pray that isn't so."

Hosea pulled her close. "To be honest, it has me worried. What if Sidney isn't happy with her change of heart? Today's conversation revealed great bitterness in Rhoda's heart. Now, hearing what the girls have said about the children, I think my sister's heart has turned cold. Don't you agree?"

"A bitter woman is hard to contend with."

"It is better to dwell in the wilderness, than with a contentious and an angry woman." Hosea quoted from the Bible.

"Oh Hosea. Let's pray it isn't true and Sidney shows up soon."

Since April, Hosea had been holding the township meetings at his cabin. The men had nominated and voted for him to be the first supervisor of the township. Since then, every third Wednesday of the month, the community's men gathered to discuss anything regarding the area surrounding Whitmore's post, the new Exchange building, and Hosea's community near the river.

Word about the meetings spread, and soon local men gathered together to discuss ways to enact laws and establish their community into a true branch of government. There weren't enough chairs to accommodate his guests. The crowd made the tiny cabin seem smaller. Yet the men continued to attend.

Aaron thought it best to start putting those laws to paper. After envisioning the type of government they'd like for their community, the men discussed the presented suggestions thoroughly, and then voted on them.

Thirty-two men represented thirty-two families. Some had children, others were alone or waiting for their families to join them from back East. As soon as Nicholas arrived, he assumed a prominent role in the governmental procedures. From experience, he knew meeting protocol and helped Hosea as the supervisor.

One of the first issues on their agenda was the formation of a school. Aaron smiled when they mentioned Betsey's attempt at gathering up parents who were interested in the proposition.

"As far as I know, Betsey can be the first teacher." Hosea told the men seated around the room.

"Sounds like a good idea, Hosea. When will it start? My two are eager to be gettin' back to school." The VanWormer family had two small children. Hosea sensed David had future leadership potential.

"Betsey has suggested that a child wanting to attend needs to be at least five years of age." Aaron offered that stipulation. "Although, our children aren't quite schooling age yet."

"Won't that bring some conflict? Not to say that Mrs. Swain wouldn't be fittin' to teach our young'uns, but having two little ones running around can be mighty difficult tryin' to teach a passel of other children. Why don't we hire an actual teacher?"

Hosea looked at Aaron for a comment.

"Betsey is capable. But I understand your concern."

The man offering the comment added, "I don't mean to sound like I don't trust your wife to conduct a proper school. Don't get me wrong, Aaron. I just know how difficult it is to have those little ones running around and have twenty or more other students to work with."

Aaron seemed to understand the concern. "I don't think Betsey is against another teacher, but just to get the school year off to a good start, she has consented to get them going."

"And we need to be grateful for her willingness." Nicholas turned to Hosea. "Let's just get the proposition up for a vote and get this school started, sooner rather than later. What do you say, Hosea?"

"I agree. All in favor, say yea!"

Murmurs of answers erupted through the crowd of men.

"Any nays?"

Silence permeated the cabin.

With a grin, Hosea announced, "Well, I say let's establish the first school for our territory on this day, October 30, 1836."

Applause and hollers filled the cabin.

"My wife will be thrilled," David VanWormer spoke. "I know that in Vernon, they've been holding school since around the middle of September. Perhaps they know of another schoolteacher in the area willing to take on our young'uns, too, if it gets too much for Mrs. Swain."

"From what I hear, Governor Mason will soon issue legislation establishing a system of free common schools here in the territory. He has even told me he plans to appoint a chief architect of the plan as the state's first superintendent of public instruction." Nicholas recited as though he'd just read a newspaper article about it.

"How do you know that?" Questioned one settler.

Nicholas cleared his throat. "It may come as a surprise to some of you, but my wife keeps up with governmental information. As we came through Detroit, upon arriving here, she visited one of her father's constituents who knows firsthand this information to be true from Mason's office. She wanted to be sure our children had proper schooling in the territory."

All the men murmured agreement.

"That's great news," Aaron commented. "As I mentioned, Betsey will start the school until we can find a proper teacher to take over, if that's agreeable to all of you."

"I'm sure one of my other daughters will be on hand to help her with her own young'uns until proper schooling can begin." Hosea took a long sip of his coffee before continuing the meeting. "We need public school available to all children, not just those in the well-to-do families, but for all."

The men voiced their agreement.

Hosea moved down the agenda to discuss all the issues brought up at the township meeting. Each meeting brought him hope that the small community next to the Shiawassee River would soon emerge as a thriving village. A united group of settlers helped to make decisions easier, but Hosea also knew that a divided community would eventually emerge. It always did.

CHAPTER SEVENTEEN

Hosea pulled his horse up in front of Ambrose's house, now occupied by Nicholas Harder and his family. He hoped they felt at home in their new surroundings. Tying the horse to a nearby fence post, Hosea climbed the stairs to the door and knocked. Nicholas's wife Sallie opened the door.

Her eyes lit up when she saw Hosea. "Hosea! Please come in. Nicholas would love to see you if he were home."

Hosea took off his cap as he entered the home. "Sallie. Thank you."

The children all gathered around to greet Hosea with smiles and hugs. "This is quite the welcome. Thank you." Hosea scrunched his hat between his hands. "Is Nicholas close by?"

Hosea had been there many times helping Ambrose with various building projects, but it was evident it was now pleasing to a woman's taste. Sallie ushered Hosea to a large mahogany table with red velvet upholstered chairs. A matching china cabinet against a far wall held matching teacups and saucers. Hosea was astonished that they'd been able to transport all of this furniture in a couple of covered wagons.

Hosea couldn't help but say, "Did all of this fit into the covered wagons you brought from New York?"

"Why, yes! I couldn't part with these pieces. I inherited them from my grandmother." Sallie ran her hand over the top of the impeccable table. "That's one of the reasons we didn't take the steamboat. I wanted to bring style to our new home. Please, won't you sit down? We rarely have company unless they need Nicholas' services."

Hosea sat, fretting that his backside was leaving dirt or horsehair on Sallie's velvet chairs. He hadn't had to worry about such things since before leaving Pennsylvania. He couldn't wait to share the details with Sally Mae. "Has Nicholas been busy?"

Sallie sat as Elizabeth shuffled the children out the door and outside to play. "Once the word got out that he was a doctor, the calls came quickly, and now, often. He goes to most places on horseback. Aaron asked him to check on some of the remote homesteads. I guess there are elderly people living there and it helps Aaron to have someone else looking in on them. So far, he's treated everything from a broken arm to high fevers. But—" Sallie raised her hands, "That is why we're here."

"I hope it isn't too much, too soon."

Sallie waved Hosea's comment off like a fly buzzing around her head. "No, Hosea. It's what he lives for. We've done our best to make our home liveable. Although I am finding it quite different here than where we came from."

Hosea felt out of place for the first time since arriving three years prior to Nicholas and his family. "It is that. Can I do anything to help?"

"Now that you've asked, I want my children in school soon. They are underfoot—"

Elizabeth entered the room with a tray laden with different teacups than those on display, and some kind of cake on plates.

"It's not that I mind, but getting together with other children will do them good." Sallie poured hot tea from a teapot Elizabeth had brought into the room, and handed it to Hosea.

Hosea tried to sip tea from the delicate purple cup, but his fingers were too large to fit through the opening of the handle. He fumbled to get a good grip and follow Sallie's conversation, at the same time. Setting the cup down so the hot tea could cool, Hosea explained Betsey's idea to get the school started and that the men in the township had approved the idea. "We'll have that, for now, until we can form a more permanent location and teacher. I'm surprised Nicholas didn't share that with you."

"He's been gone quite a bit the last few days, but that sounds lovely."

Hosea relaxed a bit from her response and addressed the possible startup date. "I'll let Betsey know of your interest, too."

"I think schooling is very important for children, don't you agree?"

Hosea agreed with gusto after raising the cup again to blow over the hot drink. "I do. Betsey has been mighty concerned about getting the school up and running. Her two will need a school soon, too."

Sallie clapped her hands. "How wonderful! I was so hoping this was a concern for our small community. We can't be raising heathens, now, can we?"

The unschooled children were far from heathens in Hosea's eyes, but he had heard other women back East refer to them in that way. A woman broaching the issue of schooling with Hosea seemed presumptuous. Sallie reminded Hosea of Margaret. Obviously, Nicholas had gained another strong-minded woman as his wife.

Sallie must have sensed his trepidation. "Forgive me for being so forward, Hosea, but you see, my father was a lawyer back in New York. He believed a child's schooling was a necessity. I often worked with him on the bookkeeping of legislative projects he began. Many people think it inappropriate to have a woman in any kind of leadership position, but my father was forward-moving, in thinking it appropriate to have a woman with strong leadership skills to be a part of the process."

The only thing Hosea could say was, "Yes, ma'am."

"With so many coming into the territory, I'm sure you also understand our need to establish a community where education, the arts, and the finer things in life are important."

Hosea preferred to take these concerns up with Nicholas. "I'm sure Nicholas will want to hear of your concerns."

"I have shared my thoughts with him." Sallie tucked a strand of blonde hair back under a sweeping bang which hung across her forehead. Sallie's beauty was striking. "He agrees, of course. His medicinal duties keep him busy, as you can see. Sometimes I need to take his place in matters such as this." Sallie smiled and sat back in her chair. "How is your wife, Hosea?"

Etta loved to take lunch down to her pa while he worked at the mill. Now that most of the crops were in and harvested, Pa had been spending more time there. A coolness filled the air, and she wrapped her scarf tighter around her neck. The trees were almost bare of leaves now. Winter would be upon them soon. Etta always enjoyed the first snowfall of the season, but she also knew that soon drifts and banks of snow would bury them inside. The path was littered with crisp leaves and branches which had fallen after a strong wind they'd had over the weekend.

As she approached the mill, she noticed a wagon attached to two large workhorses. She quickly recognized one horse. A chill, not caused by the cold, rippled through her. Should she turn around? *Don't be silly*, she scolded herself. Pa needed his lunch. She wished she'd worn a better dress to deliver Pa's meal.

Etta entered the mill, adjusting her eyes to the darkness. She shrouded her eyes with her hand, and soon she could make out the forms of four men talking over a pile of cut lumber just to the right of the saw's carriage. When she entered, the three men looked up to see who was approaching.

Charles Chalker was the first to remove his hat. "Miss Baker."

Etta felt her face flush. She was thankful for the darkened room. "Mr. Chalker."

"Etta, my girl! Do you know Charles?" Surprise marked his face.

"Yes, we met at Betsey's house."

Charles stepped closer to her. "Miss Baker, this is my brother, Chandler."

"Yes, we've met, too. You both were at our home for lunch during the mill's inception."

"That's right. You have an excellent memory, Miss Baker." Chandler reached out his hand to shake Etta's.

Etta wasn't sure which brother she admired the most. Both were tall, seemingly strong young men. And she'd also heard her pa talk about the Chalker family and what a nice farm they had close by. "It's nice to see you both again. Here's your lunch, Pa."

Pa took the basket from Etta and set it down on the pile of lumber near the men. "Etta is my third daughter. She's turned sixteen a few weeks ago."

When Charles smiled at her, Etta wanted to melt into the floor. Why did Pa have to tell the men her age?

"Well, I better get back." Etta stepped away from the group. She wasn't sure how much longer she could hide her excitement at seeing Charles again. "It was nice to see you again, Charles, Chandler."

"I thought you were going to stay and enjoy lunch with me, Etta." Her pa patted a pile of lumber stacked off to one side. It was there that she and her pa often shared lunch. Ma always packed enough for both of them.

Etta hesitated. She wasn't all together certain she could move her feet if she were to change her mind and walk away. What was causing her to act this way?

Charles was the first to break the silence. "Miss Baker, we were just about to finish our transaction. Please don't rush off on our account." Now Etta didn't know what to do. She should stay with Pa, but she wasn't sure if her legs were going to hold her up to do so. She needed to sit down. "Okay." Etta quickly moved to where Pa had pointed.

She didn't know what else to do but watch the men and their interaction with Pa. She felt like a timid child. The Chalker brothers were confident, self-assured, and utterly handsome. The men discussed lumber prices. They shook hands after depositing the required amount into Pa's hand. Charles's eyes were friendly. He stood nearly a foot taller than Pa. Despite wearing hats, both brothers' haircuts were neat, their beards trimmed. Chandler was shorter, and Etta knew she'd always be able to distinguish the differences in the brothers despite their names being similar.

Whenever Charles glanced over at her, his eyes twinkled, causing Etta to look down at her feet. She wondered if Charles had seen her staring at him. It was hard not to admire the man for his business demeanor, his charming looks, and friendly laugh. Pa seemed to like the brothers, too.

"We'll be back next week for the rest of the lumber," announced Chandler as he lifted a few slabs of cut lumber from the stack they'd just purchased. "We appreciate you getting this cut so quickly. Our barn is just about finished. You'll have to come out for a visit, Hosea. This cut lumber made the job much faster and the cows we've recently purchased will have good shelter once it's finished."

Pa seemed quite pleased with their announcement. "That's good news. Our mill is finally helping the community in big ways."

"Yes, sir. It is." Charles looked back in Etta's direction before he carried out the last few sections of lumber they'd purchased. "Nice to see you again, Miss Baker."

Etta smiled back. She longed for him to call her Etta but knew it wasn't a proper thing to have him do.

"Nice boys, aren't they?" Pa sat beside Etta after the men left the barn.

"They're men, Pa." Etta unwrapped the hot potatoes Ma had made up for her and Pa.

"Yes, they are, Etta. Men indeed." At first, Pa seemed surprised by her comment, but Etta caught him grinning at her as he unwrapped his hot potato. "The men around here seem to get younger and younger all the time. Or—" Pa took a large bite of his potato.

"Or what, Pa!"

"Or you're getting older right before my eyes."

Etta squirmed at her pa's attention. Did he know of her interest in Charles Chalker?

CHAPTER EIGHTEEN

Caroline watched Horace pull his pants on. She fed him as much as he could consume. He still wasn't gaining weight. How could she help him? As he tightened the rope on his pants for the second time, he looked up and saw she was staring.

"Caroline, I think I'm getting worse."

She pulled back the covers and got out of bed. She went to her husband and put her arms around his waist. "I think you need to talk to Dr. Harder."

Horace's face contorted. "What if it is just our imaginations? What if I'm *not* losing weight, but just growing taller?"

Should she laugh? Her heart wanted to believe there was nothing wrong with her husband. If only she could feed Horace and watch him gain weight and get healthier. "Let's just have him examine you. He's a good doctor. He knows medicine well. Perhaps he can help."

Horace pulled himself free from Caroline's grasp. "I need water."

Nicholas pulled Sallie close. He felt the beginnings of a firmer belly as they snuggled in bed; both rejecting the idea of getting out from under the heavy, warm quilts. "This territory seems colder than New York. Do you agree, my love?"

Sallie turned her head to place a kiss on his neck. "Indeed, I do, Nicholas. Despite this house being smaller than any house we've ever owned, it seems harder to keep warm against the frigid temperatures and wind of Michigan."

"The fire seems to just keep the nearest rooms warm, but our bedroom and the rooms upstairs always feel cold." Nicholas massaged her belly. "Our baby is making an appearance. How are you feeling?"

"With child."

Nicholas chuckled. "Of course you do, my dear. Watching new life grow has never failed to mystify me."

"It is a rare miracle," Sallie situated herself to see his face. "Are you enjoying your work here?"

"I don't think *enjoy* is the opportune word, but yes, it has been a challenge I'm excited to embark on. The illnesses are different here. Ague can be deadly, no matter what I do. I've also been attempting to meet with Hosea's wife, so we can discuss a few of the Indian remedies she's learned while here. Hosea said that Michigan mold helps infections. Also, some of the natural herbs and plant life have medicinal benefits as well. I need to be open to natural uses of plants to fight illness. Indians have remedies they've passed down through multiple generations. Why would they use them if they didn't bring some kind of relief or cure?"

"The Indians here appear so inquisitive."

"Aaron said many have left the area. When they first arrived, Indians were prevalent around the trading posts and now many have drifted deeper into the woods."

"Have you doctored any yet?"

"Not yet. Although I'm sure it won't be long before one will seek me out through the connection of the settlers. Hosea said they seemed to hover near his homestead when he first arrived, but he sees less and less of them now. He's been talking about a ceremony they have in the fall. The Indians gather close to Hosea's cabin and perform some kind of ritual sacrifice to appease the gods for a massacre they committed years ago."

Sallie turned her face toward him. "Ceremony? That sounds frightening."

"Hosea said there is nothing to fear. After a few days of ritualistic dancing, frivolous drinking, and fighting among the tribe, there is nothing to be concerned about."

"Do be careful, Nicholas."

Nicholas placed a kiss on the top of his wife's head. "I will, my dear. Nothing to fear."

"Has Hosea and Sally's health suffered here? They both appear thin. Do you think so?"

"This is not New York. Living off the land and having to build your dwelling doesn't seem a simple task for anyone. Hosea has literally cut down trees to farm his land and make his dwelling. That isn't easy for any man!"

Sallie turned away from him again. "I worry about the children. They're used to finer things. As I've told you, Hosea said the schooling will be at Betsey's house. No formal teacher. I hope they don't fall behind in their studies."

"They're resilient. The boys seem to enjoy being out here in the wild. Don't you think?"

"The boys, yes! But the girls—" Sallie turned her face toward him. "They need to learn etiquette and proper living."

"I think that will keep you busy training them. Do what you will. But can we start this day off in a good way?"

Sallie kissed him full on the lips. "Gladly!"

The dark room was not inviting Rhoda to start the morning with any kind of joy. Each night, it grew harder for her to keep the tiny cabin warm. The icy winds crept through the cabin's cracks. Despite the heavy quilt over her, Rhoda still shivered in her bed. She stripped back the covers and crawled out of bed, rushing to reignite the fire. Thankfully, a few embers still glowed under the heavy wood she'd added the night before. Soon she'd even run out of wood to keep the fire going. Where was Sidney? Why hadn't he arrived yet?

Trying to keep doing the laundry for the men at the mill now grew tedious. Her hands grew numb as she stirred the kettle outside. She could keep doing it inside, but having clothes strewn around the cabin to dry made their small living quarters even tinier. Although the labor had kept her and the children at least out from under Hosea's complete care, she still depended on Betsey and Sally to keep basic food supplies replenished. Once winter set in, would they be able to deliver goods to her and the children? Hosea told her that often they'd go weeks without having a break between storms. What would she do?

Rhoda watched a mouse skirt across the fireplace threshold in search of food for its family. She'd hated mice until she had to live with them here in the territory, comparing the tiny rodents to herself. Now she watched them gather food, build nests, and care for their young, as she had been trying to do since arriving in this forsaken territory. What had she been thinking about wandering this far west without Sidney?

As she piled wood onto the fire, she thought back to the time when she'd told him she would travel alone.

"You're not going alone!" Sidney scraped the floor with his broom. Small piles of spilled rice littered the floor after George transferred bags to the back of the store from the last shipment.

"Don't treat me like a child. I am completely capable—"

Sidney put the broom in a corner. "I am not treating you like a child."

"I'm capable of more things than you give me credit for. Traveling isn't difficult. I could do it. By going early, I could find us a place to live. Secure property for a store. Let me go, Sidney. I can manage."

Sidney folded his arms and looked at her in frustration. "Rhoda, you're going to badger me until I let you go, aren't you?"

Rhoda brushed a loose piece of hair from off her face with her hand. "Why are you being so stubborn? Hosea told us the land in the territory is cheap. I need to get out of this town. Away from all these customer demands. If we don't give Mabel Harlington a good deal on fabric, she runs across the street to Betty Flanders for a better price. If our corn seed is not sufficient, Lonny Mathers heads across the road to the new feed store. We have more competition than we've ever had. We can't even decide on fair prices anymore without losing customers over a few pennies. I hate it here."

"You're changing the subject. We've already decided to leave Sodus. But what has all of this got to do with you leaving earlier? I've agreed we need to move."

Rhoda stepped closer. "What if we aren't the only ones headed west? Listen to me. If I go early, I can find us a strategic place to set up a new store. Get a surveyor ready to price it for us. Get the children in school this fall."

Sidney threw up his hands. "I agree with you, Rhoda. I do. For heaven's sake, why are we discussing the advantages instead of *why* you need to go early?"

"You know. You shouldn't have to ask me that question."

Sidney sighed. "Rhoda, you can't change the past!"

They'd had this conversation several times. Multiple times, in fact. Sidney recognized how much Rhoda ached from the situation Hosea had found himself, back in New York. He knew about the scandal. But there was more to this story than even Sidney knew. Rhoda had a talent in hiding things.

"I know I can't change the past, Sidney!" Rhoda had felt the tears wanting to spill. "I have to talk to Hosea."

"Talk to him? Rhoda! What has gotten into you? Why do you think you can change other people like the devil has changed you?"

"The devil?" Rhoda spat out the words. "Is that what you think?"

Sidney looked down. "I think you're still running. And unfortunately, one day you'll stop and realize that even if Hosea comes to terms with the outcome, the scandal will continue to haunt you."

Sidney was giving up on her, too. She could feel it. He'd tried multiple times to convince her that what happened to Hosea was just a misunderstanding. She knew that Sidney, of all people, hated that she had abandoned her faith over it all.

Hosea knew enough to leave town, but Rhoda couldn't help but think that if they left too, it would give her, Sidney, and the children a better way of life. They'd be out from under the canopy of gossip that continually hung over Rhoda's head. She'd told him often that the scandal would never go away on its own. The only way to get out of it was to leave. Leave behind all the memories, rumors, and naysayers. Perhaps Sidney was right. She was running. But it didn't matter. She had to try.

"Go ahead, Rhoda. Pack up the younger ones and go before us. I'll sell off as much as I can, and then the older children and I will follow. But I need Harriet, Lucinda, and George to help me. They're staying with me."

Rhoda knew she'd gotten her way, but sadness crept into her heart. She loved Sidney. She loved her older children, but she needed to do this. Before anything could affect her heart more, she needed to leave.

Once the fire was stoked, Rhoda returned to her bed. Running away hadn't helped. It had only made things worse. She wished she'd have listened to Sidney.

A ferocious fear swept through her soul. What if he had stayed in Sodus without her? Perhaps he wasn't even coming. The cold she now felt had nothing to do with the temperature. What would she tell Hosea if Sidney never showed up?

CHAPTER NINETEEN

Feeding the chickens had always been Jillian's job. But on this brisk morning in November, Etta found her sister at the breakfast table with a cold. As she sneezed, wheezed, and coughed, Ma had decisively put her back to bed instead of sending her outside to do chores. Etta scooped up her jacket. While putting it on, she heard a horse approaching the cabin.

"I think someone's here, Ma." Etta opened the door to see Charles Chalker lifting his leg over the saddle of his horse to dismount. She wanted to slam the door shut, rush to her bed, remove the old clothes she wore, fix her hair, and tie a bow around a fresh braid, but there was no time for such frivolities. There she stood in her torn work clothes, a dirty apron smeared with yesterday's flour, and uncombed hair. Now that the door was open, she had no choice but to greet the handsome Chalker man. As Ma always said, she had a heart of gold and lots of charm, which now would be the only thing to shine. "Hello, Mr. Chalker."

Charles held tight to a lead attached to the nicest, plumpest cow Etta had seen since Pennsylvania. "I brought your pa his cow." He pulled the animal—which looked none too pleased—toward him, and rubbed her nose. "I think he'll like Myrtle."

Etta giggled, "Myrtle?"

"I mean, this cow." Charles blushed as he pointed to the cow behind him. At that moment, the cow let loose with a comment of its own. "My sister named her."

The cow's loud greeting made them both laugh.

"She sounds like she likes it here." The man took off his hat, stuffing it under one arm. "Please, call me Charles. Mr. Chalker sounds like you're talking to my pa."

Etta flashed her sweetest smile. "All right, Charles." Etta bowed her head in embarrassment. She'd never had a man ask her to use his first name.

"Can we help you?" Ma came out of the house, wiping her hands on a rag.

"Ma, this is Mister—I mean, Charles. He and Pa set up a deal for a milk cow and Charles is now delivering her."

"She's a shorthorn, ma'am. Shorthorns are gentle. She gives good milk. I think you'll like her."

Ma clapped her hands. "Milk! Oh, Charles, thank you! You don't know how much joy this animal brings me."

Charles pulled the cow closer to him. "I can take her to the barn for you. If that's what you'd like."

"Yes!" Ma exclaimed. "Please. Etta, show Mr. Chalker the way to the barn."

Etta was sure Charles could find the barn on the property, but she also knew that a few moments alone with this man would bring her about as much joy as watching her ma rejoice over the new milk producer in the family.

As they meandered their way around the side of the cabin, Charles was the first to speak. "So, your name is Etta. Is that your formal name?"

Etta turned. "My given name is Estelle, but everyone calls me Etta."

"Estelle. That's a pretty name. I have a sister named Elizabeth."

Etta felt her neck grow warm despite the cool outside temperature. "Elizabeth is pretty, too."

"How long have you been living here?"

"We came in thirty-three. Pa brought us here from Pennsylvania."

"I think I knew that. We know John Swain well. He lives near us. He's told us good things about your family."

"My sister Betsey is married to his brother. They live up on the ridge." Etta pointed to Betsey's house.

"And you have other sisters, don't you?"

"Yes, two. Caroline is married to Horace Knapp, and my younger sister's name is Jillian. She isn't feeling well this morning."

"I'm sorry to hear that. I hope she feels better soon."

"Do you have other siblings?" As the question left her lips, she remembered that she knew the answer. Her nervousness kept her from admitting her memory lapse.

"You met my one brother, Chandler. And then I have one other brother, Calvin, besides Elizabeth. We came first and my parents are still back in New York. Seneca Falls."

"You came alone?"

"If by coming with my siblings, yes, we came alone." Charles smiled.

"Here's the barn." Etta pointed out a stake. "We use this stake to tie the horse when Pa's home, but for now, I'm sure Myrtle won't mind it."

"She's not a wanderer, although this is a new home. She's used to Elizabeth and our barn, but once you milk and love her, I'm sure she'll feel right at home, quick as rain!"

Now Etta smiled. "Thank you. I'm sure we'll enjoy the fresh milk."

"She needs to be milked soon. Do you know how?"

Etta hadn't even thought about it. They'd not had a milk cow since way before leaving Pennsylvania. Betsey always milked it, because Pa said she and Jillian were too little. She could probably figure it out or Pa could show her, but the thought of having a lesson from the handsome Charles Chalker sounded much more enjoyable. "Yes, show me!"

"Sure. Got a pail?"

Before long, Etta was sitting beside Myrtle and getting streams and streams of milk into the bucket she'd provided to Charles. It was fun watching the milk sizzle and bubble into the container. The warmth of it felt good on her chilly hands. "Pa will be so pleased and excited to have a glass of milk for supper tonight."

"Well. She's all yours. I guess I best be getting home. We're busy storing apples for the winter, and my brothers will want me back to help."

"Apples?"

"Yes. This is our first crop. A few old trees were on our property when we moved in. We've added a few more, and soon we'll have an entire orchard."

"That sounds wonderful. I love apple pie."

"So do I!" Charles winked at her. "My sister is a horrible cook. Can you make pie?"

"I can make pie, but we haven't had any apples yet to make one. I used to peel the apples for Ma back in Pennsylvania. Betsey brought seeds from home and we're carefully tending the growing trees. They're just small shoots now. It will be a few years yet before we can harvest apples from them." Etta pointed toward where Pa had planted Betsey's seeds. The shoots were all that showed now. The small leaves that had developed this year had blown off.

"So, you'll have apples soon, too."

"I hope so."

"Perhaps I can bring you a few of ours."

"I'd love that. I could practice making a pie."

As they made their way back toward Charles's horse and the cabin, Etta knew she should think of something clever to say, but all she could think about was this new fellow and how much she'd like to get to know him more. "Perhaps your family could come over for dinner soon."

"We don't venture very far away from the house once winter sets in."

Disappointment filled Etta. Was he not interested?

Despite the truth of his statement, Charles added, "But if you bake an apple pie, I'll find a way."

Etta flashed him a smile. "Thanks for delivering Myrtle."

Charles stepped to one side, put the bucket of warm milk at Etta's feet, then put his hat on. "My pleasure." He put one foot in the stirrup and effortlessly mounted the enormous horse. "It's been nice getting to know you better, Etta. I'll look forward to that pie."

Thankful she had at least a charming smile for Charles, she thanked him again. She watched the giant horse trot off the property.

Opening the cabin door, she saw her sister standing near her bed with a blanket over her shoulders. Jillian sniffled. "Who was that?" She looked up as Etta removed her coat. "Your face is all red."

"It's cold outside. But look, Ma. Fresh milk." She placed the bucket down on the table.

Ma glowed with excitement. "Go get the churn. We'll have fresh butter on our bread by tonight."

A cold, damp wind filtered into the cabin as Sally held the door for Rhoda to come inside. The look on Rhoda's face caused her to step back instead of pulling her sister-in-law into a hug. "Rhoda? Is something wrong?"

Rhoda pulled off a red scarf that wrapped around her neck and removed her bonnet. "I need to talk to you."

Sally slowly remembered her manners and helped Rhoda out of her coat. How would her husband's sister keep warm this winter with such a thin coat? She and Hosea had discussed Rhoda's situation in the last few nights before going to sleep. They were both worried.

Rhoda lowered herself into a chair at the table. The pained look on her face and red-rimmed eyes told Sally that Rhoda was far from well.

Before she could ask, Sally went for the kettle still boiling over the fire. Rhoda needed to warm up before they could have a comfortable conversation. "Let me get you some coffee."

Rhoda peeled off her gloves, which were proper for a dance instead of being warm for the November day. "It's November, Sally. I don't need to tell you my concerns. Sidney is late. My cabin is ready to fall apart once the snow hits. I don't know what to do."

Sally poured coffee from the kettle into a cup on the table. She pushed it toward Rhoda, who took it into her hands to warm them before taking a sip. Sally sent up a silent prayer. What could she say to Rhoda? She knew the only solution was to impose on Aaron and Betsey, but Betsey had transformed the upper part of their house into a classroom. How would they possibly fit four children and Rhoda there? Comfortably?

Sally lowered herself into the chair across the table from Rhoda. "I can't imagine what's keeping Sidney." She enfolded Rhoda's icy hands into her own. "I'm sure he'll be here. Any day."

"I have to confess to you." Rhoda didn't look at Sally.

"What is it, Rhoda? You can tell me."

"I don't know for sure he's coming."

Sally didn't expect that confession. She leaned back. "What do you mean?"

"I haven't been completely honest with you and Hosea. I assumed Sidney would pack up the store and follow me. Right behind me. Now that he hasn't arrived, I'm assuming maybe..." She glanced up. Tears filled her eyes. "We didn't leave each other on the best of terms."

"That can't be! Why would Sidney not follow you here like his letters indicated?"

"I wanted to come. He didn't."

"What?"

"We had a disagreement before I left. It was my idea to move to Michigan, eventually Sidney agreed. I was missing Hosea. I wanted to see him. And you. The children. I missed you all so much. I was also sure a new territory would need store owners. Someone to set up a store where customers could come and get their needs met instead of having to travel to places like Pontiac. I was sure it would work. But Sally—" Rhoda covered her mouth. Tears now dripped down her cheeks.

Sally wasn't sure how to respond. She handed Rhoda a handkerchief.

"I never imagined the territory would be this desolate. I don't know what I was expecting. I knew there'd be lots of settlers who came before us. I assumed they'd have gardens, crops, animals to help them survive. I know a store would also be beneficial, but as I've told you, maybe Sidney didn't feel the same way. Perhaps he's changed his mind. He loved Sodus, and even though we had competition with other store owners, he may now feel it would be best to keep a business there." Rhoda took another swallow.

"I'm sure he's not rethought the idea. He loves you, Rhoda. Why wouldn't he come?"

Rhoda wiped her face. "I'm not the same woman you left in New York. I've grown bitter."

Sally knew a confession like this was hard for Rhoda to admit.

"I hated how people treated Hosea and you. I wanted to prove your innocence. He'd done nothing wrong. I grew even more bitter, even after the gossip died down. It wasn't fair. I never meant–" Rhoda looked at Sally with round eyes. It was as if she wanted to confess something. "Why couldn't everything go back to how it was? Hosea hadn't done anything to deserve such treatment."

"You left Sodus because of the scandal surrounding Hosea?"

"I couldn't take it anymore. These people just wouldn't stop. I felt their accusations whenever they entered our store. They looked down at us. Went to other stores for their purchases. Only because of us being related to Hosea. I could see it and feel it."

Sally leaned into the table. "Rhoda. I'm sorry you felt so betrayed by our friends. To be honest, I don't think it was all because of Hosea."

Rhoda's forehead wrinkled. Her eyes bore into Sally. "What do you mean?"

"The New York scandal had almost died away after we moved to Pennsylvania. Hosea got letters from many of the men in the church. They all repented and asked his forgiveness for how they'd treated him. Are you sure—" Sally hesitated, but it needed to be said. "Perhaps some of your feelings have gotten away from you." This was something Sally and Hosea had talked about. "Are you imagining something different?"

"You don't know what happened after you left. We didn't tell you all the details, but there were still two women in the group who wouldn't let the rumors die. They would gossip about me behind my back, even in the aisles of the store. Once a new proprietor came into town, many of them stopped coming to our store and began going to the new one. It was awful. Not only had they lied about Hosea, but they also were turning on Sidney, on me, and the store. I didn't want Sidney to have to go through what Hosea had gone through. It was just a matter of time before they started rumors about us!" Rhoda's face grew red, her eyes blazing.

The angry response startled Sally. In Sally's mind, the rumors had died down once they left town. She knew that from all the correspondence. She heard it from her own parents. Many were sorry they'd believed such lies. They hated that the scandal had forced Hosea out of town. Sally wasn't sure how far she could go with trying to explain this to Rhoda. Rhoda had turned into a bitter, angry woman. Would the truth make her worse?

"So that's my problem, Sally. I'm afraid Sidney has stayed in Sodus. He probably wants to be rid of me. I haven't been—" before she could finish her sentence, she broke down again.

Between sobs, she choked out words. "I'm desperate now! I'm out of money. The roof will not hold—" More anguish poured down Rhoda's cheeks.

Sally walked around to Rhoda and wrapped arms around her tight from behind. She knew that whatever she said needed to be said in extreme love and understanding. The only answer to Rhoda's grief was to speak the truth, but she wasn't sure Rhoda was ready to hear it. Instead, she gave love and grace. "Rhoda. Oh, Rhoda. I'm so sorry."

Suddenly, the door to the cabin flew open. Hosea stomped in, to rid his boots of the snow which covered them. "It's gonna snow big soon, Sally Mae! You just wait and see." He stopped. "Rhoda?"

Rhoda wiped at her face with her sleeve.

Hosea came to the table. "What's wrong, dear sister?"

Rhoda wiped her face off with her hands. "It's nothing, Hosea."

Sally gave Hosea a look of frustration. She knew if he had heard the conversation, it wouldn't be long before he'd be telling his sister the truth. And at that moment, Sally was pretty sure that wasn't what they needed to do. She bit her lip.

Hosea removed his coat and hung it on a peg by the door. He bent down to peel off his boots. "It doesn't sound like nothing, Rhoda."

"Hosea, would you like coffee? There's still some left in the kettle. Bring your mug and I'll fill it up for you."

"I need to be going." Rhoda stood. She acted desperate to regain her composure.

"You're not going anywhere!" Hosea lifted his mug for Sally to fill it. "Let's talk."

"I can't. I need to get home. I've left the children alone, and we need to keep the fire going."

"They'll be fine."

As Sally Mae filled Hosea's cup, she gave him an entire conversation with her eyes. Thankfully, he seemed to understand and kept silent.

Rhoda grasped her coat and pulled on her gloves. "I'll come back later. I need to feed the children dinner." Without hesitation, she hugged Hosea and smiled at him. "We'll talk later." With that comment, she left.

As the door shut behind her, Hosea glanced at Sally. "What was that about?"

"God's working in her heart, Hosea. Let Him do His will."

Caroline left the room while Dr. Harder examined Horace. Horace had grown weaker and had a yellowish cast to his eyes. It had been a long week.

While the doctor was with Horace, she went to check on the meal. Ma had brought a pot of stew, which now simmered over the fire. Opening the lid, steam misted her face as she smelled the intense aroma of venison and potatoes. She stirred the pot to be sure the meal wouldn't scorch her kettle.

She couldn't make out the murmurs from the bedroom. She hoped Horace would tell the doctor all his symptoms. Horace had a habit of denying what was bothering him. For a good diagnosis, Caroline needed him to be honest with Dr. Harder.

As much as she was thankful for the doctor coming to visit, she couldn't bear to hear his prognosis. Would it be hard news? Perhaps if she fed him better? Encouraged him to eat more? Hopefully, she prayed the doctor had a practical prescription for what ailed her husband.

Coming from the bedroom, Dr. Harder held up a small bottle.

He shook it, stopped the bottle with his finger, and then licked it.

Caroline grimaced at the thought of what he was doing. She was pretty sure the sample was some of Horace's urine. It was a deep yellow color. "What are you doing?"

"Checking for sweetness."

"What?"

Doctor Harder set the bottle on the table. "I believe I know the cause of Horace's symptoms. When a person has high sugar content in their urine, it means only one thing."

"Sugar? How can you tell it has sugar?"

"It tastes sweet."

Caroline wanted to ask if it was indeed a sample of Horace's urine, but she couldn't stomach the thought and put her hand over her mouth.

"It does." Dr. Harder put a stopper on the bottle and inserted it into his black leather bag. "How much sugar does Horace consume daily?"

"I love to bake for him. I have been trying to use more of it so it will help him gain weight."

"Well, let's stop doing that."

Caroline had a dozen questions. "Stop feeding him? Or baking for him?"

"No. He needs to eat only healthy food. His body is fighting to stay alive, and the more sugar and sweet things he eats makes it worse. It could be some sort of cancer or tumor. I've seen a few cases like it. If that's the case—" Dr. Harder pulled on his coat.

Caroline wanted to ask all her questions, but fear gripped her soul. Her heart beat harder and she placed her hand over her chest. How could she ask him the tough questions nagging her? Would he grow sicker? Would he survive? Her thoughts could not form or express the words.

"I might be wrong. This is an illness I haven't had much experience with. I am used to broken bones, scarlet fever, even gangrene and disease, but this—I've only seen a time or two. But I'm pretty sure it's either cancer or diabetes mellitus. If it's the latter, we can change his eating habits and it will help, but if it is a tumor, I don't expect anything to change. Time will tell."

"What does that mean?" Caroline asked in a whisper.

"It will probably take his life." His eyes showed compassion. "I'm sorry, Caroline."

CHAPTER TWENTY

The slight snow the territory received that November day was just enough to dampen the ground. Rhoda's prints were the only thing disturbing the fresh powder. As she made her way back to her children after talking to Sally, Rhoda found other tracks in the snow. They appeared fresh, but not from a man's boots.

Following the path to her cabin, Rhoda saw the tracks go into the woods at one place and then back onto the path at other times. Whoever was making them wasn't far in front of her.

Rhoda's heavy heart weighed on her soul. Why had she shared so much with Sally? She hadn't talked about her feelings regarding Hosea's scandal to anyone but Sidney. What would Sally think of her now? But did Rhoda even care?

As Rhoda continued down the path, the prints didn't stray too far from the trail. There were only two other homes on the path to her cabin. One belonged to the Leach family, but they'd left a few months before, and one of the mill workers now lived there. The other was the small cabin Ambrose had made for himself. He was rarely home. She scurried past his cabin and saw no smoke coming from the chimney.

She contemplated her next move. She needed more soap. The bar she'd purchased just a few weeks before had now gotten so small, she'd found it hard getting the men's clothes thoroughly clean. As she approached her cabin, she knew a trip to Whitmore's post was inevitable. She could purchase soap and ask Whitmore about any other likely places to spend the winter. She knew he'd know if anything existed.

Looking down, she realized the footprints she'd been seeing along the path led right to the front door of her cabin. The door to her small cabin stood wide open.

Fear gripped her heart as she stood still. A large person, probably a man, was inside her cabin. With her children. The silence of the forest, and in her cabin, filled her heart with dread.

Ma forced Jillian to head to the barn to gather the morning eggs, despite her cold. She wanted nothing more than to sing loud enough to hear her voice echo off the trees, but her sore throat stopped her. Ma told her to hurry so she wouldn't get sicker. She opened the bin to gather eggs. Passing the cow on her way in, she knew another chore awaited her once she got inside. Etta had filled the churn to make butter. Once Jillian returned, it would be her turn to plunge the dasher into the churn, until her arm grew tired and someone else took over. The cow would supply milk for not only Ma's cooking but also for Betsey and the children. As wonderful as the thought was, all Jillian could envision was the additional chores it would now bring her.

Soon Etta would find a husband and Jillian would be the only one left to help Pa and Ma with all the chores. Pa had cut down, considerably, the crop field, but clothes still needed mending, the animals all needed fed, water still had to be brought from the spring, and now a cow needed milked. Many of these chores fell to Etta and Jillian. Ma seemed to have never fully recovered from her continued bouts with ague, but she could still cook meals and clean. With Pa often at the mill, she looked to Jillian and Etta for help with almost everything else.

As she rubbed the dirt off the fresh eggs, she lamented over her dire circumstances. Daily life had grown monotonous. She'd love to attend school again, have afternoons set aside for visiting friends, or even go to town occasionally. For goodness' sake, she was still young! Why did the days pass so quickly without being able to enjoy them or have something fun to look forward to?

As she pined over her dismal life, Jillian looked up to see Billie coming onto the property from the south. His regular visits were now a bright spot in Jillian's toils. He'd often bring a letter from Pennsylvania or even the New York relatives to Pa. But with each visit, Jillian wondered if his visits were to see her, too.

As of late, all Etta could talk about was Charles Chalker. Long into the evenings, after Pa and Ma had gone to sleep, Etta and Jillian would share with one another their future dreams for the future. Etta often asked her what she thought of Charles. Jillian hardly knew him. She'd seen him occasionally, but she wasn't impressed. Billie was much cuter.

Jillian knew better than to tell Etta she really liked Billie. Etta would chide her for thinking about a boy. She was just fourteen; and having romantic thoughts about a boy was too mature for her, but Jillian couldn't help it. Since Caroline had chosen Horace over Billie, Jillian felt it was fine for her to daydream about him now. She continued to hope Billie would feel the same.

She smiled as she watched him look around the property after dismounting from his horse. As he glimpsed her way, he smiled. Jillian felt her body grow warm despite the cold. This time, instead of heading to the cabin, he came straight for her.

Jillian looked a mess. She hadn't taken any time to fix her hair; and now looking down at her apron, she found it covered with straw and chicken droppings. But what could she do about that now?

As he approached, Billie took off his hat and raked his hand through his hair. Jillian couldn't help but smile. That's the part of Billie she loved the most.

"Good morning, Jillian."

Jillian could feel herself blush at hearing him say her name.

"Hello, Billie."

"You know what I heard as I approached?"

Jillian didn't know and shook her head.

"Silence! Why are you not singing?" He stepped closer. "Do you know people from all over talk about how the Baker girls love to sing while they work?"

Again, Jillian shook her head.

"I wish we had a church building so I could sit close to your family, just so I could listen to your voice."

Jillian sighed.

"Are you going to say something?"

"Billie?" Should she tell him she would love to sing for him every single day of his life? As the thoughts scurried through her mind, she wondered if she should tell him how she really felt, but that would be scandalous for a woman to tell a man how she felt before he uttered similar words.

"Yes."

"Would you carry these eggs to the cabin for me?" Jillian blushed at the stupidity of her words. "I mean. I can carry the eggs. They aren't heavy and—"

Before she could say more, Billie looked around and then took hold of her hand and pulled her behind him. She didn't know what to do or say, she just followed him. The warmth of his hand in the morning chill sent tingles through her body. Where was he taking her?

Behind the barn, he leaned her up against the barn wall. "Jillian. I know you aren't of marrying age yet."

Jillian squirmed. As much as she liked Billie, she felt uncomfortable as he drew nearer to her. She could smell his breath and see into his deep brown eyes. She wanted to tell him she also had a cold. Then she changed her mind.

"Just listen for a minute. I know your age. It will be a couple of years yet before I can ask your pa for permission. But I love you, Jillian."

Jillian's breath caught in her chest. "What did you say?"

Before she could answer or tell him how she felt, Billie kissed her long and hard on the lips. Jillian's kisses were always only from her parents and never on the lips. She was unsure about what to do. In fact, instead of pushing him away, she let him kiss her.

Time disappeared as Billie pulled away and looked into her eyes. "Well, Miss Baker. What do you think?"

Jillian knew only one way to answer him. Even being inexperienced and not sure if she was doing it right, she kissed him full on the lips again. It only lasted a few seconds, but Jillian knew that after this, Billie's visits might include a little time behind the barn.

Rhoda had no weapon with her. Who was in her cabin? What did he want? Fleetingly, she thought about asking God for help.

God! Her heart was too bitter for Him to even answer. She'd neglected Him far too long. Above all, God wasn't interested in her daily needs. This was her problem. Hers alone. She'd brought her children into the territory to make a better life for them and now, if they were in harm's way, it was all her fault. She had no one else to blame.

Standing outside, she listened intently for sounds from her children. Would she cause more harm to them to go inside and then not be able to protect them? If only Ambrose were home. She'd run back to him and scream for his help, but she was sure he wasn't there.

As she crept closer to the door, she listened for any sound. Perhaps she was too late. With that thought, she impulsively offered up a quick prayer. She didn't quite know why she did it, but it seemed to be her only source of help at that moment.

Looking down, she found a large rock just outside the door. Bending over, she gently picked it up. Gripping it with all her might, she knew it would make a good battering stone, if nothing else.

As she came upon the house's threshold, she still heard nothing inside. The bright sky and sunlight reflecting off the snow made the cabin darker as she stepped inside. She squinted to see. Tiptoeing in, she could see a tall, dark figure over the bed where her children slept. Surely, they weren't still in bed, although they'd been staying in bed during the day to stay warm.

Coming closer and as her eyes adjusted to the dark cabin, she saw him. A tall man was gazing at her children, who, thankfully, were in bed and sound asleep. Just when she realized it wasn't just a man, but an Indian man, she saw his hand raised over his head. In his hand was a large hunting knife.

Rhoda sprang into action and lunged at the Indian with the rock, yelling for the children to wake up. As Rhoda brought the rock down to land directly on his head, he jumped sideways and the rock tumbled to the ground at her feet. He stared at Rhoda. The moment seemed to last for minutes instead of just seconds. Everyone stood still. Should she reach down for the rock or cover her children for protection?

As she contemplated her next move, the Indian rushed toward the fireplace, pointing to his knife. He quickly spoke in Chippewa, "Bushue, che-mok-e-mon's squaw!" As he continued to back nearer to the fireplace, he again pointed to his knife, and then toward Rhoda's grindstone. She'd found the stone just a few months before and used it to keep her own knives sharp. The Indian again pointed to the knife and then to her grindstone.

He wasn't there to harm her or the children. It seemed the only thing he wanted to do was to sharpen his knife.

At that moment, Giles woke up and screamed. When he did, he woke up his sisters. They all sat up in the bed and shrieked. Rhoda motioned for all of them to be silent. She watched as the

Indian picked up the grindstone, left the cabin, and disappeared out of sight.

Rhoda's legs gave way, and she sat on the floor. The children bounded off the bed, wrapping their arms around her and stroking her hair.

"Momma. Are you okay?" Philinda patted her shoulder.

Rhoda wasn't sure. The pressure in her bladder gave way, and she wet herself a little. "I think I need to use the outhouse."

She kissed each of her children, then walked outside. The Indian had left. She headed toward the outhouse, and as she sat, the tears and fears of the morning again erupted out of her soul. What had she done by bringing her children to this land by herself? She longed for Sidney like she'd not done in her whole life. She valued herself as being strong and independent, looking down on women who seemed to need their husbands like a spark to a fire. Despite that, she did something she hadn't done in years. She thanked God for protection over her most valued possessions, her children.

CHAPTER TWENTY-ONE

Heavy, deep snow fell that night. The pine tree branches circling the Baker property kissed the ground. Hosea didn't linger long in the doorway, gazing out at the beauty. The scene took his breath away. Although the cabin was damp and cold, no matter how hard the winter would be, from this point forward, it couldn't take away the beauty of the land with a fresh coat of snow frosting the trees. He knew he'd get the dickens from Sally Mae if he didn't shut the door, so he pulled it shut behind him as he continued to look across the river and then toward the surrounding forest.

He'd be the one to trudge through the snow to fill the inside barrel with water for his girls and Sally Mae. They worked hard to make this place their home. One or two walks to the spring was the least he could do to help.

The snowfall didn't crunch the way it usually did on a blistery January day, but his footprints left a trail from the cabin down to the spring beside the river. Lifting each bucket, he quickly filled four of them to haul back to the cabin.

As he approached their dwelling, Hosea stopped a moment to look out over the property they'd settled and had lived on for nearly four years now. The years had made his face more wrinkled, his hands less strong, and his body even more frail, but he wouldn't give up his property here in the New Territory for a thousand acres in Pennsylvania. What a blessing this venture had been for his family. Hosea set the buckets of water at his feet.

Tiny shoots of apple trees were growing deep roots in the field behind the house. A cow roamed just outside the barn and the crows of the chickens heralded the morning. A mourning dove permeated the air with his echoing songs as his mate foraged for seeds on the ground at the base of the trees, protected against the snowfall. A bouncing rabbit caught Hosea's eye as he trudged to the cabin. If he had his gun this morning... Thinking of the meal it would provide made his mouth water.

The stirring in Hosea's soul had little to do with the beauty of his property but rather his ability to see the future. He and Sally Mae would likely pass away here. They'd chosen to be the first settlers to blaze the trails, dig the first furrows in the soil, and to erect the first cabins. This would be his legacy.

Had it been easy? Far from it. The arch of his spine, the roughness to his hands, the ache in his bones all resulted from this life. Even the chore he was doing at this moment. He knew he was losing the battle of living a long life. He could barely make it through a day without nodding off on a stump after eating his lunch. Just walking to the mill made him short of breath, and each step made his knees ache. He even saw the ravages of their wilderness etched on the face of his beloved Sally Mae. Sleep came easily for them each night. It took all the energy he could muster to get out of bed each morning. He had gained a new home—perhaps a legacy someone would someday remember or acknowledge—but he was losing the battle to watch it unfold into the village he'd only dreamed about. Would anyone remember the name Hosea Baker? Above all, did it even matter?

Hosea smiled. He was just a forerunner of what would become of the cabins by the Shiawassee River. His children would remember, and his grandchildren would live past him to see the fruition of his efforts. They'd one day tell the story of his adventures and the settling of the township. Perhaps even an Indian or two would remember his name.

Remembering Alexander, Hosea still missed the boy's shadow trudging behind him everywhere he went. He'd been an angel of mercy their first year there. What would they have done without him and Waussinoodae? The two special friends they'd made helped Sally Mae and Betsey survive that first year. God had allowed Hosea to be a small part of their lives. Instead of grieving them, he thanked God for them.

Picking up the buckets, Hosea continued his trek to the cabin. There was only one more thing Hosea wanted to do for Sally Mae before his tired ole' body gave out. He was determined to build her the frame house she deserved up near the other neighbors in their growing community. It wouldn't be close to the river, which was a disappointment. He turned himself around and glanced back at the flowing waters of the Shiawassee. He wouldn't be far away, but he'd miss the sounds and the sights of the river that had brought him so far north.

Turning back, one more thought came to mind. What would it be like to live longer than any other human being? For if he could live like Methuselah, he'd see the outcome of this village. He'd give anything to see it in fifty or even one hundred years. Would it look the same? He hoped it would look as spectacular as it did on this snowy day in 1836.

Billie jumped off his horse as he came upon the tiny ramshackle cabin in the woods. He couldn't believe anyone would call it a viable shelter in the coming winter. Knowing Mrs. Seymour and the children, as he now did, he knew they didn't have much of a choice. He hoped the letter he was carrying would bring her good news.

As he neared the front door, Billie was almost afraid to knock on the door for fear it would fall apart when he did. Tapping, he heard a commotion inside.

"Yes?" Mrs. Seymour stood inside, wearing her coat, and tattered gloves revealing just the tips of her fingers.

"I have a letter for you, ma'am."

Tears pooled in the woman's eyes. "Thank you, Billie."

Billie acknowledged her with a tip of his hat. "My pleasure."

Rhoda's hands shook as she glanced down at the letter. It had to be news from Sidney. She shouldn't have any hesitation opening it, yet her recent thoughts about her behavior and temperament before she left New York made her leery. Her nightmares, as of late, hadn't helped her confidence.

Philinda approached her from behind. "Who's it from, Momma? Is it Papa?"

Rhoda knew she shouldn't pass her fears onto her children. They'd been through enough by dragging them here. They were cold most of the time, hungry at all hours of the day, and probably skeptical of why they'd traveled here without their Papa. Rhoda pulled Philinda close and rubbed her forearms. "Well, there's only one way to find out."

Philinda's eyes brightened. "I hope so. I miss him."

Rhoda was reluctant to read the letter under her daughter's watchful eye. What if he was telling her he wouldn't be coming? What if he had decided to abandon Rhoda and the younger children under her care? She couldn't bear for Philinda to hear what Sidney had to say. She just couldn't. She had to be honest. "Philinda, I think it is from your Papa, but you need to trust me. I need to read the letter to myself first."

"Why?" Philinda stepped away from her. "Do you think it's bad news?"

Her statement gave Rhoda an idea. "Perhaps." She stroked her daughter's hair. "If it is, why don't you let your Momma read it first, and then I'll best know how to share the news with your sisters and brother. Would that be okay?"

Philinda's eyes grew wide. "If you think that's best." She stepped away from Rhoda, but her eyes didn't show confidence or assurance. Only fear, like a small fawn finding itself alone at the edge of the woods.

Rhoda placed a blanket over her shoulders and left the cabin. She hated to see her children so frightened, yet she had no one to blame but herself. As Rhoda walked outside, she wondered where she could read the letter in privacy. She avoided leaving the cabin very far. What if the Indian was watching it and preparing to come back? She wouldn't leave her children alone again. Ever.

The wind blew cold against Rhoda's cheeks. She couldn't be outside for long. It was too dark in the outhouse to read well, so Rhoda wandered into the forest behind the cabin. She found a tree to lean against and opened the flaps of the paper. The uniquely folded letter revealed her eldest daughter Harriet's creativity. She could make beautiful things out of paper by just shaping or folding them in specific ways. She'd once made flowers from some old wallpaper they had at the store. Several women bought them when Sidney put them up for sale. The next Sunday, the beautiful wallpaper creations adorned several hats.

Rhoda recognized the neat cursive of her husband's handwriting. She steeled herself against the news that might reveal that she would soon find herself completely alone. Closing her eyes, which threatened to spill tears, she empowered herself to read the letter.

When she opened her eyes, she squinted in the bright sunlight. She scanned the sheet of paper. It was a long letter. Two sheets full of ink. Why would anyone write such a long letter if it were good news?

Rhoda took a deep breath.

Dear Rhoda,

This is a hard letter for me to write.

Rhoda covered her mouth with her free hand.

We've had a snag trying to get everything ready for our trip west. The first buyer for the store left town the night before we would have settled the transaction. He was a skeptical man, and I was suspicious from the very beginning whether he had the funds to buy the store, as he'd promised. Once he left town, my worst suspicions came true. That happened in August. We were packed and ready to travel once the transaction was finished, but then we realized we couldn't until a new buyer could be found.

As with many things, time got away from me as I unpacked and needed to maintain the selling aspect of the store. Before I knew it, the calendar switched to September. Knowing it would be useless to haul all our supplies so late in the year, I was frantic to find someone to buy the store. I lowered the price and tried for weeks to find a new buyer.

Whenever someone seemed interested, they'd consider the purchase but would realize we had lots of competitors for customers in Sodus. I found it harder and harder to convince tentative buyers we still had been doing well financially without them questioning why I was pulling out of town and so quickly. Despite sharing why and how we were coming to meet you, every buyer backed out of the deal at the last minute. When fall arrived, the children and I decided they should start school until we found a buyer.

Before I knew it, October arrived. I'd now unpacked all of our goods to put back on the shelves. I decided the winter clothing and fabrics would be needed for the upcoming winter, so Harriet stocked up the fabric section of the store again, and we sold many of the items that we'd planned to bring with us to the territory.

It was then I realized we'd not be able to make the trip before winter came. I needed to send you this letter and prayed it would reach you in time.

I know we didn't separate from each other on the best terms.

Rhoda held her breath.

I know this trip was important to you. I didn't quite understand it, but I now see this town depends more on the goods of Martin's store down the road. When we were packed and ready to travel, many of our loyal customers switched to his store. Understandably so. When we had to sell a bit more just to stay afloat, a few came back. But we also lost many of our faithful buyers.

Rhoda relaxed.

I'm sorry, love. I miss the children. I pray you are finding what you've been looking for. I pray it includes me and the older children. I will continue to wait for a buyer. Perhaps, if one comes in the next few weeks, I'll attempt to travel to the territory despite the weather, but I just don't know for sure what will happen.

He hoped she'd found what she was looking for? Rhoda glanced up at the ramshackle cabin which held her children. What had she been thinking about leaving the other children and Sidney behind? She should have waited. She should have listened to the wise counsel of her husband.

The only relief she'd found was that Sidney wasn't abandoning her. He knew how spontaneous and thoughtless she could be and still loved her, anyway.

The rest of the letter included things about their neighbors in Sodus. An elderly man they loved had passed away. A child had drowned at the end of the summer after getting cramps trying to traverse a local pond. She skimmed past this information until she reached his last words.

I just wanted you to know I'm doing my best to get to you. As of now, we don't have a buyer for the store, but I have a couple of leads. Perhaps even Martin himself will want to buy the store as a millenary to add to his own business. Harriet is making up some paper flowers for him and designing a few hats for him to see. She's so efficient and helpful.

The children send their love. They miss you and the younger ones, but hopefully we will see you soon. Stay well. I pray you are doing well, but if not..."

How could he possibly know that they weren't doing well? If Sidney found Rhoda and the children living in such primitive conditions, it would mortify him.

Rhoda had read enough. Embarrassment filled her heart. A grown woman who could not provide adequate shelter and food for her family.

There was nothing in the letter that would disturb Philinda. She'd let her read it. It would be better than having to tell her the news herself. Rhoda folded the letter as it had come and tucked it into her pocket. As she returned to the cabin, she looked up at the gray Michigan Territory skies and knew soon the woods would be impenetrable while snow piled ever so high. Then the temperatures would drop even more. What would she do to keep them all safe, warm, and fed?

CHAPTER TWENTY-TWO

Nicholas dropped down off the horse with a thump, his legs weak from riding so far. Another grumble erupted from his empty belly. Each step made it harder to not fall to his knees. His socks squished from walking the horse along the water's edge to get through the forest. Thankfulness filled his soul when saw the lit candle in the window of his home.

As he made his way up the steps of his house, his eldest daughter opened the door just as he was about to tap on it.

"Papa!"

Nicholas leaned against her for support. "Hold me up, daughter. Where's Sallie?" Nicholas called his new wife *Sallie* for the sake of the older children; each one old enough to remember their mother well.

"Sallie!" Elizabeth called out for her stepmother.

Sallie rushed toward them, wiping her floured hands on her apron. "Nicholas. Oh, my dear man."

He must have looked as tired and worn out as he felt. He managed a smile. "Got anything to eat?"

"Of course, Nicholas." Sallie called up the stairs. "Moses! Joseph! Come down and help."

The two boys bounded down the stairs, coming to his aid.

"Put him here." She pulled Nicholas' chair closer to the roaring fire in the sitting room. "Elizabeth, go to the kitchen and get your father some hot coffee and a slice of that warm bread I just took out of the oven."

Sallie kneeled down in front of Nicholas, pulling off his heavy boots and stripping him out of his wet socks. She immediately began rubbing his feet. "Joseph, run outside and get some snow. Hurry!"

The young man reached for a bucket by the fireplace and ran outside.

Hannah and Adaline stared at the scene as they sat on the steps. Nicholas wanted to laugh at their wide eyes and forlorn looks. "It's okay, girls. Your father is just worn out, wet, and cold. I'll be feeling better in no time. Thanks to Sallie."

"Oh Nicholas. You've been gone almost four days. How can you properly care for others if you don't take care of yourself, too?"

Nicholas leaned back in the chair and closed his eyes. "Tell Moses to bring in my saddle-bags. There's medicines in them I don't want to freeze."

Sallie issued orders to all the children. Nicholas heard the commotion but couldn't open his eyes.

Elizabeth tapped him on the shoulder. "Father, here's some coffee. Sallie wants you to drink some. To warm you up."

Nicholas struggled to obey. The steam warmed his face as he took a sip, being careful not to burn his mouth. The warm liquid soothed his mouth and throat. Sallie appointed Moses to keep rubbing Nicholas's feet. They burned, which Nicholas knew to be a good sign.

"Where have you been?" Sallie asked as she tucked blankets around him in the chair.

"The question is not where I have been, but where have I not been? I found another outbreak of smallpox in an Indian family just south of here. Many of the younger ones have it now. I did everything I could, but two children passed away while I was there."

"Oh, Nicholas." Sallie took some warm socks from Adeline, who had gone upstairs to fetch them.

"I then ventured toward a settlement just north of here, where they said a man had fallen off his roof trying to fix it for winter. He broke his leg. I set it and then moved from there to..." Nicholas took time to sip some more coffee and take a large bite out of the slice of warm bread. His mouth relished the taste, and he devoured the entire piece in just two or three bites. He handed the towel back to Elizabeth. "Can you get me some more, young lady?"

"Of course, Papa."

Sallie leaned into Nicholas. "Try to keep your whereabouts and medical affairs at a minimum. I don't want to frighten the girls."

Nicholas glanced up at the two girls still on the stairs and knew after a few more gulps of coffee he wouldn't need to worry about what he said, for as soon as he devoured another slice of bread, he closed his eyes and fell sound asleep.

"Where does Papa sleep when he is out doctoring people, mother?" Adeline asked from her spot on the staircase.

"Sometimes the settlers will allow him a place to sleep in their cabins, but mostly, he sleeps on his horse, Adeline."

"On his horse?" Hannah's eyes skeptical. "How does he do that?"

Sallie and the girls covered Nicholas with another warm blanket. "Carefully, girls." She kissed her husband on the cheek. "Very carefully." She hoped the townspeople realized how much Nicholas was doing to protect and bring health to the community. "Moses! Go take care of your father's horse, rub him down, and give him extra oats."

Philinda read through the letter her mother shared with her after coming back into the cabin. She watched her break up a small squash she had been saving on the hearth and cut it up to put into the pot hanging over the fire. They didn't have much food left. Philinda didn't remember a time when she was so hungry. It felt as if their meals were days apart instead of hours. Despite the food

Uncle Hosea and Aunt Sally brought them, it still left them hungry. Especially at night.

She wanted to complain to her mother. How could she have allowed this to happen? Back in New York, food had never been scarce, but since arriving in Uncle Hosea's part of the world, they'd faced many challenges.

Philinda pitched in to help her mother with the piles of clothing she washed each week. She knew the importance of the job. It was their only way of earning money to buy more food. But now, the men had stopped bringing their clothes like they did during the summer. Momma had told her that men don't change their clothes as often in the winter. Because of the cold, they layered clothing. They didn't care if it was dirty or not. As Philinda looked down at her own clothes, she understood it. She didn't like to take any of her clothing off, and they'd been sleeping in all they had since the outside temperature plummeted.

As she read through the letter, she wondered if they'd ever have normal again. She realized how in the past she'd taken all of her things for granted. If only they could have a clean home free of mice searching for a place to nest. Clothes that fit, instead of hanging off her shoulders like rags. A chance to sit at the table with her older sister and brothers, too. But especially Papa. She devoured his words on the page as she thought of him sitting at the desk by the window at the back of the store to write it. Closing her eyes, she envisioned the sun coming through the window and warming him as he wrote. Oh, how she missed their old house and Sodus.

She was nearly at the end of the letter when her mother asked her what she thought. "Sounds like Papa isn't coming soon?"

Momma shook her head. "I don't think so, honey. I wish it was better news."

She wanted to ask her momma the questions that filled her mind every night just before she'd drift off to sleep. What would they eat tomorrow? How many loads of laundry still needed to be washed? Could they go to the fur trading post and buy something different to eat? What Philinda wouldn't do for a piece of candy from Papa's bins by the cash register. She closed her eyes to think of the taste of some black licorice or a peppermint stick.

But the question she wanted to ask the most was too scary to even think about. Would they eventually starve to death if Papa didn't come? What would it feel like to go without food? Would the roof of the cabin finally give way and bury them all in new fallen snow? She didn't dare ask because, if she did, she might not like the answer. Instead of asking her momma, Philinda did the only thing she knew how to do well. Without her momma even knowing. She asked God for help. Help in getting her papa to them. Help for her momma to not be so sad, but more importantly, that they would find a warmer, safer place to live for the winter. Papa had told her often to not forget God was there, despite what her momma had been telling her.

As she neared the end of the letter, she continued to envision her papa writing it. His perfect penmanship always made her jealous. His bookkeeping sheets in his accounting books were neat and the numbers always balanced. Papa was a meticulous store owner.

She devoured every word he'd written. At the bottom of the page, she read the last sentence as if she'd never hear from her papa again. *I pray you are doing well, but if not, you'll find two gold coins I sewed into the bottom of the carpet bag I sent with you. I didn't tell you about them because I intended to use them when I arrived in the New Territory to buy a small building for our store. If you need to use them in an emergency, don't hesitate!*

Philinda sat up in her bed. "Momma! Did you find the coins?"

Momma turned toward her. "What coins?"

"The ones Papa hid."

Her mother looked at her with concern. "Sweetheart, you know I've used all the money Papa gave me. Remember?"

Philinda scrambled out of bed. Going to her momma's bed, she got down on her knees and pulled on the handle to retrieve it. The crumbled bag had grown dusty, but Philinda reached into it. There was nothing in it. Perhaps her momma was right. She'd used all the money on their trip here. The carpetbag had a piece of stiff fabric at the bottom to keep the shape of the carpetbag when it was being stored. Philinda used her fingernail to peel back the edge to remove it. Fingering the bottom of the bag, she searched for the hard, round coins. Sure enough, she could feel two large bumps at the bottom.

"Momma!" Philinda cried. "Come here and look. Bring your mending shears."

"Philinda! Don't you be using my shears in that bag!"

"But Momma. There's money in here."

Momma pulled back the blanket she'd put over her legs as Rhoda Ann came trotting to Philinda with the scissors. "What did you find, Philinda?"

Philinda cut a small slit in the carpetbag's bottom. As she did, she reached down under the fabric and fingered the cool coins.

Momma and the children watched as Philinda pulled out two large gold coins. She opened her palm for the family to see.

Momma sat on the bed and took the coins from Philinda's outstretched hand. "Oh, my child. How did you know they were in there?"

"Momma. The letter. Didn't you read it?"

Philinda handed the letter to her momma, who scanned to the bottom and read the words Philinda had read just seconds before.

"I missed that part."

Philinda sat back on her haunches and laughed right out loud. "Momma! That was the best part."

"These are twenty-dollar gold coins. We have forty dollars here."

"Momma. Can we get food with this?"

Tears came to her momma's eyes. "We can get more than just food. Pack up your things. Perhaps Whitmore will give us some credit on a room."

Philinda suddenly felt brave. She took the coins from her momma's hands and, without asking permission, she kneeled at her momma's bed. "Thank you, God, for saving us." For despite what her momma had been trying to instill in her heart over the past few years, she still believed in God. She wanted confidence that He always had her best interests at heart. And she was right, for He'd answered her prayers.

THREE YEARS LATER...1840

CHAPTER TWENTY-THREE

It was a sight to behold. If nine-year-old Giles hadn't seen it for himself, he wasn't sure he could convince another living soul about what he saw on this day. Chippewa and Pottawattamie Indians marching together in the procession with the early French fur traders of the village, and others who had at some time come in contact with the jovial smile and good nature of Whitmore Knaggs.

Families walked hand in hand. French traders donned their fur caps with guns leaning against their shoulders. The Indians in full regalia followed the horse-drawn travois. Never in the history of the small village in the Michigan Territory would there be such a strong sense of community to honor a man almost everyone could relate to and appreciate.

For many, Whitmore had welcomed them into the community on their first day there. For others, he'd given them a meal or a place of shelter for the night. Whitmore's meals consisted mostly of stewed pumpkin and turnips mixed with turkey or venison, but they were hot and filling. Many who called Whitmore "Old Whit" had enjoyed his kindly manner. Often he would give up his own bed for those needing a night's rest. The early settlers couldn't have sustained winters without Whitmore's help, many finding shelter just before winter. Most everyone knew they would find his trading post always open, never locked. All they had to do was pull on the rope chain to gain access to the building. Once inside, Whitmore trusted all to only take what they needed, knowing well he'd receive the goods taken back in twofold or gain another deep friendship in the exchange.

Giles's family was among those who needed to pay homage to the man who not only kept them fed in their hungriest of times, but also offered his mother, sisters, and him shelter one winter until their father could arrive from New York. Without his help, Giles's family could have perished their first winter in the New Territory. His family could have frozen to death or starved if it hadn't been for the hospitality of Whitmore Knaggs.

Many of the Indians, at the front of the procession, fought for the right to be ahead of the others, for Whitmore had helped the Indians the most. With the assistance of Whitmore's extended family and their ability to speak Ojibwa, the settlers had been able to convince the Indians that everyone wanted to pay homage to the man who had protected, guided, and fed them in their early days in the territory.

Giles watched as one of Whitmore's brothers spoke fluent Ojibwa and scolded some of the proud warriors that they needed to allow everyone in the funeral procession to pay their respects. One particular Indian appeared agitated and upset that other Indians wanted to be at the head of the line, directly behind the travois carrying Whitmore's body to the cemetery. A small fight broke out between the Indians and some of Whitmore's family. A sharp crack startled everyone. One of Whitmore's relatives fired a gun to warn the Indians to stop fighting.

The mourning procession continued to grow as settlers from Byron, Vernon, and surrounding communities joined in on the walk to the Fremont cemetery. Uncle Hosea, his wife Aunt Sally, and their daughters and families caught Giles's eye as they walked. Uncle Hosea loved to tell stories of how Whitmore had saved their lives. More times than anyone could count. The Knaggs's family had given cousin Ambrose the right to pull the travois behind his loyal horse, Nibi. Cousin Ambrose once told Giles he'd named his horse after an Indian friend he once knew.

Uncle Hosea often recounted the dealings with the Indians during his early days of setting up a farm in the territory. "If it wasn't for Whitmore, we'd have had no way to converse with the natives."

Whitmore had negotiated treaties between the Indians and the federal government. He served not only as a negotiator, but also as an interpreter communicating to the Indians the decrees, laws, and settlements of pay from the government. He gave out the money owed to them in a fair and amicable way.

The community and natives both owed great gratitude to the man now being carried to his last resting place.

As more of the settlers took their place in the procession, Momma grabbed Giles's hand. He irked him that she still considered him a child. Being nine years old, he didn't need to be led. He knew what this homage meant. Giles loved Whitmore just like the rest. He always had a peppermint in his pocket, just for him. The winter the family had spent with him at his post, Giles's mother was his cook and also kept up the post while he was gone on hunting expeditions or to fetch Dr. Harder when someone needed a doctor. Giles and his family got to know Whitmore the best while staying with him during the winter of eighteen thirty-six to thirty-seven.

Momma had worked hard that winter to help Whitmore, and she'd been able to keep them warm and fed until Father arrived the next spring. Once here, Father purchased the building near Whitmore's post called The Exchange or as it was now called The Shiawassee Exchange. It was a grand place to live, in a world where most of the settlers only had cabins for shelter. The family had lived well, ever since their father's arrival. Since then, Momma had given birth to Giles's sister, Cornelia, who was now fast asleep, being carried on his momma's back in a baby backboard made for her by one of the Indian women. Cornelia knew how to walk, but Momma knew she probably couldn't keep up with the procession, being a one-year-old.

"Giles, hurry on now." Momma scolded. Giles had a hard time keeping up with the group as he gazed at all the interesting characters around them. Some men were in full military attire. Painted faces and beaded garments were on full display among the Indians in attendance. All of it fascinated him.

"When will we be at the cemetery, Ma?" Rhoda Ann was always grumbling about something.

"Hush now! It isn't far."

Rhoda Ann took the hand of his other sister, Martha. Giles knew it would seem like a longer walk, having to listen to the annoying comments from his older sisters. Didn't they realize the importance of this moment?

Giles turned to see his sister Harriet and her husband, Alvah Laing. Alvah owned a store in a small village directly west of The Shiawassee Exchange on the Grand River Trail. His father was a doctor there and often he and Dr. Harder met to help each other. Harriet had met Alvah during her first year in the territory.

Following Harriet was Giles's sister, Lucinda, and his brother, George.

Looking up to his momma, Giles noticed her struggling to walk in the procession. She'd been extra sick the last month or so. Father told Giles not to worry about her, that it only meant one thing, but Giles felt sorry for her. Giles didn't actually know what *one thing* meant, but if father wasn't concerned, neither was Giles.

Soon, the entire procession stopped. They'd made it to the burial place. As the throngs of people crowded around the hole for

Old Whit, Giles noticed even the cantankerous Indians had grown quiet.

Pastor John Swain stood at the head of the open grave. "Thank you all for coming today to honor our friend and confident, John Whitmore Knaggs."

Giles didn't know his first name was John. He let go of his mother's grip and went to stand by his father. Father looked down, smiled, and patted his head.

"Whitmore will be remembered as a dear friend, a loyal brother, a fair trader, and a friend to the Indians and settlers of Knagg's Place."

John Swain had recently become a minister in the community north of Newburg. Newburg had finally gotten a name from Dr. Harder, who lived in a similar place called Newburg-on-the-Hudson back in New York. Even Uncle Hosea thought it an appropriate name for the growing village.

Father pulled Momma close. As Pastor Swain continued to talk about all of Whitmore's achievements, Giles thought about his parents. They were together again. He'd hated seeing them apart the year after they'd moved without Father. Boys needed their fathers. Didn't his Momma know that?

Giles disliked wearing his wool coat, but as they stood at the grave, he felt chilly. He didn't dare tell his momma for he'd begged her to not have to wear the scratchy coat to the funeral. If she knew now that he was cold, he'd have to wear it to school the next day.

As Giles glanced around the small cemetery, he saw traces of snow at the bottom edge of the trees where the daytime sun couldn't reach. Pulling his sweater tight, Giles listened, as best as he could, to all the wonderful things being recited about the fur trader. Indians joined in by standing in front of Pastor Swain right in the middle of his sermon. Other fur traders tried to dissuade the Indians from interrupting the service, but Giles had learned from Whitmore that every man was important despite how they lived or acted.

Giles thought it comical to watch the agitated natives. Some circled the grave, shaking tomahawks and rattles made from sticks and deer hide. To an outsider, it might have looked like the group would soon encounter trouble with the Indians in attendance, but everyone knew better. They just loved Whitmore like everyone did.

It was rare to see Indians on the reservation anymore. Father said disease had killed most of the tribe surrounding Knagg's Place. It was surprising to see so many today. Uncle Hosea said they'd come from all parts of the territory to take part in the ceremony.

Giles thought of a chat he'd had with Uncle Hosea about a special Indian boy named Alexander. Uncle Hosea said he thought Giles and Alexander would have made fast friends. He'd said, "You remind me of Alexander, Giles. You love being outside and imagining all kinds of wonderful adventures."

Giles wished he'd been able to meet the Indian boy. Uncle Hosea said he had been worried about Alexander due to smallpox outbreaks among the tribes. He'd said if Alexander was still alive, he'd have returned to visit Uncle Hosea and Aunt Sally. The more years that went by made Uncle Hosea believe that perhaps Alexander had contracted smallpox and died. Death always made Giles afraid. What would it be like to be dead?

Giles's thoughts were distracted by the pastor's words.

"Many loved ones have 'gone on to glory' since many of us have arrived here." Pastor Swain had lost a wife shortly after he arrived here, and he was silent for a moment, regaining his composure before continuing with the service.

Giles tried to remember every detail of the day. He would never forget it. Father told him Whitmore had died of old age. Father was seldom wrong, but as Giles stood watching the Indians chant and the other people standing quietly by the grave, he wondered if he'd just decided his job was fulfilled. Hopefully, people would never forget the name of John Whitmore Knaggs. Giles was sure he would never forget him.

Etta felt her arms grow weak from holding baby Harriet. At three months old, the baby held her head up well and seemed inquisitive about the noises going on around her. Charles looked over at her, then held out his hands to take the baby. Etta felt so proud to have a strong, dependable husband at her side and even happier to have a baby they could call their own.

She'd named her baby after her cousin, the refined and schooled Harriet. Harriet hadn't been in the territory long before she found a good man to marry.

To be honest, Etta was even more surprised Charles Chalker had chosen her to be his wife. She loved standing beside him now and lifted her chin higher, knowing they were among the new generation to make the wilderness into thriving communities.

The Chalker brothers had a farm in Vernon where Etta had gone to live after their marriage just a year before. They'd chosen a church close to Vernon to take their vows and had celebrated the occasion with a small gathering of friends outside on the church lawn following the ceremony. Within just a few months, Etta found herself with child and delivered Harriet, who had dark brown eyes. Etta reached out and brushed her knuckle under Harriet's chin. As she did, the baby gave her a smile, which took away the pain of the day. Her dark, inquisitive eyes then looked at Charles for reassurance that she was safe in his arms.

Etta glanced over at Jillian, who stood nearby. Jillian stood close to Billie. Pa had just allowed Billie the opportunity to court Jillian when she turned sixteen. Etta was sure she wouldn't make it to eighteen before she'd either run off or disobey Pa and marry Billie anyway. Jillian had confided in her frequently regarding her desire to marry before Pa's appointed date. Etta had encouraged her to wait, but she grew apprehensive about whether waiting would be the best for the couple now clinging to each other in front of them. Pa might have to change his mind, or Etta was afraid something scandalous could happen. She'd often caught them out behind the barn doing many things Etta could only imagine doing before marriage. Pa continued to insist the couple wait.

John Swain kept referring to the multitude of settlers Whitmore had helped during his lifetime. "This group here comprises many people who wouldn't have made it in the wilderness if it hadn't been for the generosity, kindness, and protection of Whitmore Knaggs. We all have a debt to pay forward to those seeking to build near us."

Etta thought about how much her pa had done for Newburg. Without Whit's help, perhaps he wouldn't have made it his first year either. Etta glanced to her right to see pa and ma. Gray hair circled the crown of Pa's head. He stooped now, probably the result of his futile attempts at being a farmer. Now that he had the thriving mill, he and Ma didn't worry about finances. The mill had been a stable business move on Pa's part.

Pa had built Ma a framed house closer to the growing village of Newburg. The tall, two-story home now stood as one of the primary residences in the village. Ma fretted that the extravagant house drew negative attention among the other residents, some still living in the log cabins built upon their arrival. But Pa wanted her to have a pleasant home, and as the owner of the only sawmill in the village, it had been an easy goal to achieve. Ma loved her home and often invited her friends over for tea. Her health had grown even more fragile during the past three years. Etta was pretty sure Pa understood this and wanted her to live nicely until God took her home.

"Whitmore Knaggs started the small community among the Indians." Most of the Indians present chanted a mourning song. John Swain waited for their cries to die down before he continued speaking. Etta believed the Indians wouldn't have coped with the territory changes as well without Whitmore's help, especially during treaty negotiations with the government. He'd strived to help in the discussions. He always wanted what was fair for his first neighbors here in the wilderness. Knowing the Indians would feel threatened and intimidated by the surge of settlers in the area, Whitmore had eased this transition for both parties. He had saved Pa from many Indian misunderstandings and he'd also given him supplies on credit their first year. He trusted Pa.

The Indians ceased their chanting and allowed John to lead the crowd in prayer. It was hard to believe John Swain was now a minister. After Abigail's death, he stayed single for a few years but had recently married a woman from a town north of Newburg.

Etta could see John's new wife, Wealthea Irons Swain, standing close to the grave opposite John. Etta smiled as she thought about Wealthea and how she really wasn't all that different from Abigail. You'd think a man would have learned his lesson the first time, yet her beauty overruled her disposition. At least in John's eyes. She had jet-black hair tied up in the latest style. Etta knew Wealthea's dress had shipped directly from New York. She'd overheard comments about it at the last dance they'd had at the Exchange.

Etta watched Betsey stoop to pick up Elisha. Betsey and Aaron's family continued to grow as they added two more boys to the family. Elisha would turn three in July and Darwin would have his fourth birthday later in the year. Ma and Pa were thrilled with all the recent births to the grandchild generation, and they frequently allowed the children to spend the night at their new home on Main Street in Newburg.

"Our village now has a name." John Swain smiled at the crowd. "Thanks to Whitmore and many of the men here in our village, it has been named and lawfully established as Newburg as of April 11, 1837." Etta smiled to think how pleased Pa and Whitmore had been that day.

As the service concluded, the mourners began to disperse. Hosea had kept his eye on the outskirts of the cemetery, hoping to glimpse Alexander among the other natives. He thought the boy, now a young man, would venture back to them for the funeral of Whitmore Knaggs. He hadn't seen the boy in years, but that hadn't dampened his hopes of one day seeing him again. Despite the years since his disappearance, Hosea always looked for him. His biggest fear was that the smallpox epidemic had taken the life of his adopted son. Hosea was sure that if he were still alive, they'd have seen him. Especially here, at the celebration of Whitmore's life. Alexander owed him a great deal.

Hosea glanced around as his neighbors greeted those around them. The families included the Devereux group, the Snell clan, the Hutchins and the Pierces and also the Harder family. He noticed Etta with her new husband, Charles.

Recently added were the Litchfield and the Beach families. Hosea's Newburg had grown, yet they'd also lost a few. Some residents had moved north, others west, some had moved on to a heavenly home. They were all dear to Hosea. He shook the hands of Isaac Banks, Samuel Whitcomb, Louis Findlay, Kibburn Bedell and David VanWormer as the group began leaving the cemetery for home.

As he walked toward Whitmore's grave, Hosea caught sight of Rhoda and all her growing young'uns. With Sidney now here, Hosea felt confident Rhoda would never have to worry about where she lived or if they'd have a meal. The couple had purchased The Exchange from Richard Godfrey and John Cushway, and it now served the community with an inn and ballroom. His glance toward the family drew a look from Rhoda, who waved and smiled. Hosea waved back. Rhoda had proved herself strong by caring for her family when they'd first arrived. Her determination was nothing short of miraculous and gracioius protection from God. If only Rhoda could see how God had cared for them and put her full trust in Him again.

Hosea knew he had to pay his last respects to his friend, Whitmore. Hosea approached the grave where they'd lowered the wooden box into the ground. Picking up a handful of dirt, Hosea crumbled the thick clay soil before he threw it atop the wooden box. "Thank you, Whitmore," he whispered. "I couldn't have made it without you."

Before he tossed in the handful of dirt, Hosea uttered a prayer. "I know you don't accept those into heaven, Lord, who don't realize the saving grace of Jesus. I did my best to show Whitmore the truth as I continue to try for all the men and woman here today. I don't dare possess the ability to see a man's heart, Lord, only You have that ability."

Hosea knew that being absent from earth meant a person was present with the Lord or, because of a man's wrong choice, suffering for eternity. It wasn't the first time that questions of a man's faith turned Hosea's heart to sadness. Questioning wasn't his job, but God's.

At the end of his prayer, he turned to find Sally Mae next to him. "We sure will miss Whitmore, won't we, Hosea?"

Without saying a word, Hosea took his wife's hand, and left their dear friend for the last time. Despite knowing he'd scanned the woods at least three or four times before this, Hosea did it again. Just to be sure he hadn't missed Alexander among the trees.

CHAPTER TWENTY-FOUR

Following Whitmore's service, Rhoda glanced down at her hands while their family headed back to the inn. Her once-youthful hands were now wrinkled and dry. Noticing them made her think back to 1836 and doing the laundry for the men in the community. She could remember looking at her own mother's hands, years before, and wondering how the normally tight, soft skin could turn so rough. Now she knew. Life did it.

Taking part in Whitmore's life celebration, she couldn't help but remember the kindness he'd given her and the younger children when she'd shown up on his doorstep that first winter day.

Thinking back, Rhoda shivered. The day had been cold, but regardless of the temperature, her shaking had more to do with the deal she'd planned to offer Whitmore. She had no clue what his response would be.

When Whit finally had shown up at the door, he motioned for the family to come into the room and to get warm by the immense fireplace in his dining area. He placed them all near the fire as he sat to talk to Rhoda.

"Whitmore."

He'd turned his full attention to her. "Yes, ma'am."

"I need help. I've waited as long as I can for my husband to arrive, but now I need help. I can't wait any longer."

Whitmore turned to light his pipe. He sucked on the end to lure the smoke into the tube. "I'm sorry your husband wasn't able to make it before the snow."

"Well," Rhoda choked back the fear that threatened to spill out of her eyes via tears. "I have currently found two gold pieces in the bottom of a carpet bag we brought from home. I didn't know they were there until my recent letter from my Sidney. I was wondering if you would allow me a room here for at least the winter? My children would not get underfoot. I'd be sure to keep them busy with schooling, mending, or jobs. I just need a solid roof over our heads. A fire, like this one." Rhoda pointed to the blazing fire in the hearth and swallowed hard, "To keep us warm and dry."

"Well, Mrs. Seymour. There is a small room at the back of the post. I've been meaning to add more things to sell at the post, but with winter coming—"

"I understand. Business is more important than a woman with children without her husband." Rhoda stood until Whitmore pulled her arm, insisting she sit back down.

"Let me speak."

Rhoda reached out for Giles's hand. She needed to keep her little boy close; it gave her the courage to swallow her pride and ask for help.

"I have a proposition for you."

Rhoda wondered if she should push the children back outside. What could this man possibly propose to her? She hoped it was proper.

"I need a cook. I also would like a woman to tend to cleanin' the place. So many bachelors live and stay here through the winter, the post gets mighty filthy. Would you be willing to take on that position for me until your husband arrives?"

The next words Rhoda heard were her own, accepting the position. The next thing she knew, Whitmore was leading them back to the room he'd been meaning to clean for a storeroom. It was even larger than the room they'd left back at the cabin.

That night, as Rhoda lay on the floor covered with furs which Whitmore provided, she could hear the prayers of her daughter next to her. The little one must have thought Rhoda had gone to sleep.

Her thankful prayer was for their new accommodations and for the kindness of Whitmore Knaggs.

Rhoda worked hard that winter, but instead of breaking her, it brought joy. The children were eager to help, and in short order, they had the post looking like a woman lived there instead of just a fur trader and a few men passing through. Giles seemed the most influenced by the man who had given up his storeroom to house the family. He soon began calling Whitmore "Old Whit," and many people followed suit. Giles followed Whitmore more than Rhoda cared to admit. Sometimes Whitmore would break out telling one of his tales from his early days as a trader, and parts were unacceptable for children to hear, but what could she do? Giles quickly developed habits which resembled Whitmore and even some of the other men at the post. There were a few words Rhoda wished he hadn't overheard, and now repeated to anyone who would listen. But Whitmore proved to Giles that good men still existed, and he would do everything in his power to help a little boy and his family. The benefits to Giles's well-being overpowered the need to learn etiquette or manners.

Sidney had arrived in the spring. Rhoda wanted to scold him, even rebuke him for making her wait, but instead she realized the lessons she and the children had learned during their months alone had strengthened her resolve to make it in Hosea's New Territory.

Two years later, the opportunity came for Sidney to purchase The Exchange. He'd moved his family there, and now Rhoda cleaned, accepted new tenants, and continued to raise her children in their new community called Knagg's Place.

"I need to fix some panes on that downstairs window this afternoon. Do you have anything else that is more urgent?" Sidney's handyman skills had come in use after their purchase of the two-story Exchange building.

"I think I can manage the inn duties. I started supper before we left this morning." The venison roast would be easy to pair with potatoes or turnips, which could boil while Rhoda and the girls made up some beds.

Sidney took her hand and squeezed it. "You look like the only thing you want to do is nap." He grinned at her.

"That would be my afternoon preference, but Martha can help me."

As they approached their business, Rhoda still couldn't believe she'd gone from a tiny, dilapidated cabin to The Exchange in such a short time. The building housing The Exchange was like no other in the small community. Guests came by stagecoach to stay at their inn. The impressive building held not only guest rooms but also an office and two additional rooms for community events, and even a place for Friday night dances. Three enormous fireplaces graced the first floor with one log which served as a mantle for all three hearths. The windows lined the entire front of the building. The floor-to-ceiling windows allowed the morning light to illuminate the main floor. Each window had eight panes. It took Rhoda most of the day to wash them.

As Sidney pulled their carriage to the front of the building, Rhoda greeted their current guests on a wrap-around porch designed for comfort and a place to wait for the approaching carriage. Rhoda and her family loved to experience the cool outdoor breezes on a hot summer night.

"Hello, Mr. Baxter." Rhoda nodded toward a man smoking his pipe by the front door.

"Good afternoon, Mrs. Seymour." She then turned to a couple sitting in chairs opposite Mr. Baxter. "Hello Marvin and Alva. Did you enjoy your lunch?"

Men tipped their hats and women smiled as Rhoda made her way into the prestigious building. They never lacked for guests, as the state had gained 144,000 residents since Hosea's arrival in 1833. Sidney and Rhoda loved welcoming others on the way to joining them in the newly established state.

Another wave of nausea filled her senses. She'd been fighting it for weeks. How could she be pregnant again? And at her age? She had given birth to Cornelia just a year before. She'd welcomed the tiny girl into their lives, but at age forty-one, surely her childbearing age would soon be over.

She'd been so ill with this pregnancy. Even worse, she struggled to make it through a day without falling asleep after lunch. It was all she could do to not just lie down while remaking a bed. Preparing an evening meal while nauseated, wasn't any better. Thankfully, her daughters helped when she just couldn't smell another piece of raw meat or clean out the guests' chamber pots.

As Rhoda entered the kitchen at the back of the building, she knew it wouldn't be long before their guests would need to be fed. As she pulled on an apron and tied it around her waist, she felt the urge again. "Lucinda!" Rhoda called out to her oldest daughter. "I need to—"

"Go ahead, Ma. I'll finish cutting up the potatoes."

Rhoda rushed to the outhouse. She longed to keep her pregnancy a secret for a while longer, despite Lucinda knowing. Her daughter wasn't a child anymore.

Walking past her desk, she knew she needed to post the records of their previous guests and their rent payments. Instead of heading back into the kitchen, Rhoda sat at her desk to work. If only she could keep her eyes open to do so.

Caroline heard the tap on the door as she removed Horace's socks. His feet were so swollen, it was a struggle to pull them off his feet. She called out for the person on the other side of the door to come in. Ma walked toward her in her best outfit, removing her black gloves.

"How is he, Caroline?"

Caroline swallowed hard and took a deep breath. "Not good. He seems to just sleep more and more."

Ma went to the head of the bed and felt Horace's forehead. "He's so warm. Let's swab him down, if only to bring him some comfort."

It would mortify Horace to know his mother-in-law was wiping down his body, but in the state he was in now, it didn't matter.

"Dr. Harder was here last night. He says it won't be long now." Caroline wiped a tear off her cheek. "He said his swollen body is a sign that everything is shutting down."

Ma glanced up at her as she removed her mourning hat.

"How was the funeral?"

Ma placed her hat and gloves on the end table beside the bed. "I saw nothing like it before. There had to be two hundred people there. Fur traders far outnumbered all the neighbors, and there were even French men who'd come from Detroit to attend. Whitmore has a large family."

"And Indians?" Caroline knew the answer would be yes. She'd heard enough rumblings from the other settlers over the past week about how many had arrived for the procession. "Any trouble?"

Ma shook her head. "None." She picked up Horace's arm and began wiping him down with the cool rag Caroline brought her from the barrel by the door. Horace winced, but his breathing went from labored to peaceful the moment she touched the cool cloth to his skin.

Caroline went to the other side of the bed. "How long do you think it will take, Ma?"

Ma whispered. "I don't know, Caroline. Horace is in God's hands. Could be hours, could be days. God appoints our time."

It had been a long four years since Caroline knew her husband would never recover from the illness he'd been suffering, despite her efforts to help him. Dr. Harder said it now had something to do with his kidneys. He hadn't needed a bedpan in days. It seemed impossible for Horace to relieve himself. He hadn't responded verbally to Caroline in over a week. Dr. Harder called it a *comatose* state.

"Do you think he's in pain?"

Again, Ma shook her head. "No child. He might feel us cooling his skin, but he probably feels no pain."

Caroline sighed. She stopped wiping for a moment. "Ma. I never thought I would be the one to bury a husband."

Ma offered her a smile. "I know, Caroline. None of us want to be left widows. You're too young to go through such heartache."

"He's been a good husband."

"Yes, he has."

"And even now, despite all that I'm going through with him, I would choose him over Billie all over again." Caroline stammered out the truthful words.

"Oh, that Billie! Etta keeps telling me about the way she keeps finding him and your sister out behind the barn. They believe no one knows and I search for ways to supervise them, but they aren't children anymore."

"What does Pa say?"

"Your pa believes none of his daughters could ever be promiscuous, as do I." Caroline's ma looked up at her and smiled. "But we're all sinners. Temptation at their age is strong."

"Will he allow them to marry?"

"If he doesn't change his mind soon, I'm afraid it will soon be a necessity." Ma wrung out her cloth and began wiping down Horace's chest. "I'm praying they just become brave, run off, and get married anyway. It would give me peace of mind. Making Jillian wait until she's eighteen will cause her and Billie to do things they wished they hadn't."

Caroline couldn't believe she was talking about such things with her ma, but the fact was, she knew Ma was correct.

Thankful for her, Caroline shared her darkest secret. "I'm afraid, Ma. I hate to be here alone when it finally happens. Although, some nights I think it will be a relief. He's suffered so much. And Ma—"

Ma stopped wiping and looked over at her. "What's wrong?"

"I almost want him to go." Tears welled up. "I feel so guilty."

Ma wrapped her in a hug. "I think that's God's way of helping us cope. Preparing our hearts." Pulling away, she wiped Caroline's tears with her apron. "I'll stay here with you, child. I won't leave you alone."

Caroline yearned to run from the room and be Hosea and Sally's young daughter again, but that would never be possible. Loss was a part of living, as they'd found out while living in the wilderness. Death sometimes came without reason and chose even young victims. Horace wouldn't grow old with Caroline. They'd bury him in the cemetery on the hill, and one day, when her time came, she'd lie beside him.

"I don't have a mourning dress to wear and with caring for Horace, I haven't had any time to sew a proper one. Do you think it would be improper to wear my wedding dress to the funeral?"

Ma took the cool rag and wiped off Horace's face. "I think Horace would like that, Caroline."

Caroline knew it to be true.

CHAPTER TWENTY-FIVE

Hosea looked out over the river from the deck of the mill. Swirling water edged higher on shore than he'd ever seen it before, more than the usual winter thaw. To the north, minor rapids were replaced by strong murky currents which covered once-visible boulders and sand bars. Hosea didn't like to see the river so full. It gave the mill an extra boost in water power for the saw, but Hosea knew many of the residents crossed the Shiawassee, and unless they did it closer to the ford in the stream at Knagg's Place, it could be deadly.

"We have a powerful flow today, Hosea. I've not seen the saw work so well." A worker came out of the mill to brush sawdust off his clothes.

"Worries me some." Hosea took off his hat, wiping his forehead. "Whitmore used to build wooden rafts to ford the river in spring. Now that he's gone, we need to revisit the topic. The rafts will be safer in this rough water than trying to forge the river without them. I need to make a trip to see Sidney. Perhaps he can round up some men to get it done."

"It looks like it could rain again today. If it does, this river will spill over its banks and soon."

Hosea spit into the powerful stream. "Ambrose will be here soon. He's building a barn for the VanWormer family. I need to see if we can get some dirt moved to block the water some. In case the flow gets stronger. When it does, it could cause the saw to seize up." Hosea showed the worker where to shift dirt to prevent an onslaught of water if the river overflowed. "We can steer the extra water behind us here, then the mill won't take the brunt of any flooding which might happen."

"I think we need to warn people who live close to the river."

Hosea replaced his hat. "I agree. Let me ride to The Exchange and let them know our concerns. The river has been rising there, too. If we get more rain in the next few days, it could cause damage to Sidney's building, too."

With that comment, Hosea strolled to his horse. As he did, sprinkles of rain wet his shoulders.

By the time Hosea reached The Exchange, dampness penetrated clear through to his woolen underwear. Even his socks were wet as he got off his horse and went inside. The grandeur of Sidney's business never ceased to amaze Hosea. Such a fine building in a tiny village like Knagg's Place was hard to believe. Newburg and Knagg's Place settlers had benefited from its rooms and community gatherings. It provided a perfect rest stop for travelers.

As he entered the building, he had to garner Sidney's attention. He didn't waste time bringing up the subject. "I haven't seen it this high since we arrived, in the spring of thirty-four. We have more residents now. You'll have stagecoaches delayed. I think we need to prepare for any flooding that might occur."

Sidney placed a piece of stationery on the counter between them. "What do you suggest?"

"Either we get busy and get a few rafts built or do what Whitmore always pushed for."

Sidney's facial expression held a questioned look.

"We build a bridge."

"Whitmore always said it was a need."

"We can get the townspeople together to help. Newburg residents, too. We need a safe route to the west side of the river. Right at the ford in the stream here. That would be the best location." Hosea's attention went to Rhoda, who came to the counter to greet him.

"Rhoda!"

"Hosea. What brings you here on this rainy morning?"

"He's suggesting we get neighbors together to build Whitmore's bridge."

Hosea pointed through one of the tall windows at the front of the building. "We can start on this side of the river. It won't help us through the spring of this year, but in future years, we'll thank Whitmore for the idea and the gumption to get it done."

"We can name it after him." Rhoda placed a quill and inkwell on the counter so Hosea could sketch out the idea for her and Sidney.

"My artwork isn't all that great." Hosea dipped the quill and drew lines. "We'll need quite a few logs. Sawn in half. I can do the mill work for free. If everyone donates a portion of their property logs, we should have quite a bridge. Strong enough for even the heaviest of coaches." He pushed the paper toward Sidney.

"Looks great, Hosea. When can we get started?"

"As soon as the rain stops, and the river goes down. Until then, I think we need to warn everyone that the spring thaw will make the water higher. I've never seen it this high. Put up a notice here and I'll alert the community through the message chain. We need people to know at these dangerous levels, bad things could happen."

"Will do, Hosea."

"Now come back here and get dry by the fireplace. I have lunch almost ready." Rhoda went around the counter and helped Hosea out of his coat.

Giles glanced out the window of his bedroom. The droplets of water hadn't stopped running down it for days. Every morning, Giles and Rhoda Ann would get out of bed to see if they could go outside to play. Plenty of chores kept them busy, but going outside to the woods or to find crawdads down by the river gave them reasons to finish them quickly. When it rained, their parent's rule of "being seen and not heard" made for boring afternoons. During the past few days, it had been too dangerous to cross the river to get to school.

Martha and Philinda thought it their mission to teach the younger children. Unfortunately, Momma agreed. Their teacher, Miss Post, demanded less than his sisters. Giles hated not being able to see or play with his cousins at recess. They never had recess at home. After finishing schoolwork, Momma expected them to bring in wood, sweep the porch, or fetch water from the spring. The only playtime for the Seymour children remained at the conclusion of the evening meal or when Momma scratched everything off her list. The size of Papa's building often matched the chores on Momma's long list.

Rhoda Ann and Giles loved the walks to school. Each afternoon, they found extraordinary things to do on their trips home. *Extraordinary* had been Giles's longest spelling word that winter and he loved using the word—all the time. Rhoda Ann knew the meaning, so when Giles discovered something extraordinary, His sister knew their afternoon walk would turn into an adventure or a reason to peel off their knee-high socks and dip their feet into the river. There had only been a few days that spring when it had been warm enough to take off their shoes.

Without school, the extraordinary moments remained few.

Giles pressed his nose to the cool window. "Will it ever stop raining?"

Rhoda Ann finished making their bed. "Stop wishing and get over here and smooth the wrinkles out of your side of the bed. You know what will happen when Martha finds it with wrinkles."

Giles knew. He turned and pulled at the bedsheet.

"Just don't pull the covers too far on your side. I'll have to fix it."

Giles often wondered what his life would be like without sisters. Momma had just told them about having another baby. Perhaps this time, it would be a boy. Except by the time he came of age to play and take extraordinary adventures, Giles would be too old. He'd have to work like his oldest brother, George.

Both children finished their chore and headed out to the table for breakfast. Giles pulled out a chair at the long table which had just been hosting the inn's "special guests" as Momma and Pa called them. He hoped the leftovers included a pancake overflowing with maple syrup. How he loved maple syrup.

Momma came to the table and placed clean plates before Giles, Philinda, Rhoda Ann, Martha, and George. The toddling Cornelia just went from chair to chair, getting her fill by begging her siblings to give her a bite. She'd take a small bite, cram it into her mouth, and then toddle to the next sibling's chair for more. Uncle Hosea had promised to make a highchair for Cornelia, but he'd been too busy trying to watch the overflowing river lately to get anything made for Momma. Cornelia probably wouldn't enjoy being confined to a chair, anyway.

"What's for breakfast, Momma?" Giles's mouth watered just thinking about the syrup.

"Rhoda Ann, go wipe off the flour from your apron before sitting down to eat. You'll get it on the tablecloth." She turned to Giles. "Biscuits and gravy today, Giles."

Giles tried hard to not show his disappointment but got a scolding from Momma.

"Giles! Stop pouting. We can't have pancakes every morning. You know that."

Giles lifted his fork and sighed while Martha passed him a biscuit and the bowl of white gravy. "Can we have pork soon?" Giles missed the delicious sausage that went into the gravy back in New York.

"You know the answer to that, young man."

Momma spooned some of the hot gravy over Giles's biscuit. She popped his head with the bottom of a wooden spoon. "Now eat and be thankful."

They didn't say grace unless Philinda was at the table, because Momma never wanted to talk to God, even though she'd stopped protesting when Philinda did it.

"Dear God. Thank you for what we are about to partake. Thank you for Momma and her hard work to make it for us. May you give her health and strength. In Jesus's name."

All the children said, "amen."

Giles said it late, because he couldn't get his mind off the rain still streaming down the window beside his chair. As he spooned in a mouthful of the white gravy complete with a buttery biscuit, Giles saw his father blowing off a sheet of paper with fresh ink on it. He watched him grab a nail from under the counter and a hammer.

Swallowing a mouthful of milk to wash down the pasty gravy, he watched Pa nail the note to the front door. "Philinda? What's Pa nailing to the door?" Cornelia was now by his chair, wanting just a portion of a biscuit he'd put beside his plate. He handed her a small bite.

Philinda looked up to see. "I don't know, Giles."

Giles needed to know. He struggled with reading and if he didn't ask someone, he'd stand at the door for hours trying to decipher Pa's handwriting.

"Momma. What is Pa nailing to the door?"

Momma glanced toward Pa. "It's a flood warning. Uncle Hosea stopped this morning and said the river was very high due to all this rain. He wanted our guests to be careful."

"Careful of what?"

"The river water. And that especially means you and your sisters."

"Does that mean we can't cross again today?"

"That's exactly what it means. Getting near the shore is dangerous as well. As soon as you're finished with your breakfast, I have a job for you and Martha."

Giles couldn't help the tremendous sigh he let escape in his exasperation.

Momma gave him a scolding look.

He lowered his head and concentrated on his meal.

"I have lots of spices to sort from the shipment that came from back East this past week. You'll be putting labels on all the bottles and helping me sort them today."

"Spices make me sneeze!" Martha said, before Giles could voice the same complaint.

"Until the river descends, that is exactly what you'll be doing for a few days. Now finish your breakfast."

CHAPTER TWENTY-SIX

Horace died on a Friday. Few attended the funeral because of the high river levels up and down the stream by Hosea's property. The Newburg residents stood by Caroline to pay their respects, but even Etta and Charles couldn't cross the river to attend. In fact, it had been two weeks since anyone ventured across the strong, rapid river.

Raindrops dripped from the brim of Caroline's hat as she stood close to the open hole where the men would soon lower her husband into his final resting place. The pain in her heart felt as sad as the dark clouds hovering overhead. Newburg hadn't seen the sun in days.

"Ashes to ashes, dust to dust. Please take into your care the soul of our beloved husband, friend, and brother, Horace Knapp. May he rest in peace here on the cliff above the Shiawassee River with the other souls who have gone before him."

Caroline knew Reverend John Swain was thinking of Abigail. Her grave was just a few feet from where she'd decided where to place Horace. Abigail and Horace were among the first ones buried in the cemetery north of Pa's property. It sat near the blackjack oak tree Pa loved so much.

People took handfuls of dirt and threw them into the hole in front of her. The usually dry dirt was replaced by rock-solid clay after all the rains. Each handful ricocheted off the wooden box, causing a loud crack each time. Caroline couldn't take her eyes off Horace's casket. She could shoot a deer or wolf from yards away, manage for months to support her and Horace with additional sewing jobs, but her courage evaporated in thinking she'd leave Horace here in the ground. Forever. She'd no longer feel his muscular arms around her at night. He'd never arrive home from work to share a warm meal with her. Their life together was now over.

Caroline had Pa design Horace's coffin with precise details. Her explicit wishes included ornate carvings and specific dimensions. Pa met all her expectations. Horace's tall frame needed a long casket. She wanted Horace to wear his shoes, for no one else could fill them. Horace had always wanted to look his best at special gatherings, and his next greeting included meeting God. He'd have wanted to wear his good shoes. She'd also been meticulous about mending his best shirt and even sewing in a nice handkerchief inside his chest pocket.

A widow. Caroline had been a happy wife, and her longing to become a mother hadn't gone away. But how would that happen now? Society often gave little regard to widows. Sometimes even shunned them. How unfair that was! She hadn't wanted this, especially at her age, but she hadn't had a choice.

She loved Horace with all of her soul. As the men began lifting shovels of dirt to fill in the grave, she felt like a part of her had died with Horace. She'd vowed to stand beside him, but death had robbed her of that duty. 'Till death do us part!' Knowing the words only brought a brokenness to her heart. Horace was young. He had so much more love to give. To Caroline, to children of their own. Over the past two years, he'd told Caroline many times he felt robbed.

Among his last words to Caroline were, "Promise me you'll marry again." At the time she chided him for even asking her such a difficult question. Marry again? Why? Why fall in love with another man if it only meant more heartache or even another loss if he were to die early, like Horace? Trying to comprehend this made Caroline's heart break in two. To love another would mean her half heart would be broken again because as long as she lived, the other half would be inside the coffin with Horace Knapp.

People walked by her and either touched her shoulder or squeezed her hand. Through her tears she wanted to acknowledge everyone who stood in the rain to pay their condolences, but she couldn't take her eyes off the dirt now accumulating in piles on her husband's coffin. What she wouldn't do to go back to the day he'd helped her haul water up from the river to her house with Pa and Ma. To experience their first kiss on the trail.

As Jillian kissed her cheek, she glanced at Billie, who tipped his hat to her. What if she'd have chosen Billie? She wouldn't be standing here today as a widow. But instead of making her wish she'd chosen Billie instead of Horace, it did something else.

Caroline stood up straighter. She lifted her shoulders and her head just as Pa came toward her and wrapped her in his arms. Thankfulness filled her heart as she thought of how much Horace had loved her. Even for just a few short years.

"My sweet Carrie girl. Your ma and I are surely sorry for your loss." Pa kissed the top of her head but didn't let go of her. "Blessed are those who mourn, for they shall be comforted."

"Thank you, Pa."

Ma leaned in to kiss her cheek. "We love you, Caroline."

And just like it was when she was a child, her pa took her hand, her ma wrapped her arm around her shoulders, and they left Horace all alone under the earth. Caroline's life with Horace was over.

The grief in Caroline's soul came in waves, just like the swollen current of the river. It had rained so much that laps from the river neared the corner of Pa's first cabin. Something drew her to go to see it. The deserted little farm stood empty. Pa stored implements in the barn and also a few crops from last year's harvest, but most of those were now depleted. The chickens, the oxen, and Myrtle the cow now inhabited her parents' new barn closer to town.

Coming around the front edge of the cabin, Caroline thoughts drifted back to their first years in Newburg. She felt the log walls and, turning toward the river, found the path which took her to the spring to gather water. It brought her heart back to the simple life she'd led there. Where her biggest worry included whether she could find enough berries for a pie or whether she'd find a snake on the path to the spring. She'd lived such a carefree life. Then she smiled. Or had she?

She thought about the frost which killed Pa's early crops, the lack of food their first winter, and having to fight off the torrents of mosquitoes with the stinky Indian ointment. Watching Indians come toward the cabin from out of the woods and wondering if they were friendly or cruel. She remembered the windstorm that came up when the only people home were her ma and sisters. How frightened and alone she'd been, loading a rifle in the dark and then praying it hit the target of her first wolf. Their life at this cabin hadn't been easy either, but they'd survived. Perhaps her parents had been gracious and careful to not share their heartaches and fears with her while she was young.

Walking toward the front door made her think of her wedding day in 1834. She'd been so happy to become the wife of Horace Knapp. He'd come into her life like a whirlwind, just like the spring days this year. It had rained continuously for weeks. Was heaven shedding tears of its own? She never imagined what kind of outcome it would be for her when she'd accepted Horace's hand on that wonderful day in June. It hadn't rained that day. The sun shone bright and promising.

But today, as she roamed the property, Caroline wondered if the sun would ever shine again.

Rounding the corner to return home, Caroline saw a man on a horse approaching her from the south. He rode a beautiful white workhouse, and Caroline knew right away it was Etta's husband, Charles.

"Caroline!" He waved at her as he approached.

"Hello," Caroline called out as the horse came toward her.

"What are you doing here?"

Caroline sighed. "I don't know. I guess I just wanted to see how close the river now rose to Pa's cabin."

Charles got down from the horse. "It is close."

"That it is." Caroline wiped off the moisture from her cheeks. She hadn't realized she was crying. "I must look a mess."

Charles looked at her. "No. You look fine. Are you all right?"

Caroline decided lying about it didn't help. "I will be..." was her new answer.

"I'm sure you will. Losing anyone, is never easy, even more so a spouse."

Caroline nodded. "I don't think anyone really knows until it happens to them. How did you get across the river today?"

"I took a raft. They're solid, but these waters are so unpredictable. I let Butch here—" Charles patted the side of his horse's head, "–forge it on his own. He decided he'd just as soon swim across, which was good because he didn't fit on the raft with the rest of us." Charles laughed, then looked toward Caroline.

"What will you do now?"

"I don't know yet. I need to find work. I think I may go see Uncle Sidney and see if I can be some kind of maid at the hotel. I've also heard Ambrose is looking to build a store again. Perhaps I can help him."

"Those sound like excellent prospects." Her sister's husband looked down at his feet. "You know, Etta would love to have you close to us. You are more than welcome to find a place near Vernon township."

Caroline smiled. "Thank you, Charles. That is very kind. I will consider that."

"The baby would love to have her Aunt Carrie close."

The comment regarding her niece made Caroline grin that much more. She loved her nieces and nephews. "I would love that, too."

"Once the calving season ends, I'll have some time. We could build you a small home near us and you would be more than welcome to live there."

"I have so many options." Caroline patted Charles's horse. "I need to decide soon."

"You'll make a wise choice." Charles mounted his horse.

Caroline loved Etta's choice of a husband. Charles was thoughtful, noble, and kind.

"Thank you. I need to be getting back. I left meat cooking over the fire. I wanted out of the house and needed a walk." Caroline rubbed her arms. "If only the weather would turn."

Charles tugged on the horse's reins. "This rain is getting monotonous. I needed a tool from Hosea, and he said I could find it in the barn here. I'd best be getting it and heading back to work."

Caroline smiled. "Thank you again for your kind offer. Maybe I'll take you up on it. I'd love to be closer to Etta. I miss her."

Charles tipped his hat. "Please do. We'd love to have you closer. Etta gets lonesome for her family."

Rhoda woke from her dream with sweat dripping down the sides of her face. As she sat up in bed, she wiped off her forehead. Her nerves felt like they'd burst right out of her skin. Her hands throbbed. Was she sick?

Looking into the dimly lit bedroom, she felt for Sidney. Her touch interrupted his snoring for just a moment. Thankfully, she hadn't fully awakened him as she'd done in the past. Her heart raced. She breathed out through her mouth and then in through her nose to calm her throbbing heart. As she did, she could still hear the thrum of raindrops dashing against the windows. The rest of the house was silent. Rhoda glanced over at Cornelia in her makeshift bed in the corner, her arm over her head and mouth open, thankfully asleep.

Once she could breathe easier, she lay back against her pillows, clasping her chest. She hated the nightmares. Why did they torment her, interrupting what little sleep she could get before needing to get up to fix breakfast for the guests and her family?

This dream had been about Cornelia. Her wandering youngest child. Several times lately, they had found the small child roaming the house in search of people. The toddler longed for attention. Rhoda often found her sitting on the lap of the guests as they sat before the fire. She'd also find her tapping on a guest's door after putting her to bed at night. Rhoda knew most of it derived from her lack of attention for her daughter. She frequently put Cornelia's siblings in charge of caring for her. In finding Giles or Rhoda Ann, Cornelia was typically found trailing behind them.

In the dream, Rhoda discovered Cornelia missing from her bed and went through the house in search of her. Rhoda went to ask her children to help but they were all sleeping. She'd wanted to rouse Sidney, but he was nowhere to be seen.

Rhoda searched not in their present house, but in the cabin which had been their home that first summer in Newburg. How could she lose a child there? There were hardly any places to hide.

Mice skittered across her feet as she looked. The roof sagged over her head as if, at any moment, it would cave into the house. That's when panic gripped her heart. Would she and Cornelia be buried? She had to find the child.

Rhoda closed her eyes in fear. A rumble of thunder erupted from outside. As she went to the door, storm clouds rose from the east and rapidly covered the sky. Her other children were playing tag outside. Asking each of them if they'd seen Cornelia, none of them acknowledged her question, but continued to avoid the hand of a sibling, and even her own, trying to touch them. Growing exasperated, Rhoda approached Giles and turned him toward her. He stopped, but deftly escaped her grasp as if she were playing the game with him.

Someone grasped Rhoda's arm. It was Sidney. He' was telling her, "Rhoda, don't get caught—", a smile on his face. She tried to explain to him that Cornelia was missing in the cabin and if they didn't get her out, she'd be trapped when the heavy rains came. Each time Rhoda tried to speak, she had no voice. Leaving the children to play their game, she ran back into the cabin to find the baby.

Once inside, the thunder intensified. As she looked under beds, behind chairs, the rooms of the small cabin intensified, and somehow she was inside the inn. Looking down a hallway, the doors seemed endless. Stopping to see if she could hear the child, she noticed rain hitting a nearby window. The sound growing louder, a flash of lightning lit up the room. Rhoda felt hopeless and then realized she needed to save herself from the sagging roof as it crushed her from above. She put her arms above her head to hold it up.

That's when she woke up.

Rhoda stopped thinking about the dream and wiped off her forehead with the back of her hand. But then she remembered Hosea. Hosea had tried to save her. He'd reached his hand through a window. He hadn't said a word, but just before touching her, he stopped. Looking at her with pity in his eyes, he turned, leaving her all alone. It was as if he knew he couldn't save her and had easily given up. Without speaking a word, his eyes told her what he thought of her situation.

Rhoda closed her eyes. Remembering Hosea's eyes made her flinch in pain. She'd had scary, sad dreams for years now. Ever since they'd left New York. Sidney would awaken her from them. She'd sometimes find herself wrapped tightly in damp sheets or at other times screaming. They were horrifying nightmares. Each one.

What did it all mean? She reached down to touch the bulging belly under her nightdress. Did it mean something about the baby? Why couldn't she just get a restful night of sleep? The long, working days made her so tired and her queasy stomach made it impossible to eat. Was that it?

Rhoda lay as still as she could, listening to the raindrops against the windowpane. She wished the rain would stop, along with the nightmares.

Did God want to frighten her? As her father used to say, "fear is not of God." But as the nightmares continued, there were some nights she'd be afraid to go to sleep. Did it have something to do with her guilt? Remorse which had lived in her soul since New York?

She closed her eyes. If that was the reason, the nightmares wouldn't end. They'd continue until she succumbed to a confession—the very reason she'd come to Michigan. Could she ever confess? God knew she wanted to, but guilt had fangs gripping her soul like a rabbit in the jaws of a wolf.

CHAPTER TWENTY-SEVEN

Watching the Shiawassee River flow northward, Hosea related a tumultuous river to an estranged heart. The churning seeming to never end. Each drop of water striving to reach a destination, continuing downstream in search of a calm pond, only to find more rapids, and the strong current dividing the ground when it got in the way. Danger lurked at every curve. A wayward heart seemed to have everything in common with the powerful force of an overflowing river.

As he stood on the bank, Hosea contemplated his heart. Was he righteous? Did he fret during the night? If so, it could mean he didn't trust God fully for his future. Each day brought new temptations of its own. He knew he lacked the ability to live a perfect life; that's why he needed Jesus.

Joy filled Hosea's heart to know that someday his struggle with daily sin would be over. He longed to be with God, and knowing that a sinless life awaited him in heaven seemed to draw him even more. Life on earth brought a constant heart battle. Despite that daily battle, he had peace. Peace that overwhelmed him, because he knew that Jesus's blood covered all his feeble attempts at a sinless life.

What joy had a Christ-filled life on earth given him! Although he had moved his family to unfamiliar places, had been wrongly accused of something he hadn't done, and faced death more than he desired, there were days on earth that had brought him great joy. As long as he chose it. He reflected that thinking of self, often leads to frustration. Earthly desires take a person away from God instead of toward Him. Hosea wanted his needs to be met only by God. Only He could stop the cravings for money and power, and overrule his prideful heart.

His thoughts turned to Rhoda. She hadn't changed. Bringing God up to her wasn't an option, despite him having tried several times. A wedge of bitterness separated their once close relationship. He felt it every time he was around her. What would it take for Rhoda to allow God to draw her close? Hosea knew it had to be a choice Rhoda would make, but he also knew a stubborn heart could be too hard to break. And Rhoda's stiffened heart toward God was stronger than most. Would God choose to soften it?

Hosea looked down at the trench to the west of the mill. He stood at the edge of the strong flowing stream which divided his mill from the brunt of the forceful water flowing upstream. The rain hadn't ceased. It had rained every day for weeks. Some days it poured; other days brought light rain and bulky, dark clouds which appeared to want to give way to more rain.

Sally Mae hadn't been able to hang the laundry outside. Hosea had built her a lean-to on the new house where she could wash clothes without dripping dirty water throughout the entire kitchen. Their clothes dried there now. Every night, she lamented how all she wanted to do was hang her laundry outside to dry. "Nothing smells better in life than a towel hung out to dry in the spring air," she'd said for weeks.

Looking back to the churning river, Hosea thought of Caroline. She'd come home to be with them after Horace's death. Sadness etched her face. Creases were forming in the lines of her eyes and mouth. She was way too young to mourn. Thankfully, Jillian brought her comfort. His youngest daughter continued to fill their home with laughter and music. Now that Caroline had returned, the singing would often go long into the night as the girls would sing each other to sleep. Hosea loved having his daughters home. One day their laughter and singing would be gone, so he cherished each day he had with them.

"It's not going to stop overflowing the banks if it doesn't stop raining soon."

Hosea turned to find Billie getting off his horse behind him.

"Billie! How are you?" Hosea shook the young man's hand.

"Hello Mr. Baker."

"I think you're old enough now to call me Hosea, Billie. It would be fine with me, if you did."

Billie nodded. "Thank you, sir. Do you think the river will rise more?"

Hosea looked up at the sky. "If it doesn't stop raining soon, it will."

Both men stood near the bank, which seemed to lose inches of ground every day.

"Never seen it this high."

"I came across on a raft and I'll tell you, it made me nervous."

"I'm sure. As soon as it lets up, we need to get a bridge built."

"That's what I've come to ask you. I'd like to be a supervisor on the job, if you'd let me. I've always dreamed of building a bridge. I'm curious about your plans."

Hosea patted a stump just inside the mill's door. "Let's sit and I'll tell you."

After going over his plans on how to get the bridge built, Billie seemed even more excited. "I think I can help. Would you allow me the opportunity to try? My father was influential in building bridges at home. I've helped him often before."

Hosea liked the idea of handing off the bridge construction to someone else. "I think that would be a possibility. Why don't you search for other interested and daring builders?"

"I have a few people in mind."

"Good. We need it sooner rather than later. Who knows when this rain will stop, and we can get to work? The stagecoach will need a safe place to cross without having to trust the path Whitmore made long ago."

Billie picked up a stick and began drawing in sawdust on the floor. "This is how I see it."

Hosea watched the young man's plan emerge from a pile of dust.

"What do you think?"

Together, they sorted through the bridge details.

"As soon as the water subsides to about four feet, we'll get started." Hosea smiled. "I'd be proud to promote your abilities at the next township meeting. It will be good to have safety for the travelers, a dry way for the children to get to school, and a safe, permanent solution, no matter what time of year."

Billie set down the stick. "Sir, I have something else I'd like to talk about."

"Surely. What is it?"

"Jillian."

"Jillian?"

"I want her to be my wife."

Hosea took a deep breath. He knew the boy had been pining for Jillian for years. The conversation about "her hand" was eminent. He knew it. "She's mighty young, Billie."

"Many women have married an even younger age than Jillian. We love each other. I don't want to wait much longer. If you can trust me to build the community a stable bridge, surely you'll trust me with your daughter."

Hosea knew his widened eyes probably gave the man an answer before any words did. "Trust comes with works and marrying my baby girl is quite different from building a trustworthy bridge."

Billie blushed.

Hosea knew Billie had waited long after proposing to Caroline to get himself a wife. That had been six years ago now. "Can you wait until summer?"

Billie's face brightened. His eyes grew wide. "It all depends. Early or late summer?"

"She won't be eighteen until October."

Billie sighed and was about to say something, but Hosea stopped him.

"Okay, then. I think an August wedding would be nice. Can you wait that long?"

"If that's your answer, I'm good with it."

"Thanks for understanding and being respectful. And as far as I'm concerned, you'll be the foreman at the new bridge."

And with that remark, Billie mounted his horse. "Thank you, sir."

As Billie's horse trotted back south, Hosea knew his days with daughters under his roof were truly numbered.

"August?" Jillian whined just like Billie wanted to.

"I know. But it will go quickly."

Jillian took his hand and kissed the back of it. "Can you wait that long?"

Billie knew better than to talk of such things with Jillian, but he didn't want to be dishonest. "It's better than having to wait a whole year! It'll go quickly."

Jillian pulled him behind a tree and kissed him like she'd been doing now for almost a year. It didn't help his determination to honor Hosea. His entire ached to follow a kiss from Jillian with other things. Billie pulled away. "Perhaps—"

Jillian took his face in her hands and began planting kisses on his forehead, his cheeks, and even in the crook of his neck.

"Jilly, you gotta stop this! We need to get through spring and almost through summer, and if you keep—"

Her mouth met his, and his words stopped. He pulled away again. "Jilly—you gotta help me and this—" he pointed to her lips, "—is not the way to do it."

Jillian giggled and put her head on his shoulder. "But I love kissing you. I'm tired of waiting."

Billie pulled away from her. "You don't think I am, too? I want nothing more than to make you my wife." Every muscle in his body tensed with desire.

She grabbed his hand. "I'm sorry. I just can't help it. Don't you wonder what it's like?"

"Every single night."

Jillian laughed again. "Me, too."

"Would you dishonor your pa by getting married earlier?"

"What do you mean?"

"Let's find a local preacher. What about John?"

"John Swain?" Jillian's bottom lip protruded out. "He would tell on us."

"What would it matter? We'd be married by the time he told."

"What if he wouldn't do it?"

"Then...we'll find another. There isn't a lawman around who wouldn't let us get married. My ma got married when she was fifteen."

Jillian turned away.

Billie knew better than to force Jillian into marriage. If he did that, Hosea would kill him for sure. But if she willingly came with him, knowing good and well what they were doing, would it be wrong? What would rushing it mean? They'd been playing the hide and seek kissing game now for over a year. Often, after his visits, he'd leave more frustrated than if he stayed away."

Jillian turned back and into his eyes. "We wouldn't have to wait."

"What do you mean? Get married now?"

Jillian traced his face with her finger. "Let's not wait for—"

Billie stepped back. "For what?"

"You know." Jillian blushed.

"And how and where will we pull this off?"

Jillian nuzzled up to him and again laid her head on his shoulder. "I wouldn't mind it. I think we could. Maybe when Ma leaves for town or goes to help Betsey."

"Oh Jillian. I don't know."

"It would be our secret. What's a piece of paper, anyway?"

"It wouldn't be..." Billie stuttered. "Legal. You know..." He could feel sweat dripping down his torso. He never thought Jillian would agree to something like this.

"Waiting is for children. We aren't children anymore." Jillian held his face between her hands while she kissed him with force.

Billie pulled her near, feeling her soft figure against his. "When?"

"Come back some afternoon. Next week, Ma plans on helping Betsey while school is in session. Pa will be at the mill."

"What about Caroline?"

"We'll figure that out, too. I'll make it work."

"Oh, Jillian. It's all I'm dreaming of—"

"Then let's not wait any longer. Okay?"

Billie couldn't believe what they were talking about. But he loved the idea. How would anyone know?

Giles woke to silence. Jumping out of bed, he scurried to the window to look outside. The normal splats on his windowsill had stopped. Perhaps today they'd have sunshine instead of rain.

Gathering up his clothes, he pulled on his pants. Lifting his nightshirt off, he slipped his arms into his shirt. He couldn't wait to get out onto the porch to see if it had indeed stopped raining.

Tiptoeing out of his bedroom, he carefully pulled the door shut behind him without making a sound. He carefully avoided waking his sisters. They would just give him a chore.

Looking around the main room, he noticed a slit of light coming from underneath the kitchen door. Momma was up fixing the guests their breakfast. He could smell flapjacks, but today, he needed to find out if the rain had finally stopped. The mouth-watering pancakes would have to wait.

The front door was unlatched. Pa must be out doing chores before the first stagecoach arrived. A slight squeak from the door caused Giles to stop. He listened carefully to be sure his momma hadn't heard. Like his sisters, Ma would put him to work, too.

He inched the door ajar enough to slip outside unnoticed. As he did, he could feel the cool morning penetrate his clothes, but as he got out from under the porch roof, he knew—the rain had stopped. Off to the east, Giles saw a streak of daylight rising above the horizon. Looking up, he saw stars. The rain had really stopped. After counting thirty-two days of rain, today looked promising. What wouldn't he do for a day of sunshine.

Giles tiptoed to the end of the porch and looked west. He could hear the roar of the river but he couldn't yet see it. If today held even a few hours of sunshine, Giles would persuade Martha to follow him to the river's edge. It seemed like a long time since they'd been able to dig in the mud to find crawdads, slimy worms, and Indian arrowheads. How he missed their fun adventures. He longed to take off his socks, plunge his feet into the mud by the river, and dig. It was all he could think about for days.

"Giles! What are you doing out here?"

Giles jumped at his pa's voice. "Pa! Has it truly stopped raining?"

Giles pa stepped up onto the porch edge beside him and looked off to the east. "I believe it has. It's chilly this morning, but yes, I do believe the rain has stopped. What are you doing up so early?"

"The rain stopped. The quiet woke me up, Pa."

Pa transferred the bucket of water to his other hand and laughed. "I suppose you're right, son."

"Can I stay out here for a bit before having to fetch more water for Ma?"

Pa smoothed down the hair on Giles's head. "Sure, you can. But don't take too long. We have guests to serve."

Giles nodded. "I just want to hear the silence."

"But, son."

Giles turned to his pa. "Yes, Pa."

"You stay clear of the riverbank. That water needs to descend more before you and your sisters go there to play. You hear?"

Giles watched his pa disappear into the inn. He couldn't wait. He wondered how close he could get before it was too close, like Pa had warned him. Even if he could just throw rocks into the river, that would be better than sitting inside deciphering numbers with Philinda.

CHAPTER TWENTY-EIGHT

"Another dream last night?" Sidney brushed past Rhoda as she cracked eggs in the sizzling pan near the hearth.

"How did you know?"

"You seem even more tired this morning than usual."

Rhoda sighed. Rarely did Sidney not sense her mood or her lack of sleep.

"Who was it about this time?"

Rhoda couldn't answer. Rhoda hated recalling her dreams the next day. Sometimes she couldn't. But the dream about Cornelia missing lingered in her thoughts.

Her silence caused Sidney to ask, "What are some of God's attributes?"

Rhoda stared at her husband. He ignored her look and kept piling wood onto the stack beside the fireplace. "Why do you ask?"

"I'm just curious. What do you believe anymore?"

"I'm not sure why you feel the need—"

"Just answer me!" Sidney hadn't talked about spiritual things with Rhoda in years. Her lack of faith didn't stop him from reading his Bible each morning.

"His attributes?"

"Yes, you know. He's loving, eternal..." Sidney motioned with his hand to have her continue listing them.

"He's kind. The creator. Holy."

Sidney looked up with a smile. Now he pulled up a chair and began stirring the eggs in the skillet for her.

She went to a nearby table to find a knife. "What are you getting at?"

"Have I ever done anything to aggravate you?"

Rhoda now laughed. "Of course."

"You answered way too quickly." This brought smiles to both of them.

"Sorry." Rhoda adjusted her apron strings. She'd tied them too tight that morning. "As I've done to you, too."

"Hmm, interesting."

"Sidney. You know I'm not comfortable—"

"Is God good?"

"Hosea would think so."

"Do you?" Sidney tapped the wooden utensil he was using on the side of the skillet. The eggs sticking to it slid into the pan.

"I'm far too busy this morning to talk to you about any of this."

"Rhoda, just answer me. Is God good and in what ways?"

At that moment, Rhoda felt her unborn child move. She knew the answer to her husband's questions. She hated that she couldn't leave the room, go off, and do something else. She had to get breakfast ready for the guests. "He got you here." Tears welled up in her eyes.

"I wasn't sure I wanted to be here."

Rhoda stopped slicing bread. "What?"

"I'd grown angry with your refusal to believe that God even exists. It not only had affected me, but it had begun to affect the children. You wouldn't even allow them to pray for their meals. And then you got this idea of going to Michigan early and dragging the younger children along with you from New York to this wilderness. And I believe you knew, down deep in your heart, that if you'd have left without the younger ones, I would never have followed you. Is that true?"

"Would you have stayed in New York if I hadn't taken them?"

"I thought it better if the children weren't around you as much." Sidney swallowed hard. "Or at all, for that matter."

"Then why did you come?"

"For the same reason. I need to be near all of my children. Not because I need them, but because they need a godly example and influence in their lives."

This time Rhoda swallowed.

"You're about to have another baby, Rhoda. How many will it take for you to realize running isn't good for you, but it's devastating for our children?" Sidney gave the eggs another stir. "How much longer will you run? I need to know."

"I'm not running."

The look Sidney now flashed frightened her.

Tears welled up in her eyes, dimming her eyesight. She dropped the knife she was using to cut the bread for fear she'd cut herself. "I'm not worthy of God's forgiveness."

"What are His attributes, Rhoda?"

She wasn't sure she could answer Sidney through her tears.

"Good. Gracious. All-knowing. Forgiving?" Sidney counted them off on his fingers.

"He's holy, Sidney. Without sin. He's perfect."

"But is He forgiving?"

"Only to those who ask for forgiveness."

Sidney stood. "When I do something wrong. Whatever it is. Do *you* forgive me?"

Rhoda nodded.

"Then why wouldn't God, who is everything we've listed, not forgive you? Are you special, Rhoda? Is your sin any different than mine, or even Hosea's?"

Rhoda slowly shook her head.

"Then, sweetheart!" Sidney took her into his arms. "What are you waiting for?"

Caroline placed a stack of her clothing into the chest at the end of the bed. She'd packed most of her house up and now only had to add clothes. Looking around her bedroom that she'd once shared with Horace, she couldn't believe that today she would leave their dream home to venture closer to Etta and Charles. They lived a fifteen-minute wagon ride from Pa's house. Pa would be here soon to help her pack up the rest of their belongings and take her to the cabin just outside of Etta's house.

Charles had shown her the cabin last Sunday when she'd visited their family after church. She loved envisioning living near Etta again. She missed her sister. This move was a wise thing to do. She could sell this house and use the earnings to pay for daily needs until she decided about what to do next.

The cabin was a part of Charles's property. He'd lived in it before they built the frame house that he and Etta now lived in. By being close, Caroline could help Etta care for Harriet.

Caroline tucked her winter coat into the side of the chest. It was frail and ripped, but she'd need it again when the snow flew in Michigan. As she looked around the room, Caroline thought of all the memories she'd shared here with Horace. She'd have to pack those away, too. He wouldn't return. Her husband was gone, yet his memory would last forever in her heart.

Before she could get completely packed, she heard a wagon outside. Going to the door, she glanced out to see if Pa had arrived.

She found a stranger instead. She went out onto the porch to greet him. "Hello!"

"I'm looking for Caroline Knapp. Is that you?"

"Yes." Caroline shielded her eyes from the bright sun that clouded her vision.

The man got off the wagon and held out his hand. "Good to meet you. My name is Kavenaugh. Jason Kavenaugh."

"Mr. Kavenaugh. How can I help you?"

"Folks here say you are trying to sell this place. Is it still available?"

"Why, yes! It is. I'm moving closer to my sister today. Near Vernon."

"I was wondering if I could make you an offer?"

Caroline folded her arms. "Of course. Let's talk."

"Is your husband home?"

Caroline wrestled with the question. Couldn't a woman sell a home? Why did it always have to be a man who needed to do it? "My husband passed away. Earlier this year."

The man removed his hat. "My condolences, Miss...I mean Mrs. Knapp."

"Thank you."

After that comment, the negotiation for Caroline's home started. She stood strong with the price Pa and Ambrose had suggested. The man seemed perturbed that he couldn't get her to budge on the price, but Caroline knew if this man didn't purchase it, others would be just as interested and would pay handsomely for such a pleasant home.

Soon they settled on a fair price. Caroline had asked way above what she wanted but was thankful that she had. Caroline held out her hand. "It's a deal!"

"I suppose you want cash."

Caroline cringed. Why did he ask her that? "What else is there?"

"I have a nice carriage. My wife made me bring it from back East. I also have a fine mare to go with it. The mare is getting old, but she can still pull a carriage well. It'd be a fine unit for you to have to get around these parts. If you'd take some off the price of the home."

It would be nice to have a team to get from Vernon to Newburg whenever Caroline would want to come back for visits. And having it to make a trip to the cemetery from time to time would also bring her comfort. She wouldn't have to ask Charles to bring her back and forth. Caroline stood taller. "I think that would be a fair trade, sir."

"I'll bring it by this afternoon, along with the money for the house."

Caroline felt independent again, much like she felt after killing the wolves at Pa's cabin. As much as she missed Horace, she knew she could take care of herself well, with God's help. Horace would be pleased.

It took another long week before Giles could venture to the river again. He knew to get close would be dangerous. He'd watched the men maneuvering the rafts across the river even after the rain had stopped. Pa was right. He needed to be careful.

He loved to dig in the dirt. Finding treasures brought him joy. Daily, he would find old Indian tools or arrowheads, but Giles also wanted to find Whitmore's treasure.

A legend had been told that Whitmore Knaggs buried a jug full of gold near his trading post before he died. An Indian girl loved to tell the story about how she'd seen Whitmore leave his house one night and venture down the river.

Supposedly, carrying a lantern, Whitmore stopped close to a large rock in the river. There, he buried a "pile of gold" as the squaw said. What if Giles could find it one day? He'd be rich. Whitmore would love it if *he* were the one to find it. He'd share with his family, of course, but the rest he'd save to spend on all kinds of things. While he dug, he thought of the things he'd buy. Perhaps a good rifle to go hunting with his pa. For his ma, he'd buy her a new stove. Like the ones they'd had back East at the store. He'd buy himself a nice new pair of leather shoes. Ones that fit and weren't "hand-me-downs" from George. A horse would be nice.

He'd always wanted one of his own. He could ride it anywhere he wanted. Even to school.

But first, he'd buy himself a new hoe. A steel one. Pa used to sell them in the store back East for about sixty cents. Thoughts of what he'd buy with the gold he found filled his mind as he dug and dug and dug in various places around the edge of the riverbank. At each large rock, he'd dig around it thoroughly as to not miss the jug which held all of Whitmore Knagg's gold.

He had often wondered why Whitmore had buried his gold. Pa and Momma had a desk at one end of the inn where they did transactions for the residents of the village. The settlers would bring Pa their money and then he'd give them a tiny book to keep track of their amount until they returned with either more money to add or needing part or all of their money back. Giles thought it was genius of Pa to think of such a good business. He could keep the money until the settler needed it. Pa would even give them a little extra money back if they kept their money with Pa long enough. Pa said he was the first bank in this part of the wilderness.

Perhaps Giles would create a bank of his own. He could keep people's money for them. They could trust him as much as they trusted Pa. He'd make sure of it.

"Cornelia!"

Giles stopped digging to find his Ma standing on the porch of the inn. Cornelia must have wandered off. Being so little, Ma was always finding her upstairs or in the pantry pulling out pans. She was always underfoot, somewhere.

"Giles!"

Giles stood to his feet, "Yes, Ma!"

She looked angry and somewhat frantic this time. "Have you seen Cornelia? I've searched the house. I can't find her anywhere."

Ma looked pretty in the sun. Her belly was growing with the child inside. Giles could never figure out how a baby, growing in a woman's belly, could get themselves out of there. "I haven't seen her Ma."

His ma went back into the inn. Before Giles went back to his digging, he took one look around the property. He didn't see the toddler anywhere.

Suddenly, he heard a loud splash!

Martha must have heard it, too, for now she was running toward the river. Giles looked up to see Cornelia floating down the river, splashing frantically.

Dropping his stick, Giles knew he could get to the baby first, before even Martha and he took off running toward where she'd gone in. Martha soon caught up to him and together they started following the floating baby down the river. Every few feet, his baby sister would lift her head and cry out.

"Giles, we have to get her. If she gets caught in the current—" Martha was now screaming for help from anyone who might hear her.

Giles knew what to do. He didn't care that he would get his play clothes wet. He knew he needed to get his little sister out of the river as fast as he could.

Martha screamed again. "Ma! Pa! Cornelia's in the river!"

Giles heard Martha scream again as he headed into the stream to attempt to rescue his baby sister. The current caught his legs just as he waded in, and before he could catch himself, he bobbed in the water just behind Cornelia. If he could just catch her, he could pull her to the bank and to safety. He paddled with all his might, but the current kept taking him under.

He'd suddenly remembered what Pa had told him many times. "If you find yourself in water and you can't swim, try hard to float. Just relax and float." But try as he might, the current was too strong. Soon Giles could no longer see Cornelia in front of him. He gulped a whole mouthful of water as the current kept pulling him under. What would he do now? How would he rescue his sister if he had to rescue himself, too?

Giles could hear men screaming behind him. Splashes of water made it sound like some were jumping into the water to rescue Cornelia. Gustus, the raft driver, strained to hold out an oar to Giles. Giles stretched as far as he could to grab hold of the oar, but also looked down the river to see the pink outfit of his sister still bobbing in the water. He needed to help her. She was too little to know to float. She wouldn't know what to do, and she must be even more scared than he.

Instead of grabbing hold of the oar, Giles decided he wouldn't get out of the water until he rescued Cornelia. Giles turned his body to see if he could get his bearings and maybe even find a small sand mound to climb on, but when he did, he saw a log coming straight at him in the current. He paddled to get away from the log. He then decided if he got close, maybe he could lift himself on it, and then grab Cornelia, too.

As he watched the log come near, a lot of things went through his head. Would he be successful and help his sister? Pa would be so happy and proud if he did. The current twisted him around and he could no longer see the log until it hit him on the back of the head, and everything went dark.

Dragging a log from the river, Hosea prevented it from blocking water to the mill. Sticks and logs piled against the mill needed to be removed. As he transferred the log onto a nearby pile, a galloping horse and rider came toward him on the path from Knagg's Place. The rider and horse were coming at a breakneck speed and soon Hosea could hear the rider yelling something. Before he could make out what he was saying, he saw it was Billie.

As the horse skidded to a stop, Billie rushed down to the river calling out to him. "It's two of Rhoda's children. They've fallen in the water. They're drifting in this direction!"

Did Hosea hear him correctly? "What happened?"

Before he could repeat himself, Billie jumped into the strong current, scanning the river as he entered. "Go get the rope on my horse and I'll tie it around me."

Hosea ran to Billie's horse, unhooked the rope on the saddle, and unwound it. Running to the river, Hosea threw out one end of the rope to him. Billie yanked the opposite end of the rope around his waist and cinched it tight. "Tie the other end to my horse."

Hosea unwound the rope as he trotted back to Billie's horse. He slipped the rope around the saddle horn and tied a tight knot.

Billie called from the shore. "Hold tight to Brandy."

Hosea grabbed the horse's halter, watching Billie struggle to get farther into the stream. Two or three times, the water knocked him off his feet. Holding his arms out of the water, he edged in deeper and deeper. Soon he was swimming. He motioned for Hosea to pull back on the rope. Leading the horse away from the water, Billie quickly regained his footing, planting himself at the drop-off edge, only a third of the way from the riverbank.

Hosea called out. "What are you going to do?"

"Stop those bodies before they get by."

Bodies? Oh God, no. It can't be. Hosea prayed as he held tight to Billie's horse. He still didn't know what had happened, but he thought he'd heard something about Rhoda and her children.

Billie fought the current to stand erect as the river cut around him. Hosea watched as he looked one way and then the other. Soon more men arrived. One man took off his coat, grabbed the rope holding Billie, and worked his way toward him. Another man leapt from his horse and, tied another rope around his waist, just as Isaac Banks arrived. He held the third man's horse for him. The four men staggered into the water, each one carefully searching the water as it flowed past.

Hosea wanted to help more, but if he let go of Billie's horse, it might bolt and take Billie with him. He held tightly as more people joined in to watch.

"Pa, what's happening?"

Caroline pulled up alongside of him in a horse-drawn buggy.

Hosea shook his head. "I don't know any details, but by what others are saying, I think two of Rhoda's children have gone into the river downstream. The men are here to see if they can rescue them.

"Which of her children?"

"I don't know Carrie, but please pray."

Nicholas arrived just a few minutes later.

As more people gathered on shore, the mill workers each carried out boards to direct the water flow into the makeshift canal beside the mill. Their efforts were tedious, but finally the stream went directly past the others on shore. They didn't catch all the river water, but enough so the men in the water were able to sift through what was left before it flowed past the mill. Men and women lined the small stream. Surely, someone would spot a small child.

The men in the river called back and forth to each other. On shore, other men gathered wood to start a fire. Once lit, the first four men who went into the river came out to get warm. Other men took their place. After nearly an hour, a man pointed out something bobbing in the water. A small pink dress floated toward them. People on shore shouted and pointed to the clothing for the men in the water.

A tall man next to Billie was the first to reach the child. He grabbed for her swirling dress. Soon he was lifting the tiny girl's limp body out of the stream. Another man reached him and carried the girl to shore.

As the man placed the tiny body on shore, Nicholas kneeled down beside her and cradled her head with his hand. Besides a few scratches on her arms and face, the child didn't appear injured. He rolled her onto her stomach and hit her on the back several times. She didn't respond with a breath or even a cry. After several attempts hitting her back and lifting her belly off the ground, Nicholas stopped. He looked up at Hosea with tears in his eyes. "We're too late. She's gone."

It was Cornelia. Rhoda's youngest baby.

The men on shore shouted to the men in the water that there might be another. Hosea stroked the side of Cornelia's pale cheek. Nicholas closed her eyes. As others came to see the child, Hosea knew what Rhoda would want. He took off his coat and placed it over the tiny child's body.

Hosea could envision the curious toddler heading into the water on her own. But who, out of Rhoda's other children, would follow her? And why? As he stood, he prayed fervently that they would find the next one, too. If not for the child's sake, for Rhoda and Sidney. Surely, that child had drowned, too, having been in the river all the way to the mill.

A few moments later, Sidney and Rhoda arrived on the scene. Rhoda was sobbing uncontrollably. She stopped and looked at Hosea's coat on the ground, and then at Hosea.

All he could do was shake his head.

Rhoda fell to her knees as Sidney made his way toward his daughter's body.

After hours of searching, men continued scouring the river in shifts. Some of the first men who went into the water left to go home for dry and warmer clothing. Billie went back into the water for his third attempt.

A shout echoed over the water. Billie struggled to grab something brown in the water. As he lifted it out, it was a brown shoe.

Just then, Hosea saw something in the stream beside the mill. He pointed and hollered, "Look! Right there!"

A man in the crowd waded into the stream. Bending down, he lifted another child from the current.

It was Giles. Nicholas ran to the edge of the stream and collected the boy. He tried the same life-saving procedure that he tried on Cornelia but without success.

Rhoda left Cornelia's body and ran to sit on the ground next to Giles. She lifted the boy's head into her lap and let out the most mournful cry a woman could utter. The people watching all either bowed their heads or simply stood in silence. Some men removed their hats. The only noise to be heard were two nearby crows, the rustle of wind through the trees, the weeping of other women, and the wails of a distraught mother. Hosea's heart ached.

There was no evidence of life. Two children had died. Hosea pulled Caroline in for an embrace and whispered. *"The Lord giveth, and the Lord taketh away—,"* he stammered but continued, *"Blessed be the name of the Lord."* Caroline sobbed into his shoulder.

People turned to leave the scene. Whether out of respect for Rhoda and Sidney, or to not have to listen to the weeping of a mourning mother, Hosea couldn't tell.

Sidney picked up his daughter's body, cradling her in his arms, and wept into Hosea's coat.

Hosea felt a hand on his shoulder. It was Nicholas. "Are you okay, Hosea?"

Hosea nodded, wiping tears off his face with his sleeve. "What do we do now?"

Nicholas whispered in his ear, "Give Sidney and Rhoda time to mourn. Then, let's get the bodies of the children into the mill. Coffins need to be made."

CHAPTER TWENTY-NINE

Hosea patted Sally Mae's back as she sobbed on his shoulder. "Oh, Hosea! Rhoda and Sidney must be devastated!"

"Nicholas told me to come tell you before you could hear the news from someone else."

"I need to go to Rhoda." Sally pulled away to look at Hosea.

The look on her face made Hosea pull her close again.

"Where are they?"

"I left them at the mill with the bodies. I think they'll need us to make the arrangements for the children's burial. I don't think Sidney can do it." Hosea sat at the table. "That boy was such a good boy. Everyone said they think he went into the river to save the baby. I think they need to have a little time for it all to sink in. Losing one baby is bad enough, but two. I don't know how Rhoda will get through this without God's help. She might just blame Him more."

"What can we do? How can we help them?"

"We need to pray. Rhoda is in no condition to take such a shock."

Sally Mae looked up with questioning eyes. "What do you mean?"

"Nicholas told me, she's expecting again."

"Oh Hosea!" Using her apron, Sally Mae wiped her eyes.

"Let's get some things together. We can stay at the inn for a few days. That way, we'll be there when they need us. We can help with whatever guests they have. Food will still need to be prepared.

Sally Mae sighed. "Yes. Anything they need. Let me get a satchel packed."

"What do you say to someone who has just lost not one but two children?"

Putting a hand on his shoulder, Sally Mae kissed his head. "I don't know. God has never made us handle such heartache."

Hosea turned to look up at his wife. "But we have."

Sally Mae gave him a questioning look. "Can we use Alexander's life to comfort Sidney and Rhoda? He wasn't legally our child."

Hosea looked down at his hands. "In my eyes, he was just as much my child as Betsey, Ambrose, and the girls." Tears filled Hosea's eyes. "There isn't a day I don't mourn that boy. He brought me so much joy, even for the short time he was with us. How can I say his loss wasn't slightly similar?"

Sally Mae sat beside him. "How will you approach Rhoda?"

"I don't know exactly, but I know that when we suffer loss, God sustains us. I don't know any words which can be adequate, but I'm willing to be God's mouthpiece, if He so wishes."

Sally Mae patted Hosea's hand.

Rhoda went right to bed once they got back to the inn. She couldn't think of the next second, minute, or hour of her life. Feeling lost, she longed to go to sleep...to pretend nothing had happened in the last few hours. Her gaze turned toward the corner of the room, Rhoda could see Cornelia's bed in the corner. Crawling out of bed, Rhoda went to it and bent over to pick up Cornelia's blanket. Putting it to her nose, she breathed in its scent. Sobs racked her body.

How had this happened? But more urgent was why?

Returning to her bed, Rhoda lay down and pulled blankets over her shoulders. Stifling sobs, she cried into her pillow. Thinking of Giles brought even more heartache. Her loving, adventurous boy hated being inside over the past few weeks. He'd been miserable. He hated rain, storms, or snow, which kept him from going outside to explore and dig. Why had he thought it best to go into the water after Cornelia? Rhoda had told him, and Sidney had reiterated the dangers.

Sidney came to her bed. He stroked her hair while she sobbed. He whispered prayers in her ear. For once, Rhoda tried to listen to his words and gain comfort from them, but her heart didn't know how. Nothing could help her. He asked her to remember she was carrying a child and her sorrow wouldn't be good for the unborn baby. But Rhoda couldn't think of new life right now. Mourning two of her children was more than she could bear. How could she get control of herself over a child she'd never seen while mourning those she'd had for years?

Rhoda tossed and turned for hours. If only she could fall asleep. Squeezing her eyes tight, she wanted the world to fade into non-existence. Perhaps she'd dream again. For a few moments, she slept. A dream took her back to New York. She had just ordered material for the store. One of her favorite things to do. She'd take time to pass her hand over each bolt, feeling the texture, breathing in the aroma of new cloth, and dreaming of the garment she could create from the beauty of new fabric. The fresh fabric reflected bright colors, no holes or worn edges, and the jealousy it would create among the customers always made Rhoda feel rich as she sported a modern, new-styled dress. Being a store owner had its advantages. Her children would always wear new clothes instead of hand-me-downs from older siblings.

Once awake again, if Rhoda thought about a new arrival of fabric at the store, the pain of her loss could dim. Despite it seeming trivial in comparison, it somehow brought Rhoda a temporary relief to the massive pain of her current situation. But even trying to distract her thinking brought black colors, which then led to her wondering what a mother should wear to a funeral for her children. How could she place the bodies of her precious Cornelia and Giles into dark graves?

When Sidney came into their room a few hours later, Rhoda asked him if they could bury the children in the same coffin. He mumbled an answer, but she insisted that was how it needed to be. "Cornelia won't be afraid then. Giles will take care of her."

Once she'd told him that, he agreed. He promised to ask Hosea.

Sometimes the tears gave way to nausea, which took her pain to a whole new level. She'd retch into a nearby bucket but not bring up any food. She hadn't eaten since breakfast and it was nearly dark. She knew the new baby needed nourishment, but Rhoda couldn't think of eating.

In the moments when sleep eluded her, Rhoda could do nothing but stare at a frame on the wall. Inside the gold frame was a wedding sampler that her aunt had stitched for her. Perhaps she should never have married Sidney. If the marriage wouldn't have happened, she'd have never had Cornelia or Giles. Today's pain would not have happened.

Hours turned into days. Despite dark curtains covering her bedroom windows, during the day, somehow light brightened them.

"Rhoda." A voice came from the doorway. "Can I come in?"

Rhoda recognized her brother's voice. She'd been able to ignore everyone who'd tried to get her to eat or even speak, but she knew Hosea wouldn't let her ignore him.

She turned her head toward the voice.

The dark room smelled awful. Hosea wasn't sure why it had such a horrid odor, but he knew Rhoda probably hadn't even risen to use the outhouse. Perhaps the chamber pot beside her bed needed emptied. He would get Sally Mae into the room as soon as he could. His sister shouldn't have to live like this.

"It's Hosea, Rhoda. May I come in?"

There was no response from the mound in the bed. He needed to light a lamp. It was hard to see in the dark room.

"Rhoda. I'm coming to your bed." He wasn't sure if she could even hear him, but he'd been advised by Nicholas to tread lightly. "I'm gonna sit right here. I don't want you to be alone any longer." Hosea lowered himself into a nearby chair.

His vision adjusting to the dim room, he noticed Rhoda's eyes focused on him. He'd debated for hours what he could say or do to help his sister through such an ordeal. He knew he'd have no words to comfort her, but he knew Who would. He'd prayed that whatever he'd say would be words from God. He'd relied on the Holy Spirit for years as to what to say in difficult circumstances and, this was one of those moments.

"Rhoda. I know God hasn't been of much comfort to you lately. I also know this trial He's brought to you is more than any woman should have to bear." Hosea coughed into his hand. "I'm so sorry, Rhoda. It's awful what happened to your children."

Hosea paused for a response, but there was only silence.

"Rhoda, do you remember the kitten you had back home? The one Pa brought you from town one day?"

He waited again for an answer, but heard nothing.

"You loved that kitten. I believe you named her Penny cause Pa said he'd spent a penny to get her from a local farmer."

The door to the bedroom opened and a slice of light from the front room of the inn filtered into the dark room. For a moment, the light helped Hosea make out Rhoda's face. Dark circles around her eyes made her look almost dead herself, but glassy eyes stared back at him. He continued.

"You took that kitten everywhere. You were three or four, but you cared for that cat like she was the only thing that mattered in your life." Hosea chuckled. "Ma said she never found you without finding the cat who followed you everywhere. You slept with it, nursed it, and carried it into the tops of the trees when you climbed. When you started school, Pa scolded you for taking it with you. You cried and cried every morning when you had to leave it. He told you the cat would be at home waiting for you to return."

Hosea saw Rhoda blink. She was listening for her eyes grew moist. The sister he loved so dearly gave a glimpse of her emotions.

"Penny was a wonderful cat and, if I remember clearly, a good mouser."

"I remember." It was a mumble, but Rhoda had responded.

Hosea sighed with relief but continued his story. "I said before, losing a child is horrifying to go through. But I do believe God prepares us for what's to come. And as a small child, losing a pet is a tragic thing to endure. Penny didn't live forever. Pets never do. And the day she died you would barely allow Pa to put her in the ground. You wanted a nice place for her to rest, and it took you all day to find just the right spot. You chose for her to go under the hickory tree in the backyard. It had been a happy place for you to remember all the fond memories you'd shared with Penny."

Hosea could see Rhoda smile.

Hosea looked up to see Sidney in the doorway. He was silent and stood behind the door, so the only person to see him was Hosea.

"You went to Penny's grave every day to put flowers there. You'd often sit for hours patting her grave. You surely loved that cat. Do you remember?"

Rhoda began to cry. Tears wet her cheeks.

Hosea prayed for strength. "What's happened to your babies is heartbreaking. There used to be a small Indian boy named Alexander." At the mention of his name, Hosea looked to the floor, and tears formed in his own eyes. "He wasn't my flesh, but he was special to me." Hosea took a deep breath. "I loved that boy. He followed me everywhere. He was there when I planted corn and there to enjoy eating it with me at the end of the season. That boy had a part in saving my children and Sallie Mae from death. I didn't think I could spend a day without him...until God decided it was time for him to leave me.

"I don't want you to think I understand the pain you are having because I don't. Alexander didn't live with me long, but while he was here, he brought me great joy. That's what I cling to, Rhoda. I try hard to remember the wonderful memories of our time together. If I never would have met or grown to love Alexander, I wouldn't have those cherished thoughts. God allowed him into my life when I needed him most. He'd been a gift, just like the gift of your kitten from Pa. Would you rather have not had Penny, or would you desire to cherish the moments you had with her?"

Rhoda turned her face away.

Hosea thought he'd lost her. He'd said too much. He prayed an urgent prayer for God to show His love to Rhoda through him. Hosea kneeled by the bed. "Rhoda. These children have been a loving gift from your Heavenly Father. He chose for them to live brief lives, but their memories will live forever in your heart.

"I can't take away your grief or heartache, but remember these babies' lives. Remember the joy they both brought you. Do that now. Cherish the sweet lives of Cornelia and Giles, as we will all be doing in the days to come. As the years go by, you will slowly and gradually go on, with the joy of your memories to encourage even your worst days."

Rhoda turned a tear-streaked face to him. "I want them buried by Whitmore. Giles loved that man. I don't want them alone by people they don't know."

Hosea patted her damp cheeks. "Whatever you want, Rhoda. We'll bury them wherever you'd like."

"I've been horrible to God, Hosea. I've left Him out of my life for so long. I've done wicked things to you and to others. I'm still trying to convince myself God forgives me, but do you think He is now punishing me because of it?"

Hosea had prayed that the discussion would lead to this. "I don't know God's heart or His intentions. As close as we are, He never reveals His plans to me or asks for my advice on any matter. I don't know why He's presented you with this excruciating trial of your life, but I know He's there! He doesn't abandon us in our pain. He wants you to return and accept His love for you. Of that, I am certain.

"As for what you've done to others, we can never drive God away by doing bad things. That's not how the Bible says it works. It's us who leave God, not the other way around. Like a parent, he wants us to return to Him. Welcome Him back into our lives—no matter how we've treated Him. He never stops loving or caring for us. It wasn't He who turned His back on you. So just return to Him, Rhoda. He's waiting with open arms."

Rhoda nodded.

"Giles was a wonder. Wasn't he? That child was such a busy one. Always curious, always searching, always exploring. And Cornelia—what a sweet baby she was. She looked like Ma, don't you think?"

Rhoda pushed herself to a more seated position in the bed.

Hosea stood and plumped up the pillows behind her as she leaned back into them. "I don't know how to go on without them."

"No. That's a hard thing to do, but you know what? The sun will come up. A new day will dawn. And as each day passes, so does the intense grief you feel. It won't take a day, a month, or even a year to get over this heartache, but gradually, just like with Penny—you'll learn how to live with it. And what it will leave will be their sweet memories to cherish. You'll see Cornelia's smile in Martha or Giles's adventurous spirit in your new baby. No one can ever take those thoughts away from you."

As Hosea left Rhoda's room, he patted Sidney on the back. "I don't know if I said anything right, Sidney, but she's a strong woman. Lean on each other. Support one another. Give yourselves time to recover from such a hard loss."

"I worry about the baby she is carrying."

"Everyone is concerned about that, too. God's will is perfect in life and in death. Some people claim the Bible says God won't give us more than we can handle, but that's not entirely true. For God never wants us to handle anything like this alone. The Apostle Paul wrote, *'God's grace is sufficient for thee; for my strength is made perfect in weakness.'* He carries us through it, not on our power, but in His.

"I'm praying for a peace that passes all understanding for you and Rhoda. It's a supernatural calm He gives us. Something we can't explain to others. I've had it many times in my life, and I can tell you right now, it's a power only God can give."

CHAPTER THIRTY

"She's gone three days without food, Nicholas. Will it harm the baby?"

Nicholas shook his head. "I don't know. It isn't good. Babies are resilient with lesser things, but this grief business is tricky. It seems unborn babies don't do well when traumatic things happen to the mother. I've seen it often."

"Could the child come early?" Sally Mae asked him as she placed a slice of rhubarb pie on his plate after dinner.

"I would suspect. Possibly. I just need to be here with her to be sure everything is all right."

Sally Mae sat next to Hosea and took his hand. "We'll stay here for her and Sidney."

"Rhoda mentioned to me she wanted the children buried up by Whitmore. Is there space near his grave?" Hosea turned toward Sidney. "Is that what you'd prefer for them too, Sidney?"

Sidney wiped tears from his eyes. "Whatever Rhoda wants."

"I'll head up there in the morning to check. I'm putting the final touches on the coffin now. One of my workers knows how to carve wood and has offered to put the children's names on one end. He does beautiful work."

"I think we need to have the funeral tomorrow, if Rhoda can handle it. The children need to be buried soon." Nicholas took a long swig of his coffee.

Sidney nodded. "You're right. Can you pass the word? I'll let Rhoda know the next time she's awake. Do you think she'll be able to handle a funeral, Doctor?"

"No one knows. Not even me, but it needs to happen soon. Perhaps getting her out of bed will do her body some good, but I'll be near if she needs me."

"I've prepared her a plate again. Perhaps after talking to Hosea, she'll eat something." Sally Mae took a tray and left for Rhoda's bedroom.

"Let's pray she eats. That's what's most important now." Nicholas sat back and crossed his arms.

Almost the entire village of Newburg turned out to attend the funeral of the two drowned children. A wagon carried the casket holding the children to the cemetery where they'd buried Whitmore.

Rhoda had allowed Sally Mae to help her get dressed. She'd chosen a black dress with a dark veil over her face.

Rhoda clung to Sidney and Hosea's extended arms as she descended off the inn's porch and into Caroline's new buggy. She'd offered it to the family to use. Rhoda greeted Caroline when she handed the reins to Sidney. Philinda, Martha, George, and Rhoda Ann walked behind the carriage with the rest of the family following them.

Rhoda looked up to see the carvings of the children's names on the end of the casket in the wagon in front of them. Fresh tears sprang to her eyes. Sidney grabbed her hand and gave the horse a cluck to follow the wagon.

She'd had a dream like this. It had been years ago, but Rhoda remembered it now. It was as if God had somehow prepared her for what would happen. Instead of being angry at Him, she decided her anger toward Him had gone on long enough. She thanked Him in her thoughts for giving her a glimpse of what she'd have to do in the future. It almost felt comforting to her.

Along the way, entire families joined the procession as the wagon and buggy traveled to the cemetery in Fremont.

Traveling along the river, Rhoda felt the cool breeze filter through the veil over her face. She decided the breeze felt better on her skin than the rough fabric of the veil. Pulling the dark covering up and off her face made her sigh. Since the day the children drowned, the river had slowed considerably. The once-tumultuous water now flowed easily, and there were even calm parts of the river.

The sun warmed her shoulders. The grief in her heart still felt raw. Tears formed easily. She wondered if she'd ever run out of them.

The long procession wound its way to the cemetery, and soon John Swain's voice echoed through the crowd. He spoke of grief. He told stories about both children, which Rhoda tucked into her overflowing memory bank. The scriptures he shared brought hope and peace.

"We never want days like this to happen. Our community is in mourning for the lives of Giles and Cornelia Seymour. Tragedy strikes many families, but losing a child is an excruciating pain; a grief made deeper by the lives they never had a chance to discover and fulfill."

John talked about the children, and then asked Gustus to come forward. It surprised Rhoda that the man who manned the rafts at the river would even want to say something at the funeral of her children.

The old man stood beside the children's grave. As tears flowed down his face, he recalled the day. "I watched both babies go into the river. Cornelia had gotten to the edge of the water and I heard the splash as she slipped on the mud and landed face down into the river. She never had a chance, but her brother decided it was his responsibility to save her." The crowd gasped. "He ran right into the river and made an endeavor to paddle toward Cornelia, but the river was mightier."

Rhoda wasn't sure she wanted to hear more, but she knew the man well. He was usually quiet and soft-spoken. There must be something he wanted to say which might bring the family comfort.

"I watched the boy bob up and down as the river took his futile strokes and began surging him down the river toward Cornelia. He never gave up trying to reach her. His little arms flaying and his legs kicking. As he came near me—" the man stopped talking and wiped off his mouth. Tears were streaming down his face and he could barely talk. "—What happened next was nothing short of heroism."

What had he said? Rhoda squeezed Sidney's hand.

"I held out an oar. He could have easily grabbed it. He was within inches and then I saw that young boy's face. He wanted nothing to do with saving himself. He looked down the river for his sister and refused my offer of help. I've never seen a child with more determination and stamina than Giles Seymour. He will forever live in my memory as the boy with grit—" Then the man smiled up at Rhoda and Sidney. "—just like the person whom that little boy admired more than anyone else: Whitmore Knaggs. The boy was determined to save his sister. His bravery will never be forgotten. He should be an inspiration to all of us."

A single grave held the casket of her children. While it slipped into the ground, Rhoda felt the pain start. It had grown through the day, but now she couldn't deny what was happening. She gripped

Sidney's arm as she felt a trickle of water slip down between her legs.

She wasn't sure if she should tell Sidney. Her skirts were full enough that no one would notice, but the squeeze of pain that gripped her middle now almost sent her to her knees. This pain was familiar. There would be no denying it.

Upon leaving the cemetery, Rhoda told Sidney to be sure the doctor followed them home. Sidney pulled Nicholas aside. Nicholas nodded and borrowed a man's horse. Rhoda had been the center of attention too much, so now she sought only privacy for what would soon happen.

As the pain grew worse, Rhoda couldn't forget Gustus's words. If Giles had purposely given his life for his baby sister, the least she could do was keep his example and be brave now. She wasn't nine years old, but she knew that bravery came at all ages. Without hesitating now, Rhoda said a prayer of thanks for the lives of her children. She knew the hole they left behind would be enormous, but she took Hosea's advice and dwelled on the memories and the joy they both had brought her and Sidney. She reflected that even those who pass away at young ages have an eternal impact on other's lives. By mimicking a person's admirable character, their memories would be kept alive.

Despite all that she'd just gone through, Rhoda knew the next few hours would be even worse. However, instead of being afraid, she relished in the physical pain. For some odd reason, it brought her relief. Would God give her strength? Would He even listen to someone who'd ignored Him for years? As another pain shot through her abdomen, she knew this day would be remembered as one of the worst of her life. She'd most likely end this day with another loss, but it was just one day of her life. Far more time had brought her immense joy and thankfulness.

Gripping the bars of the carriage, she closed her eyes. This day would define her. It would either send her on a course of complete denial of a god who could allow such heartache or open up a light to a path back to Him. She wanted to use this day of excruciating heartache as an instrument of healing instead of piling her mountain with more anger. If she walked the path back, Hosea would be an instrumental part of that. She wanted him to be the first one to know.

When the pain subsided for a moment, Rhoda spoke to Sidney. "Can you send for Hosea?"

CHAPTER THIRTY-ONE

"I just want to be here for you." Sally Mae wiped the sweat off Rhoda's brow.

"Please Sally. You need to understand—" Another hard pain gripped Rhoda. She bit her lip to keep from screaming out. "I need to be alone. Please!" She then prayed that her pleading would work.

Sally backed away. "Only if you promise to call for me if you change your mind."

Amidst the horrific pain, Rhoda nodded.

As Sally left and shut the door, Rhoda allowed grief to take over. Sweat dripped from every pore in her body. She kicked the heavy blanket off.

Nicholas had also stepped outside the room. He told her it could take all night to deliver the child, but Rhoda knew her ninth child would enter the world as easily as Cornelia. Sweet Cornelia told the world in a boisterous way that she'd arrived in less than two hours of labor.

Yet as the night wore on, the anguish only intensified. It didn't feel like the labor of Rhoda's other children. Unbelievably, Rhoda welcomed each pain. Not because she wanted to suffer, but somehow it lifted her out of the grief that encompassed her over the past few days. She could concentrate on this experience instead of seeing the faces of her dead babies on the shore at Hosea's mill.

Nicholas came in to check on her, and again she pleaded for even him to leave her alone. He protested that it could be a hard delivery, but she told him she'd given birth to many children before this. She'd call him if needed. Not being sure they'd leave her, she used an angry tone to force them from the room. Even when the door shut after they left, she knew she wasn't alone.

As Jacob in the Bible had once wrestled with God, Rhoda decided this was her time. She allowed the pain of giving birth to fight through much of her anger. As the pain grew in intensity, Rhoda asked God questions. Why had he allowed her older sister to die at such a young age? Why did she question His motives? How could Hosea have such faith and her efforts seem so futile? Each question was answered by Bible verses her father had taught her, which brought comfort and understanding. As each verse entered her thoughts, she recognized from whom Hosea had gained his Bible verse recitation. It had been their father.

For the first time in her life, Rhoda experienced God. Through her pain, she could sense His presence. It was as if He were right in the room with her, wiping her face, holding her hand as a pain grew intense, and enveloping her with His love. As she felt the tiny body of her baby slip from her womb, she asked God to never leave her alone. A memory flashed into her mind of her father quoting, *"And the Lord, it is He that doth go before thee; He will be with thee, He will not fail thee, neither forsake thee; fear not, neither be dismayed."* When most men utter swear words, Hosea and her father replaced them with Bible verses.

As she called for Nicholas, Rhoda picked up the tiny baby from off the bed. The little boy struggled to catch his breath, but Rhoda could see he would be too tiny to live for long. She cradled the infant at her breast and gazed at his tiny hands, which were no bigger than her thumb. His feet, a mere inch long. His eyes were too big for his little head and for a moment, he gazed up into her eyes as if he could draw strength from her.

The door opened and Nicholas rushed to her side.

"Please give us a moment." Rhoda couldn't take her eyes off her tiny son. She knew that today she would lose her third child in four days. Rhoda didn't see death at that moment, but real life. For even though this baby wouldn't live longer than a few minutes, he would always remind her how precious life is. God created him for this moment. And although tiny, he was perfectly made and given for a special purpose in Rhoda's life. Bringing him into the world had renewed her faith in God. She now knew all things sent from God were for her good. Not only did she know it by heart, but she also believed it with her whole heart.

As Nicholas tended her, Rhoda snuggled the tiny body. She kissed the small head and thanked God for allowing just a moment of time to hold him. As she'd remember Giles and Cornelia...she'd cherish this moment the same.

"Rhoda, please allow me to see him."

Rhoda held out the now limp baby to Nicholas who took a look, wiped out the baby's mouth, and then placed Rhoda's arm back around him to cradle. Shaking his head, Rhoda knew the baby wouldn't have had a chance of survival from the expression on Nicholas's face.

"It's okay, Nicholas. Now I have three reasons to desire heaven."

As Nicholas finished the delivery, he placed the blanket over her again as Rhoda asked, "Can you ask Hosea to come in?"

Hosea entered the dark room. Why hadn't his sister asked for Sally Mae? What could he do for her now?

Nicholas stopped what he was doing and excused himself from the room.

"Hosea." Rhoda called out to him and extended her free hand to him.

As he neared the bed, he could see the outline of a tiny body against Rhoda's chest, the small creation was covered with a small piece of cloth.

"Sit beside me."

Hosea sat on a chair near the bed. "Rhoda? Are you sure you don't want Sidney? Or Sally Mae?"

Rhoda smiled and shook her head. "No. I need to talk to you."

Hosea didn't know what to say.

Rhoda looked down at her baby and patted his back. "It's a boy, Hosea. I want you to build another tiny coffin for him and place him atop Giles and Cornelia's casket. Will you promise me you'll do that?"

Hosea choked back tears. He couldn't stop them from streaming down his face. "I promise."

"But that's not why I wanted to talk to you. I have to ask for your forgiveness."

Hosea blinked back the tears from his eyes and wiped them with the back of his hand. "My forgiveness?"

"Yes." Rhoda held up her hand so he wouldn't ask another question. "Please let me finish."

Rhoda's face reflected a change to Hosea. He wasn't sure what kind of change, but something was different.

"For years, I've watched your life. I don't remember a time without you. We've endured the death of our sister and also our parents. We did it together. I cherished you. I missed you so much when you left New York for Pennsylvania. Every single day I thought of you and hated that we weren't together."

"I missed you too, Rhoda."

"But you also need to know. I was ashamed to be near you."

"Ashamed?"

"Yes. For there is something you don't know. All that caused you to leave New York—" Rhoda took a deep breath. "—was my fault!"

Hosea shook his head. "Rhoda, you've misunderstood. I didn't leave New York because of you. It was the scandal. I knew I'd never have the confidence of the church or any of our friends if I would have tried to stay and plead my case."

"Hosea." Rhoda now spoke through tears. "You wouldn't have left if it hadn't been because of what I did."

"I don't understand."

"I started the rumor."

Hosea sat back in his chair.

"It was me. I started the rumor that you'd stolen money from the church." Rhoda exhaled and her shoulders relaxed.

"You? But why?"

"I was jealous."

Hosea didn't know what to say. He gave Rhoda a puzzled look.

"Ever since I was small, I've watched you. I envied your strong faith. No matter what happened, whether it was being teased by kids at school or even after receiving a severe scolding from Father, it only made your relationship with God stronger. Your faith never wavered. You never turned your back on God in spite of the hard things that happened to you." Rhoda transferred the baby to her other arm and squeezed Hosea's hand harder. "I wanted a relationship with God like that. But I have always been a 'doubting Thomas.' Faith has never come easy for me."

"There are many people like you, Rhoda."

"But many people don't act in such a harsh way. One day at the store, I hinted to Martha you'd been purchasing things from the store that it astounded me you could afford. You remember Martha Whitfield, don't you?"

Hosea nodded.

"She asked me where I thought you'd gotten the money from, and I told her that the only place you had access to that much money would be from the offerings you counted at church. I thought Martha would just go to you and accuse you in person, but by the next Sunday, she'd gotten the whole church involved. I was too ashamed to stand up and tell everyone the truth. I'd done something as horrible as accusing my dearest brother of something he would never do.

"Over time, I kept telling myself that God would never want a relationship with someone who had done such an awful thing. Instead of confessing, I withdrew from Him. I decided I'd be better off trying to punish myself for the terrible things I would say and do."

Hosea couldn't believe what she was saying. "But Rhoda, you didn't know the lie would cause such harm."

"No. I didn't. But Hosea, that's the worst part. I didn't stop it, either. I never imagined you'd leave the church and the community you loved because of a rumor. By then, it was too late to confess. You were gone. The consequence has lasted for years."

Again, Hosea remained speechless.

Rhoda looked him straight in the eye. "Hosea, can you ever forgive me?"

Hosea knew his answer would be the steppingstone to help his sister continue a healing process. How could he ever deny someone the right to forgiveness? Especially knowing what Jesus did to pay for Hosea's sins. "I forgive you." Hosea also knew that along with his words, his actions of forgiveness needed to follow.

"I meant you harm. At first, I pretended I had done it in jest, but it wasn't true. It was evil. If I hadn't have started all this, we'd both be back in New York. We'd have never been apart for as long as we've been during the last few years. Everything would have turned out differently. Even this." Rhoda looked down at the small, lifeless body of her baby.

"But don't you see?" Hosea now regained his voice. "If it hadn't of happened in New York, I would have never come here to start this community. I would have never had the amazing opportunity of watching a tiny village appear in the wilderness of Michigan or to be a part of it. I would have never met Alexander and been able to love him. Yes, it's been hard, but the rewards have been even greater. Don't you see now how all things work together for good for those who love God? Even the trials we face. Don't you understand that now?"

Rhoda's eyes shone bright as she looked at him. "It's hard to admit out loud, but yes, I do. Now I do. My grief for my dear children will never go away, but as you said before...they have brought memories I will never forget. My life, from this point, will never be the same. In fact, with God by my side, it can only be richer and better—whatever happens, because now I understand."

They buried baby Guy right on top of Giles and Cornelia's grave. If a child showed bravery in trying to save his sister, he'd take the hand of this tiny one, too. The image was a figment of Rhoda's imagination, but it brought her comfort, as she knew all three children were now in God's presence.

The loss of three children passing away within four days of each other seemed a life-shattering event, yet it had brought Rhoda immense peace. As Hosea said, it was *"a peace that passeth all understanding"* and that's how she felt. Her heart also felt extreme relief that the truth had been told and she'd received Hosea's forgiveness.

The peace didn't take away her heartache or loss, but it sustained her to endure it. She found comfort in Giles's courage, Cornelia's curiosity, and Guy's hope—which only a baby can show—that the world can go on. She'd live with their memories for the rest of her life. She didn't hate that they'd been born, or that she'd had to experience their deaths so early, but she cherished the blessing that they had lived and influenced her life for even a short time. Each one was an indescribable gift. Her roots in God were no longer shallow, but deep and, hopefully, stronger.

CHAPTER THIRTY-TWO

Caroline wiped down the mantle before she placed a few meager kitchen supplies on it. She'd settled into her new home just a few weeks before, but because of the drowning deaths of Aunt Rhoda's children, she'd lived with the family at The Exchange for the first part of the summer to help with the other children. This gave Rhoda time to rest and recuperate from the ordeals.

Caroline delighted in her small cousins and loved to care for them. Each one, even the older George, had struggled with the deaths. Rhoda Ann especially would often cry herself to sleep because of the loss of Giles. The situation helped Caroline to feel useful since her own loss. It seemed as if death hovered over the small community. Everyone needed time to heal.

As Caroline returned to her new home close to Charles and Etta, she knew it would take time. She loved to visit Etta and share in caring for baby Harriet. Harriet was a joy to watch. She could stand now and loved to jabber a variety of sounds. Caroline watched Etta mothering, and she again longed for the day she could have a child of her own. But until that time, she adored Harriet and her other nieces and nephews, now five in all.

Caroline placed a kettle of water over the fire for tea. Setting a cup on the table, she spooned in some tea leaves Ma had prepared from the summer's rosemary and mint crops. Caroline loved the fresh aroma of her afternoon beverage.

A spirited knock sounded at her door. From the outside, Caroline could hear Jillian's voice. "Caroline! Are you home?"

Caroline went to the door, but before she could open it, Jillian swung it wide and marched in. "I have to talk to you."

"Jillian! You're very bold today!" Caroline folded her arms.

"I'm sorry. I don't mean to bother you." Caroline's sister stood in traveling clothes, carrying a garment bag.

"Jillian? What on earth? Are you going somewhere?"

Jillian seemed winded as she placed the bag on Caroline's table, nearly knocking off her tea cup. "I'm eloping!"

Before Caroline could ask, Jillian poured out her plans.

"We can't talk long. Billie will be here soon. I didn't want to leave without telling someone where I was going."

Caroline sat so she could take in everything Jillian was telling her. "And where might that be?"

"First, Big Rapids. Then, we'll probably stay with Aunt Rhoda at the inn." Jillian looked down at the floor but twisted her hands in what appeared to be nervous tension. "I didn't come here to have you stop me, but I wanted to be mature and let someone know our plans."

Caroline forced a giggle down with a gulp. "Mature, huh?" She tried hard to not display skepticism in her expression, but Jillian knew her too well.

Now it was Jillian who folded her arms. "I'm mature. I'm about to run off with my boyfriend and finally get married. That's a very mature thing to do."

Caroline looked down at the floating herbs in her tea. Picking up a spoon, she stirred the mixture. "Why yes, Jillian. Going against Pa's wishes or permission is quite the mature thing to do."

"Stop it!" Jillian sat across from Caroline. "You know how much Pa wants us to wait, but we just can't. We love each other. We want to start our life together. How could Pa understand such a thing?"

Jillian was right, of course. Pa would never understand a young woman's heart, but he understood common sense. "And how will you two live? Winter will soon be here. Do you have crops stored for winter? Can Billie support you financially?"

The questions surprised Jillian, by the look on her face. "Billie has more money than most of the settlers coming into the village. We'll figure it out! Best of all, we'll figure it out together. We don't want to wait until the end of summer."

Caroline sat back in her chair. "Jillian. August is not the *end* of the summer. You know Pa wants what's best for you. There are reasons he's asked you both to wait. Why can't you trust him?"

"Because." Jillian lowered her eyes to her hands.

"Because?" Caroline picked up her sister's chin so she can see her eyes.

"Caroline. You've been a married woman. You know men have needs."

"Jillian! I'm surprised at you."

"But you do. You've been with a man. You know they push to be married as quickly as possible. It's been four years now that Billie has wanted to marry me. We've waited long enough. Please don't stop us."

"I can't possibly stop you other than tying you to a chair here in my home. And that would be impossible. I know you, Jillian. You'd manage to get free."

Jillian gave Caroline a grin of satisfaction.

"Just be reasonable. Listen to Pa. We can plan a nice wedding. One you'll be happy with and will please you and our parents."

Jillian fiddled with a button on her sleeve. "I can't wait any longer, Caroline. Billie will be here soon."

Caroline knew whatever she had to say would not stop her sister. Billie was a good man. She'd wanted to marry him herself. He and Jillian were a good match. They'd have a rough few years if they married early, but if they did go ahead now—they'd still be fine. She'd also seen how eager Billie was to be married. Being older, it was probably hard to wait. He'd planned to marry Caroline almost six years ago now.

Caroline rose from her chair and went to her bedroom. Opening the chest at the foot of her bed, she dug through the winter clothes and bedding stored in it to pull out a garment wrapped in cloth. She brought the package back to the table. Opening the cloth, Caroline found the veil her ma had allowed her to wear on her wedding day. Ma had given the veil to her. She'd worn it on her day and loaned it to Etta for her wedding, too. She placed the veil across Jillian's open arms. "Wear this. Ma wore it, then Betsey, me, and Etta. It was our something borrowed. But do me one favor." Caroline squeezed her younger sister's hand. "Bring it back to me. I want to pass it down to Julia and Harriet some day."

"Do you think it will last that long?"

Caroline giggled. "If not, we'll figure something out that will allow them to at least carry it down the aisle."

Jillian looked into Caroline's eyes and whispered, "Thank you."

Caroline nodded. "But if you tell Pa that I gave you my permission, I'll find you, and it won't be fun to endure a tongue lashing from me." Then she smiled. "I still wish you'd wait for Pa's timing."

Just then, a knock startled the sisters.

"It's Billie."

Caroline patted the hand of her sister, who was no longer the silly little girl who followed her everywhere. "I hope your day will be as special as mine."

As Caroline closed the door behind the excited couple, she breathed a prayer that they would be as happy as she and Horace had been. Caroline knew every moment counted. Perhaps that's why she was giving Jillian her blessing. One never really knew what tomorrow would bring. A person should live one's life, learn from mistakes, and keep going. She prayed she had just made the right decision to let Jillian follow her heart.

Nicholas pulled his buggy up to the Bakers' house. Ambrose had come for him earlier in the day, but he'd been out checking on a sick baby just north of the village.

After mounting the steps of the Baker residence, he knocked on the door, calling for Sally. "It's Nicholas, Sally."

Ambrose was at the door in seconds and opened it for him.

"Where is he?"

"In here."

Nicholas found Hosea in a chair by his bed. Sally was awkwardly spooning broth into her husband's crooked mouth. Nicholas sighed. He knew what this was.

"Hosea. Don't you know I'm a busy man?" He knew that being serious right now would set Hosea off on a tangent about

Sally making a big to-do over nothing and, by the look on the man's face, it was far from that.

"I tried to..." Hosea tried to talk, but his speech was nothing more than a shaky attempt, at best.

"Save your strength, my friend."

A teary-eyed Sally stepped out of the way as she allowed Nicholas to take her seat, wiping her eyes at what appeared to be relief at the sight of him.

"So, what's happened, Hosea?" Nicholas took out a listening device to perform an auscultation.

Hosea waved him off with his left hand. "It is not'-ing."

Nicholas noted the absent *h* in the word. "Hosea. Hold out your tongue."

Hosea gave him a half-sided expression and did as Nicholas asked him. The signs were all there. His friend had, or was having, an attack of apoplexia. How he could sit in a chair was beyond Nicholas's comprehension.

"What is it, Nicholas?"

The panic in Sally's voice made Nicholas wish it was as simple as just a cold or even ague, but instead it was much more serious.

"Well, Hosea. I think you need to rest and not be sitting up in this chair. Let me get you to bed." Before Hosea could object, Ambrose came close, and together they maneuvered Hosea into bed. Nicholas hovered over the man, who was not only a patient, but one of his best friends. They'd been through so much together, especially in the past few years. Tragedy was never a timed event. He couldn't lie to Hosea. "Hosea, I believe you have apoplexy. Not a serious case, but one, nonetheless."

"What does that mean, Nicholas?" Sally pulled the blanket up to her husband's neck and eased his limp arm underneath.

"Hosea has been through lots of heartache and stress this past year. It's a body's way to tell a man to slow down. Take it easy." Nicholas placed the earpiece back into his doctor's bag. "I've been suggesting to Hosea to do just that."

Hosea waved him off with his good arm. "I'm needed." Hosea took a deep breath. "Everywhere."

"That's the problem. You need to let the younger ones take some of the load now. And for today and the next few months, you need to rest."

Hosea shook his head. "I caa-nnot."

"You don't have a choice, Pa." Ambrose spoke now. "I will take over the workings at the mill until you're better."

"Too many peee'ple need..." Hosea seemed to grow exhausted from speaking and instead pointed to himself.

Nicholas nodded. Hosea was right. He was the lifeblood of the community. Everyone wanted his assistance, help, and prayers. Since arriving in Newburg, Nicholas had seen it firsthand how many depended on him. If Hosea were to die, it would be yet another tragic loss in for the whole community. A community which had repeatedly experienced exhausting trauma over the past year. "I don't think this will be crippling to you, Hosea. You can still put weight on your leg, although only time will tell how it will affect your everyday life. But for now, you need to stay put and rest." He winked at Hosea. "Doctor's orders!"

After getting Hosea settled and almost asleep, Nicholas followed Sally and Ambrose into the main part of the house, leaving Hosea to rest alone.

"Will he be okay?" Sally offered Nicholas a cup of coffee, then sat.

"Yes. I believe so. He'll find it hard to talk and also to get function back into his arm, but it appears to have been a mild case. He's a lucky man."

"Blessed, Nicholas."

Nicholas sat and used the cup to warm his hands. It had been a long afternoon, and he had several more calls to make. Thankfully, nothing serious enough to avoid sharing a cup of coffee with Sally and Ambrose.

"I'll be back in the morning to check on him. I'm sorry this has happened, but as I've been trying to encourage Hosea to rest more, I knew this could be possible."

"He's been running himself into sickness since he arrived here. Helping so many people, running a new village, helping Rhoda and others who are trying to make their way, as well as being in charge of the largest-producing mill in this area. I knew it might hit him soon." Ambrose stirred his coffee. "I'll do my best to help."

"The next few hours are crucial in an illness like this. He could have another attack or even more. He just needs to rest. Keep giving him liquids. In a little while, we'll get him out of bed to see the extent of damage the apoplexia has done to him. It might take a few weeks to assess it."

Sally and Ambrose nodded their understanding.

"I'm glad you're here with us now, Nicholas." Sally poured more coffee into Nicholas's mug.

"Isn't it remarkable? I never knew how much a doctor can mean to a community until I came here."

Hosea made his first attempts to get out of the house and to the mill within a month of his apoplexy attack. His struggle to be normal eluded him. He'd gained a permanent twist in his left leg and he couldn't lift his arm higher than his waist. Hosea just wasn't the same. He knew even his best efforts to remain normal were gone. He needed to continue to trust the Lord for his next steps.

With Ambrose and Sally's help, Hosea functioned as best as he could. Most all the townspeople had urged him to keep moving but also volunteered themselves for some of Hosea's daily tasks. Ambrose had become the new supervisor at the mill. Nicholas assisted Hosea with many of the township duties, and prepared meals came to the house regularly. To Hosea, it seemed as if all his efforts to help others were coming back triple-fold in the kindness of his friends.

One evening, Rhoda stopped by the house.

"Rhoda, please come in." Sally Mae welcomed her sister-in-law in with open arms. "How have you been doing?"

Tears sprung to the woman's eyes, but she smiled. "Our house is quieter. I miss Giles's antics and Cornelia's demands, but we're managing. I can't say it's been easy."

Rhoda pulled a chair up close to Hosea and sat next to him. "Hello, Hosea."

Hosea patted her hand. "Rhoda."

Rhoda must have seen the twinkle in his eye because she smiled at him. "How are you feeling?"

Because of his illness, Hosea couldn't finish a sentence without frustrating stops and starts, he nodded instead.

"I've come to share something with you. I'm not sure if it will change other people's minds, Hosea, but I've written a letter to the church in New York. I want them to know the truth about you."

Sally Mae sat opposite the siblings. "Do you think that's necessary, Rhoda? Hardly anyone who went to the church while we were there is attending anymore. The last letter I received from Marvis Compton said as much. Why send it now?"

Rhoda took a deep breath. "I know I can't change the past. I know that what I did was awful, but if only one member has been a part of the former congregation...I want to make things right. Please allow me to do this."

Hosea had so much to say to his sister. She didn't need to send a letter back to the church. He'd forgiven her. Rhoda needed to move on and let the past remain there. As far as helping Rhoda's conscience feel better, that was God's job—not Hosea's. If only he could fully communicate that to her.

"Hosea. Will you read it? Let me know if it is clear and concise."

Hosea took the letter and read it through carefully. Rhoda was an excellent writer and her words touched him. Upon finishing it, he realized how many things he'd done in his lifetime which deserved letters of repentance to others. He didn't think the New Territory had enough trees to make the paper for such a feat. Pride at his sister's attempt to make things right touched his heart and tears filled his eyes. He'd always been emotional, but since the apoplexy, even more so. He wiped at his eyes with his shirtsleeve.

"So, it's okay if I send it?" Rhoda looked straight into his eyes.

Hosea smiled.

"Thank you."

Hosea stood and shuffled off to his bedroom. He lifted his Bible from its place beside his bed and brought it into the kitchen. Placing it on the table, he used his good hand to flip through the pages. He came across the verse he wanted to quote, pointed to it, and handed the Bible to Rhoda.

Rhoda read the indicated verse aloud. *"But as for you, ye thought evil against me; but God meant it unto good, to bring to pass, as it is this day, to save much people alive."*

Hosea hugged his sister. "Your sin. Gone!"

As Rhoda and Sally Mae conversed during the next few minutes, Hosea delighted in the renewed relationship with his sister. He'd seen considerable change in her since the death of her three children. She had terrible moments which brought sudden tears, but her face radiated a renewed spirit. Her hateful comments about God had disappeared. Her love for Him rekindled. Those signs were enough for Hosea to know for the rest of her life, Rhoda would lean on the One who could sustain her. Hosea prayed he was right.

FALL OF 1842

CHAPTER THIRTY-THREE

Hosea startled awake. His focus roamed around the silent room. He could hear a soft snoring beside him. Sally Mae had been working so hard over the past year and a half, and now they were trying to prepare for the coming winter. Even with Ambrose's help, she worked long into the night and often came to bed with Hosea unaware. Hosea disliked that much of his work now fell on Sally Mae's shoulders. His wife had been, and even now was, his greatest gift.

Hosea eased himself out of bed and, surprisingly, Sally Mae didn't stir. He went to his clothes, hanging on hooks on the far wall of their bedroom, and put on the clothes with great ease. As he walked out into the living area, he pulled the bedroom door shut with a gentle tug. He didn't want to disturb his wife.

Ambrose had been sleeping at their house, but he was upstairs, and Hosea knew even a massive earthquake wouldn't wake him.

Looking around the room, Hosea admired his home. Sally Mae always made their dwelling neat and tidy. Homemade curtains hung from each window and now fluttered in the breeze coming through them. This appeared odd to Hosea, as just yesterday they'd had the first frost of the approaching winter. Why had Sally Mae left the windows open?

Hosea went for his coat by the front door, took it off its hook, and opened the door. The warm air from outside brushed against his face. He didn't really need a coat, despite the October calendar date. So instead of trying to push his numb arm into the coat, he placed it back on the hook beside the door.

Looking out over the houses still dark from sleeping inhabitants, Hosea started down the path leading to the mill and the river. He wanted to pray by the river this morning. As he walked, he noticed his usual stumbling gait was gone. He walked freely and with little exertion. Stopping at the end of the lane, he turned again to face the multiple houses and businesses now lining the roads of Newburg.

He could see the doctor's house where Nicholas and his family now lived. Oh, how he loved his friend. They would be friends until the end of time. Nicholas was a shining light in the community where they resided. He not only worked tirelessly to meet the medical needs of the village, but he was also helping it grow into a vibrant and friendly community.

There were plans in the works for two new inns to be built soon, as well as a blacksmith, a market, and even a possibility of a cheese factory. Before long, a fine school building would give the children a place to learn. A real town loomed in the future for this growing location near the Shiawassee River.

Hosea still remembered what it had looked like when he'd stumbled upon the area in 1833. A small clearing along the river had caught his attention. He longed to not only build a cabin there, but also to bring his family back to see what kind of land he'd chosen for them to live. God had been his navigator. He thanked Him for leading him here.

As he neared the river, it no longer raged. The soft gentle flow of the stream reminded him of the lazy days of summer when he would remove his shoes and wade in up to his knees. He decided that somehow the warm morning lent a perfect time to do that. Hosea sat on the bank and removed his shoes with ease. Funny, he didn't even remember putting them on.

Pulling off his socks, Hosea dipped a toe into the stream and felt the coolness of the water. It felt heavenly, just like it did on those scorching hot August summer nights. His thoughts went back to the moment he and Alexander had waded in to catch fish. He laughed at the memory of Alexander stumbling backward and landing on his bottom right in the stream. Putting his hands on his hips, he wondered if he could now do the same thing as he'd done way back then to help the boy not feel so clumsy. Could he fall backward and not drown trying to stand back up? He decided not to try it, but instead he stood right in the middle of the river. The water meandered around his legs, cooling them.

He sniffed the air. The pine scent reminded him of the boughs they brought in each Christmas to adorn the house. A musty odor mixed with the pines filled his nose with a familiar smell. The scent of his river.

The Shiawassee River was his home. He felt more alive and happier here than anywhere else. Yes, it had brought difficulties: cutting down trees that fell across the road, using those same logs to build a home, breaking through the soil which had never been tilled before, and raising Ambrose and his girls where no White man had ever trod. They'd endured tornadoes, wolves, Indians, and those tormenting mosquitoes and even the possibility of starvation. Surviving in this land was nothing short of miraculous. He had God to thank for that.

Hosea raised both hands in the air to praise the Creator, who had allowed him the opportunity to experience such joy. He supposed that as time went on, no one would remember the name of Hosea Baker. His children and grandchildren would, but in fifty or even a hundred years from now...who would want to know his name? Would they know him for the scripture verses he quoted? He might have a line or two in the history books of the area, but even that seemed a stretch for the simple and ordinary man from New York and Pennsylvania.

Hosea's legacy remained in the deeds and acts he'd done to make this place a village. He felt satisfied with his attempt. He'd endeavored to honor his father's name and as the head of his family. He hoped his grandchildren knew how much he loved them. But did it really matter?

His good deeds were just rags when the credit all belonged to the God he served. Jesus deserved all the glory, not Hosea. Hosea prayed that everyone who knew him understood this. He wanted his life to be a reflection of the God he served.

Looking down the river, Hosea saw a man standing on the shore across from him. The silhouette was hard to see against a bright light behind it. It must be the sun rising on another day. Hosea put his hand over his eyes to block the brightness and to see who was standing there watching him.

Hosea gasped when he realized who it was. He had to get across the river and to the young man. He knew him. He was sure of it. He strode against the current to get a closer look. Putting his hand down, Hosea now recognized him. He waved to him. Without even looking where he walked, he strode around rocks and across the river to reach the boy, now grown into a man. As he drew near, the man stepped away from the river. He nodded to Hosea.

"Alexander!"

The frown on the young man's face changed to a familiar smile. "Pa!" As if he was as surprised as Hosea to see him.

"Where have you come from? How did you get here?" He'd said the words without stuttering.

"I've been waiting for you."

Hosea wanted to reach out and touch him, but for some reason, he couldn't. It was as if Alexander was a mirage of sorts. Perhaps a delusion.

"I've come for you, Pa."

"Come for me? Where are we going?"

"The place you've waited to be for many moons. You will love it there. There are many waiting to see you."

"Really? Where is this place exactly? I would hate to not tell anyone where I'm going. They'll worry."

Alexander raised his hand to Hosea. "Follow me, Pa. There is nothing to fear. Everyone in Newburg will know where you are. They'll be along soon."

Hosea didn't quite know what to think, but he trusted Alexander. Alexander would never lead him to harm, or off to an unknown place. So with that, Hosea lifted his once-numb left arm and took Alexander by the shoulder. Alexander pointed down a narrow trail.

"We just need to follow this trail." Alexander patted Hosea's hand on his shoulder. "Together."

"Will you go with me, Alexander?"

"Yes. I know how to get there because you once told me the way."

"Thou wilt shew me the path of life: in thy presence is fullness of joy; at thy right hand there are pleasures for evermore."
Psalm 16:11

HISTORICAL ACCURACY NOTES

Have you ever come across a treasure? That's what happened when I was researching for the Newburg Chronicles series which had me reading newspaper articles based on the establishment of Hosea Baker's North Newburg.

While reading a newspaper from the Owosso Argus-Press dated Saturday, September 14, 1963, a title caught my attention. 'In 1836, People Began to Stream into the Area'. The writer reported about the early fur traders and also mentioned John Whitmore Knaggs. As I continued to read, I learned more about Hosea and Ambrose and how Julia Swain had been the first baby born in Shiawassee County.

Buried right in the middle came this treasure:

Sidney Seymour was preceded to his 160 acres by his wife and four of his children. She traveled by stage from their home in Rochester, New York, to Pontiac and then hired a teamster to take her to the home of her brother, Hosea Baker.

Hosea had a sister who followed him to Michigan! I continued to read.

She arrived with 10 cents left and, not wishing to put her brother out, she moved into a vacant cabin in the yard of her brother's mill. She then walked to Shiawasseetown, bought 10 cents' worth of soap and set about to do the washing for the three men employed at the mill.

So, readers, this part of the *Shallow Roots* story is accurate regarding the life of Rhoda Seymour. The article further reported that three of the Seymour children are buried at the Fremont Cemetery and their deaths were within three consecutive days. I based my story of the children's passing, within three days, on that one paragraph.

I have visited the grave of these children and they are all buried under one stone. The newspaper article reported them as Giles age 15, Cornelia age 8, and Guy age six. Yet the dates on the tombstone do not reflect this. It lists the children having passed away in 1840, except for Cornelia.

Find a Grave, a cemetery research site, lists the dates of the children's deaths as Giles in 1840 at nine years of age; Guy in 1840 at just under one month; and Cornelia in 1846 at eight years of age. Why the newspaper information is different, I do not know.

Upon viewing the tombstone in person, the dates look as though all three children passed away in 1840, within three days of each other. If this is true, Cornelia would have been just under two years of age.

Once I read Rhoda's story from the newspaper, I expanded my research to include the Seymour family. Rhoda arrived in Michigan alone with four children, and Sidney followed later. They purchased The Exchange building in 1839 and began business there. It sounds unlikely that is was a store, but The Exchange building served as an inn and ballroom around the time the Seymours owned it.

Rhoda's story gave me a fresh character for *Shallow Roots* from the treasure I found in the 1963 newspaper article. Hosea was the oldest in the Baker family, and Rhoda was the eldest daughter and closest sister to Hosea. This might be why Rhoda followed him to Michigan, because they shared a close relationship.

Caroline's husband, Horace Knapp, passed away not long after the couple were married. I found no record in my research indicating why or how, so I imagined perhaps he could have passed away from diabetes. Diabetes was not well understood at the time, and no effective treatment existed. The couple did not have children during their marriage. They buried Horace at the Newburg Cemetery and despite Caroline remarrying, she was later buried next to him.

Hosea built the first mill in Newburg. The account of Stephen Sergeant and his dream is true. Sergeant was traveling north to help his Uncle Frank Sergeant and James Ball and had a nightmare that someone would pass away while building the mill. James Ball is the name of the man who passed away building the mill.

Hosea indeed left New York because of a scandal and moved to Pennsylvania before coming to Michigan. The exact details of the scandal are unclear. Rhoda being a part of the scandal came from my imagination.

In my beginning research of the Baker family, I was unaware of how many daughters were actually in the family other than Betsey and Caroline. I added two more because research said Hosea had daughters (plural). I chose to name Etta and Jillian because nothing was written about their given names. Upon further investigation, around Caroline's grave at the cemetery, I found a grave marked Susan Black. I soon found out that Susan was Caroline's youngest sister. Another sister, Eliza, is buried elsewhere. You'll soon be learning more about Eliza in the last book of the series.

Next to Susan's grave is a stone engraved with her husband, William Black. I had named a boy interested in Caroline by the name of Billie, before I knew who Caroline actually married. So now I had a dilemma. I made up the part regarding Billie arriving to find Caroline. I incorporated that Caroline didn't marry Billie but Horace, and then I thought up the idea of having Jillian fall in love with him instead. This fulfilled the fact that Jillian did marry a William Black. Whether he went by the nickname Billie is another part of my made-up story. The idea to have them elope was mine, but it is recorded that William and (Susan) Jillian did not get married close to Newburg, but out of the county. So perhaps an elopement did take place.

Doctor Nicholas P. Harder arrived in the village in 1837 from Sullivan County, New York. He was the first physician to practice in this section of The Territory. Nicholas' first wife, Margaret, did pass away before he arrived, and it lists his second wife's children as coming into the territory with him, so he had remarried by the time he arrived in the New Territory. His wife was pregnant when she arrived in Newburg.

Nicholas became a doctor when he was twenty-three years old. Further information from the Harder family says he was a man of fine physique and stood six feet in his stockings and weighed 180 pounds. It said he often slept on his horse while caring for the community near Newburg. All the children's names that I've listed as coming into the territory with him and his new wife are accurate.

Hosea does build a sawmill, but whether he gave up farming is an assumption. As he grew older, perhaps the overall toll of maintaining a farm in the 1830s became too great. With all that Hosea had to do to start the community in Newburg, I think his health probably suffered for it.

I do refer to a town, north of Newburg, as Big Rapids. It was later named Owosso after the Indian Chief Wasso.

The research and details of the Exchange building are accurate. It's reported that the building was extraordinary for the era. They brought most of the supplies in on oxen carts from Pontiac to build it. The log which went the entire length of the building is also accurate. (Please find a photo of the building after this history section.)

To add further drama to the story, I added the fact that Rhoda's husband arrived late, despite the fact that he did arrive the same year as Rhoda.

John Whitmore Knaggs died and was buried in 1840. It is reported that many dignitaries, military men, Native Americans, and settlers from the area attended the funeral. No one is sure where Knaggs is buried, but some believe it to be under or near the schoolhouse in Newburg and was moved later. This has not been confirmed either way. I have also read that he was buried in Fremont, but there is no grave marker or stone to verify that fact.

Etta does marry a man named Charles Chalker. The Chalker brothers and their sister, Eliza, are a part of the early settlers in a village near Newburg. Vernon is just east of Newburg and is a small community to this day. The Chalker brothers built a cider mill, so that is why I have them planting apple trees.

The story about a settler finding an Indian over a woman's children is a true story. It happened just as I wrote it, but I took the liberty of writing it as if it happened to Rhoda.

John Swain does remarry Wealthea and soon becomes a Pastor. It is my imagination that he was the Pastor to reside over the funeral of John Whitmore Knaggs.

Rhoda's children dying in a flood is also my imagination. It wasn't unusual for families to lose multiple children in the 1830s because of illness, accidents, or even drownings. I'm sure there were many times that the Shiawassee River had flood issues, especially in the spring months.

The idea of having Rhoda responsible for the scandal in New York is a liberty I felt fit the story well. As I've previously written, Hosea's New York scandal is a mystery.

I do not know Hosea's cause of death. His tombstone reads that he passed away in 1842. Hosea would have been just fifty-two-years young. In this generation, that is a young age, but for all the trials and heartaches that Hosea endured even before he arrived in

Newburg, as well as what he experienced once he arrived, it is possible that he died early from exhaustion or disease.

As far as Alexander goes, I have had someone say that Alexander just moved away from the family and perhaps took a job and raised children. As far as him passing away from the smallpox epidemic, between 1833 and 1836, is my idea, only because I had him return to live with the Indians in Crooked Paths Straight. As I wrote in the history details of that book, Alexander's name appears in the records of living with the Baker family at one time. Why he was there continues to be a mystery.

To have Alexander as the first person to greet Hosea on his journey toward the light of heaven brought me joy. I hope it did for you, too.

Elizabeth

THE SHIAWASSEE EXCHANGE

Perhaps, one day, someone can name, for me, the individuals in this photo. My dream is that they are somehow related to the Seymour family, if not the family themselves, or maybe it is just travelers heading west through the Michigan Territory.

The Shiawassee Exchange of 1831 was known first as a business. B.O. and A.L. Williams built the Exchange as a place to conduct their trade as the Jacob Aster Fur Trading Company. For some years, the place was known as a wayside inn and ballroom, which occupied nearly the whole of the second floor of the story and a half building, and was the scene of many a winter night's gaiety.

The initial Exchange was added onto in 1835. Supplies for the enlargement were hauled into Knagg's Place by oxen teams and wagons from Pontiac. The lower rooms were used as business and living areas with three fireplaces, deep as they were wide. Small window panes made up the floor to ceiling windows. Gables at the building's edges were made of black walnut with elaborate fan shaped carvings in them. The building was an amazing feat of architecture for its time.

It was also known as a bank for a time. To this day, paper money is circulating among antique collectors with The Exchange name printed on it. It was one of four banks in the area. They included: Ypsilanti, Howell, Knagg's Place, and Flint. Many claimed that it was built on the most beautiful and charming areas of the Shiawassee River.

If buildings could talk to us, this one would have much to say, I'm sure.

About the Author

Elizabeth's first book titled *Under the Windowsill,* is a coming-of-age story about a young woman named Kenna who runs away to Mackinac Island in search of a better life.

Elizabeth's second book titled *Promise at Daybreak,* has a Durand, Michigan setting and is about two elderly sisters who are forced together due to illness. They meet again to fulfill a pact they made at their mother's grave.

Elizabeth's third book titled *Just a Train Ride,* highlights a love story from the 1940s. An elderly woman recalls her love story for a frustrated fellow passenger on a train from Chicago to Michigan.

A sequel to Just a Train Ride is Elizabeth's fourth book, *Mere Reflection.* It is the continuing story of Blaine, the young girl on the train. What kind of life got Blaine to the place she is now and why is Callie's help so important?

The first book in the Newburg Chronicles series is *The Year the Stars Fell.* It covers the first nine months of the adventures of the Hosea Baker family as they embark on the mission to settle in the Michigan Territory. The second book in the series is *Crooked Paths Straight* and gives a glimpse into Caroline's life.

For more information on where to find Wehman's books, check out her website at **www.elizabethwehman.com** or like her on Facebook at Elizabeth Wehman/Author for new and upcoming books. Also, become a fan of Elizabeth's historical series by joining the *North Newburg Chronicles* page on Facebook.

Elizabeth lives in Owosso, Michigan with her husband. You may email her at elizabethwehman@gmail.com.

Made in the USA
Monee, IL
03 May 2024

57828828R00236